For R.R.A.

'I had never before seen the countries of warm
temperature, nor the country of Hindustan.
Immediately on reaching them I beheld a new
world. The grass was different, the trees different,
the wild animals of a different sort, the birds of a
different plumage, the manners and customs of the
wandering tribes of a different kind. I was struck
with astonishment, and indeed there was room for
wonder.'
Memoirs of Baber – for the year 1504

Birds of a
Different Plumage

Birds of a Different Plumage

A Study of British-Indian
relations from Akbar to Curzon

Peter Mudford

COLLINS
St James's Place, London, 1974

William Collins Sons & Co Ltd
London · Glasgow · Sydney · Auckland
Toronto · Johannesburg

First published 1974
© Peter Mudford 1974
ISBN 0 00 216061 7
Set in Monotype Fontana
Made and Printed in Great Britain by
William Collins Sons & Co Ltd Glasgow

Contents

Illustrations

Each section depicts a stage in the development of the relationship between England and India. IOL indicates the picture is reproduced by kind permission of the India Office Library; NPG by kind permission of the National Portrait Gallery.

MAPS

Acknowledgements

I would first like to acknowledge the encouragement given to me throughout the writing of this book by John and Sheila Auden. Their help and suggestions have been invaluable. In the initial stages I was kindly assisted by Rajeswiri Datta and Attia Hosein. In the course of my research D. A. Richards has, as a historian of Indian and Company history, directed my attention to several works which have had a shaping influence on the development of my own ideas; Dr Michael Slater provided me with scholarly assistance in relation to *Household Words*; and Dr P. V. Neuss has helped me with innumerable improvements to the accuracy and consistency of the script. Finally, and in particular, I should like to thank Philip Ziegler whose encouragement and interest in this book have contributed a great deal to its completion.

All that I owe to my wife is acknowledged in another and different form elsewhere.

In the course of writing this book I have been given invaluable assistance by the staff of several libraries: Birkbeck College in the University of London, the India Office Records, the Royal Commonwealth Society, and the London Library. Although they are mentioned in the notes, I should like also to record here my particular debt to the work of three previous writers on India: Philip Woodruff, David Kopf and Anil Seal. In relation to their research, as to the assistance given by those mentioned above, the defects of this book remain only my own responsibility.

I should like to thank Mrs George Bambridge for her kind help in giving me information about her father, Rudyard Kipling, and his attitude to India, as well as permission to quote from his works. Macmillan & Co. have granted me permission to quote from Rabindranath Tagore; and the Oxford University Press to reproduce the maps from C. Collin Davies, *An Historical Atlas of the Indian Peninsula*, Oxford, 1959.

The illustrations are the product of generous assistance given by Mr and Mrs Lennox Money, G. Eyre, Esq., and Mrs Mildred Archer, to whom I should like to express my thanks.

I should also like to acknowledge here the patient and persistent help given by Jennie Chisman in typing this book, which has been subject to much revision and alteration.

Lastly, I should like to acknowledge two debts of a rather different kind: first, to my colleagues in the English Department at Birkbeck who relieved me of my duties during a summer term, and so enabled me to write the first and essential version of this work. Secondly, to my parents whose warm and affectionate interest has constantly encouraged me in this project.

Introduction

On 15th August, 1947, the Indian flag replaced the Union Jack on the Red Fort at Delhi. Since then the realignment of world-power has brought about far-reaching changes in the relation-ship between Eastern and Western worlds. The involvement of the United States in the Far East, the growing influence of China, the Treaty of Peace, Friendship and Cooperation between Russia and India of 1971, as well as the increasingly independent voice of India herself, have served to remove the last vestiges of the Imperial scene. Between England and India the pace of separation has also been rapid. The economic pressure upon England to join the Common Market, the erosion of the Commonwealth, the decline of British influence east of Suez, and the introduction of immigrant quotas have worked to dissolve that association which lasted for more than three hundred years – first in the period of the East India Company, and later of the Empire. But though the Raj has now passed away 'like early morning mist before strong sunlight', it still represents a unique phase in the development of the relation-ship between Eastern and Western worlds; it is of interest now not merely or solely because of its contribution to imperialism, but much more importantly because it involved large numbers of people, both Indian and English, over a considerable period of time in contact with a culture that was alien and often incomprehensible to them.

With India's population now forming a sixth of the world's population, the need for understanding of mutual differences, of the causes of prejudice and dislike, and the attitudes which have led to friendship and trust, remains an indispensable part of the struggle to create one world. At times, the power of technology, of economic and material growth make it look as though the old differences between cultures are fast disappear-

ing. That is not my belief. Technology makes it possible for
more men to live better, or to live at all; but it does not solve
the differences between them. Local variety, whether within a
nation, or between nations, forms a central part of the world's
vitality, but it is also the origin of some of the more blatant
misjudgments and misunderstandings. Within the records of
Anglo-India is lodged the evolution of a relationship not
marked by high civilisation, but full of the signposts to where
narrowness of vision, and arrogant or impatient dismissal
came to do irreparable damage.

Many people remember one line from a famous ballad by
Rudyard Kipling: 'Oh, East is East and West is West, and never
the twain shall meet . . .' Few recall how the poem goes on to
qualify this seemingly pessimistic statement:

Till Earth and Sky stand presently at God's Great Judgment Seat;
But there is neither East nor West, Border, nor Breed, nor Birth
When two strong men stand face to face, though they come from
the ends of the earth.[1]

In the complexities of the twentieth century the old belief in
strong men, however sympathetic, scarcely seems to mean very
much – or at any rate to leave too many questions unanswered.
And so it is in search of an answer to the problem which
Kipling's ballad raises as to the nature of the differences between people of East and West that this book has set out. Taking
the Anglo-Indian* relationship as a specific example, I have tried
to formulate a view of the conflicts in ways of life, attitude and
belief which have acted as a barrier in the past. What kind of
differences proved most intractable? And were they peculiarly
the result of Empire, and the kind of place that Empire was, or
the product of deeper and less ephemeral divisions? The traveller to New Delhi cannot help but be aware of the alien spirit
that inspires Sir Edward Lutyens's Imperial Capital: it is grand,
assertive, spacious but with few enough traces of that subtle
assimilation apparent in the sculpture of the Gandharan school.
It recalls to mind the question asked by W. D. Arnold in his
novel, *Oakfield; or Fellowship in the East* (1854): '. . . Is the

---

* Anglo-Indian is used here, and throughout this book, to denote simply the
British-Indian relationship. It is never used to mean Eurasian.

language about our common brotherhood as false in theory as in actuality or is there really some common ground of the same human nature discoverable, though as yet not found, scarcely looked for ?"[2]

The nature of the relationship between people and civilisations, like that of individuals, is inevitably the product of their individual time-scales. And this is particularly true in the case of England and India. Had the encounter between them occurred at other moments in their evolution, its course would inevitably have been very different. This does not invalidate the interest of its records as an example of the problems of international understanding. But it does mean that a chronological account of them, with all the inevitable omissions it involves, proves essential. I have begun from the journals of the first English travellers to India in the seventeenth century, and followed their isolated steps into the immense records of the nineteenth and twentieth centuries. It is a long journey on a huge landscape; and on it I have tried not to lose sight of the fact that there is not one India but a massive sub-continent (climatically, ethnically, linguistically and now politically divided) which renders untrue almost all generalisations about it. Similarly, for the English the whole story could never be told, because it would in fact be the story of every English man and woman who had been in India, and the kind of contacts and experiences, of whatever value, they had lived through. In this volume the story has only been taken as far as the first decade of the twentieth century, and the Viceroyalty of Lord Curzon. The complexity of the patterning of events in our own time, and the increasingly political nature of the problems which presented themselves to the minds of men and writers, as the Empire neared its end, would demand a somewhat different organisation of material to that used here. The fragmentation of society, its codes and beliefs, which began to remould European life after the First World War, had its inevitable effect on those who went out to India and on their relationships with the Indian community, which was itself being fused and unified by the struggle for *swa-raj*.* That, however, did not silence the dialogue between East and West;

* swa-raj: self-rule.

rather it brought to the surface certain aspects of the difference, and charged them with particular life. Since 1947 the problem has been transformed once again - at least on the surface. But the basic human and cultural conflicts still flash out of the past as reminders of what can all too often and quickly be forgotten.

Two further ideas lie behind the writing of this book. The first results from the legacy of English on the sub-continent of India. This has imprinted many historical records with examples of differences in attitude and feeling that would not have been apparent, or at least been far less accessible, without this legacy. But its importance too is not merely historical. Among the hundreds of languages and dialects which the people of the Indian sub-continent speak, English acts as common denominator. As a Congress of Indian writers at Simla in 1971 revealed: 'The inescapable reality is that English continues to be the only expedient language throughout India . . .'[3]- It is also a major link with that outside world from which the solution of many of India's technological problems will come. But as in other parts of the English-speaking world, the instrument of potential communication is also dangerous. It can lead to a false assurance about understanding, which does not in fact exist. The problem of language will never be far from the central themes of this book.

The second idea concerns the concept of civilisation, which now seems difficult to define. In the mid-nineteenth century a good many people accepted without question that the civilisation of Europe was superior to that of the East. It represented - to use Matthew Arnold's phrase - a more advanced example of the 'humanisation of man in society'. The events of the twentieth century have made it impossible to believe in that superiority which was used to justify an imperial mission; and there is nothing to be regretted in the disappearance of such attitudes. But as with all gains there have also been losses. A state of civilisation still implies the opposite to barbarism; and if civilisation is to survive, not merely as a theoretical ideal, but as a way of life which is to be aimed at, then the question of what we mean by it becomes a vital and important issue. It is difficult to preserve something unless you know what it is. But the daily strife of our time does not make it easy to retain a sense of perspective or balance. The period of the British presence in India from 1579 when the first Englishman, a Jesuit missionary, arrived in Goa does, however, present a cleanly separated slice of time in which it is possible to watch the growth of a particular relationship; and to trace the way in which the values brought to it by Englishmen affected the kind of civilisation it became, just as the changing state of India determined the response to increasing British power. In this context, it is possible to see something of the points at which assimilation and rejection on either side worked - and to indicate what values came closest to creating a shared civilisation, and what proved damaging and divisive. In the developing course of Anglo-Indian relations it is not difficult to see when and how actions and policies of a particular sort served to limit the kind of civilisation which could result from them.

The story of the contact between Eastern and Western worlds in the particular case of British India contains, I believe, a unique account of the difficulties which stand in the way of understanding between people of different cultures - though obviously not a uniquely important one. The battle for any improvement in communication needs to be fought on many fronts; and the records of the past - the ideas, feelings, and visions of men in their particular situations are marked by those conflicts in the human situation which change only very slowly. Communication is a day-to-day business; but a knowledge of the causes of break-down and break-through in the past - an understanding of some of those differences which the written word records, has its contribution to make to the future. As the great Akbar said:

To light a candle is to commemorate the rising of the sun.
To whomsoever the sun sets, what other remedy hath he but this?

Chapter 1

A Kind of Permanence

... the European leaves his wife and children in the midst
of a crowd of a hundred thousand persons, all strangers
to them, and all speaking a language and following a
religion different from their own, while he goes off
the whole day, hunting and shooting in distant jungles,
without the slightest feeling of apprehension for their
safety or comfort...

W. SLEEMAN, *Rambles and Recollections of an
Indian Official*, 1844

Life is so uncertain, disease so rapid; there are such
lengthened separations and so many uncertainties in
the conveyance of intelligence, that I feel quite
bewildered at the startling occurrences I hear of ...
The frightful rapidity of death and all belonging to it,
in this climate, obliges immediate interment.

H. LAWRENCE, *Journal*, 1837

THE coincidence of often haphazard forces which led to the
creation of a British Empire in India are no less striking
than its anomalies as a civilisation. But before turning to the
particular, some recurring characteristics of the relation
between England and India need to be mentioned: they form
the setting in which the action was played out, and provide a
commentary upon it.

The quotation from Colonel Sleeman at the head of this
chapter which vividly indicates the isolation of the European
face in the multitudinous Indian community remains the most
striking single fact about the English relationship to India. The
correspondent of *The Times* in 1858, W. H. Russell, referred to it
as a 'numerical nothingness'[1] which made the English survival
of the Mutiny as surprising as their conquests in the previous
century. Until the development of sophisticated weapons, the
English in India could easily and quickly have been exter-

minated by any concerted attempt to bring this about. The proportion of Indians to Europeans varied from place to place, and from time to time; but the discrepancy was consistently huge. In 1752, in Calcutta, there were approximately 1000 natives* for every European; in the 1870s in an administrative district of Lower Bengal twenty Europeans lived among a native population of more than two and a quarter million. Even in Simla, at the zenith of Lord Curzon's administration in 1901, there were 40,000 natives and under 2,000 Europeans. These figures are interesting in several ways. They illustrate, in the first place, a truth in the comment of Lord Metcalfe, Governor-General in 1834, that British 'power depends solely on our military authority'.[2] Metcalfe, like many other realists, had no sentimental illusions about the affection in which the British were held; and this in itself involved a certain kind of psychological strain which Emily Eden, the sister of Metcalfe's successor, Lord Auckland, outlined effectively in her description of an open-air entertainment - with music from *Puritani* - for the English at Simla. There were 105 Europeans to 3000 mountaineers who 'looked on at what we call our polite amusements, and bowed to the ground, if a European came near them. I sometimes wonder they do not cut all our heads off and say nothing more about it.'[3] These were conditions likely to bring out the best and the worst in men; and often they did.

The small size of the English community also meant that only a microscopic proportion of the Indian population had any direct contact with them - and then most often in an official or servile capacity. Even in the former, the degree of mutual comprehension was often so slight as to make any significant contact impossible. The problems presented by English law to the Indian villager, which will be taken up in more detail later, exemplifies this disadvantage in a critical form. As Colonel Sleeman discovered on his journey through Oudh shortly before Dalhousie's annexation of that unruly kingdom in 1856, there were many people who preferred the law of the sword which they did understand, to the prospect of being ruined by litiga-

---

* The word 'native' recurs frequently in the literature of all periods. In many instances it means no more than the opposite of foreigner. On this basis I have used the word, where appropriate, in this book.

tion in the Company's courts which they did not. But the ramifications of mutual incomprehension that inevitably resulted from paucity of contact went far deeper than public issues of this sort. John Beames, a recently appointed Assistant Commissioner in the Punjab, was surprised to be asked in the early 1860s how much he had paid for his wife. The Punjabis for their part rejected as incredible the assertion that he had not paid anything at all for her.[4] Another young 'bearer' or servant reasonably believed that the English worshipped Queen Victoria because he had seen her image in their churches; and a native officer in the Indian army of the same period recorded his failure to understand the mercy shown by Sahibs to their enemies: 'If your enemy is not worth killing, he is not worth fighting with . . .'[5] Such examples could be continued at length. They serve to illustrate that, where customs and attitudes were so different, only a very large English population living in close contact with Indians in their own villages could have started to make any significant difference to Indian civilisation; and such numbers did not exist. On the other hand, the majority of Europeans found too much in Indian life inaccessible or unappealing to attempt orientalising themselves; and the examples of those who did was not on the whole an enticement.

'The census of 1921 found only 8·2 per cent of the population over five years of age able to read and write.'[6] Out of every hundred men, only fourteen were literate; and of the same number of women, only two. This was more than a century after the grant of the first lakh* of rupees by the Company for the purpose of Indian education. Even where contact and communication were desired, they could often only occur at an elementary level owing to differences in educational background. Again, the results of this in terms of practical issues like medical and material progress were of great significance, and will be returned to later on. Here, it is more necessary to stress the particular kind of isolation in which these differences in educational background meant that many of the most dedicated civil servants had to live. A collector, administratively

---

* A lakh – 100,000 Rupees: in the early nineteenth century the equivalent of about £12,500.

responsible for an area of 30,000 square miles, inhabited by villagers with their own ancient and traditional ways of life, would not be lacking in work, but inevitably remain aware of the few points of mental contact between them and his own classical, Christian background.

Equally significant were the numbers of educated Indians, in the larger communities, who had little or no personal contact with the English or English civilisation. Again, the size of the population – together with differences in language to which we must shortly come back – was a controlling factor, as well as personal tastes. Rabindranath Tagore in his *Reminiscences* (1917) leaves a memorable picture of the manner and degree to which the educated Indian preserved his own kind of civilisation in the capital of the Empire, Calcutta. Srikantha Babu was among the earliest admirers of the young Tagore's verse, and the poet writes of him: 'He was of the old school of Persian culture, and knew not a word of English. His inseparable companions were a hubble-bubble at his left, and a *sitar* on his lap; and from his throat flowered song unceasing "[7] As with everything in India, the pattern was not neat. Babu H. M. Thakur who lived in Calcutta in the early part of the nineteenth century was attracted to the scientific experiments and political ideas of Benjamin Franklin. He adopted a European style of living that enabled him to converse with those who shared his interests. But even in rarer cases like this where understanding and contact was actively sought, the possibilities for it were limited by the predominantly commercial interests of the Europeans in Calcutta. This situation improved during the course of the nineteenth century; but in relation to the total numbers which composed either community, only marginally. Differences in educational background, and the cultural context that implied, acted as a powerfully restrictive influence upon the growth of a common community.

Also divisive was the difference in the conditions and style of living between the two communities. Almost every critic of the British way of life, especially in the period of Empire, commented on its aloofness. Some came to regard this as a necessary attribute of the ruling race; but its justification on imperial grounds must not be confused with its historical origins in a social situation that was significantly different. The manner and time at which the British presence in India was established, and the rigorous conventions in Muslim and Hindu life, contributed to the kind of society which developed in the future. As with much in the growth of the Empire itself, where imperialism counts for less, and chance for more than is often supposed, the possibilities open to the early English traders were limited. The collegiate life of the Company's servants in the factories of the early seventeenth century resulted directly from their scarcely tolerated presence in a land where lawlessness and war daily threatened their survival. At Madras, for example, the establishment of a fort on a deserted but defendable strip of beach led quickly to the growth of a black town outside the walls. In Calcutta, on the other hand, the communities were to a large extent juxtaposed because the Nawab of Bengal did not initially allow the English to build any fortifications. In the isolated circumstances of early Company life, where survival and good trade relations with the local powers remained the ambitions of the English merchants, it was only natural that they should make themselves comfortable so far as possible in their own way, and according to their own style. This did not prevent, in the first two centuries of the Company's existence, a good deal of social and friendly contact between the merchants and their Indian neighbours. Within their own factories a disciplined and rigorous life was a means of improving the chance of survival. As Charnock, the founder of Calcutta, remarked, 'a fort was worth more than an ambassador' in seventeenth-century India and the improvements the English made to their settlements were only the result of prudence and common sense. In 1674 a young doctor, John Fryer, on a visit to Bombay described how the English, whose life expectancy was reckoned at two monsoons, had attempted to make their lives a little more endurable: 'About the house was a delicate garden, voiced to be the pleasantest in *India*, intended rather for wanton Dalliance, Love's artillery, than to make resistance against an invading foe.'[8] On the Governor's bowling green at Madras or in the pursuits of fishing and fowling, the Company men did nothing more questionable than recreate themselves with simple and customary pleasures. But by 1871 the same scene has taken on a wholly different moral tone:

As to the Native Town, no Irish village of the worst kind has a look of greater poverty, confusion, and utter discomfort. The low huts covered with palm leaves, the open drains, the naked children with their naked fathers and miserable looking mothers, together with the absence of all attempt to give a decent look to the houses, present a most remarkable contrast to the wealth and luxury of the neighbouring city . . .⁹

The English as rulers now have responsibility for that squalor; before they were only visitors. But still those early settlements indicate the origins of differences which only became offensive when their context was changed. In the Bombay garden we are aware of a good attempt to hold things together in adverse circumstances; in the later description of the city, it is impossible to avoid the awareness of failure to construct any common civilisation from two communities long since living together. With the conflicts of attitude and idea between the garden and the city, the following chapters will be much concerned.

In Fryer's description of the Bombay garden another type of difference suggests itself - not altogether easy to define, or place in importance - but which often enough plays some part, either as symptom or cause, in the kind of civilisation that Anglo-India became. I mean some radical difference in aesthetic temperament and taste. It would be as hard, and fruitless, to try to suggest how large a factor this was in the average person's response to situation, as to indicate its origin in different cultural (or economic) backgrounds. But without any doubt differences in taste did exacerbate the estrangement between the communities. On the whole, the English responded better to the Muslim than the Hindu temperament and taste, finding them for obvious reasons, less alien and remote. Few travellers express any great admiration for the majority of Hindu temples; practically none fails to find the Taj Mahal one of the wonders of the world. This preference for the Muslim was equally common in human relationships. Lord Morley, the Secretary of State for India in 1909 typified a common attitude when he said: 'I am an Occidental, not an Oriental . . . I think I like Indian Mahummedans, but I cannot go much further in an easterly direction.'[10]

The importance of differences in taste emerges with particular clarity in cases where Indians, usually Hindus, have adopted an English style of living. In 'Wanderings in India', a series of articles published by Dickens's *Household Words* in 1857, the author remarked:

There is something peculiarly quaint about the arrangement of European furniture in the house of a native gentleman . . . in the dining, or drawing-room, you will find a wash-hand stand, and a chest of drawers, and a toilet table, while in the bedroom you will, perhaps, discover an old piano, an organ, a card-table, or a chifonier. The furniture has, for the most part, been purchased at various sales, and has belonged to officers of all grades, civil and military. On the mantelpiece you will find a costly clock of the most elegant design and workmanship, and on each side of it, a pair of japan candlesticks not worth half-a-crown . . . I sat down to a table twenty feet long . . . which was covered with a damask table-cloth of European manufacture, but instead of a dinner napkin, there was a bed-room towel . . .[11]

His English taste for propriety is offended by this; and the contrast with the delicate garden is at once apparent. Here, the aesthetic difference expresses itself in something not much stronger than a kind of unease, as though a desire for the predictable and expected has not been fulfilled. But often the more characteristically Hindu things become, the more violently the Englishman wants to reject them. Victor Jacquemont, a Frenchman who travelled in India between 1829-32 saw this indifference and hostility to things Indian as a basic defect of the English. This was in many respects so; but in matters of taste the impulse ran deep. E. M. Forster whose *Hill of Devi* concerns two visits to Dewas in 1912 and 1921 records not only a common distaste for Hindu music, but for the general aesthetic effect of their religious festivals: 'What troubles me is that every detail, almost without exception, is fatuous and in bad taste. The altar is a mess of little objects, stifled with rose leaves, the walls are hung with deplorable oleographs, the chandeliers, draperies - everything bad.'[12] On a more everyday matter, J. H. Grose had made precisely the same comment a hundred and sixty years before Forster about the Mahrattas:

Tastelessness . . . is so thoroughly rooted in them, that though no people are fonder of decking out their women with rich jewels, yet they would prefer those of their own workman's coarse and clumsy setting, to those of a Robertson or a Lacam . . . purely for the want of a relish for perfection, which makes them contented with what they have a habit of daily seeing.[13]

Tagore makes an interesting comment on Hindu aesthetics in this respect which goes some way towards explaining the kind of distaste felt by many of the English; he is writing of standards in performance:

In our country the understanding portion of the audience think no harm in keeping the performance up to standard by dint of their own imaginations. For the same reason they do not mind any harshness of voice or uncouthness of gesture in the exponent of a perfectly formed melody; on the contrary, they seem sometimes to be of opinion that such minor external defects serve better to set off the internal perfection of the composition . . . This feeling seems entirely wanting in Europe . . . In our country the virtuoso is satisfied if he has heard the song; in Europe they go to hear the singer.[14]

These are sophisticated distinctions; but the literature of Anglo-India provides many instances of customs which at an aesthetic level were capable of causing estrangement: the 'prevalence of obesity which [the Hindus] imagine adds to the dignity of their port',[15] the discolouring of teeth by the chewing of betel, the smell of oils used to anoint the body, the use of cow's urine as holy water, or the smearing of the body of the fakir with excrement. At this level questions of aesthetics also become on the one side, matters of godliness, and on the other, of cleanliness. Nirad Chaudhuri has written succinctly of this difference between the European and Indian mentality in *The Continent of Circe*:

Occidentals come from a clean and tidy material world, in which dirt, squalor, and disorder are sins . . . I would say that no man can be regarded as a fit citizen of India until he has conquered squeamishness to the point of being indifferent to the presence of fifty lepers in various stages of decomposition within a hundred yards, or not minding the sight of ubiquitous human excreta everywhere, even in a big city.[16]

At one extreme of this difference in taste, we encounter irritation at the absence of perfection, and the presence of slovenly informality; at the other, a disgust at habits which appear unclean, and, as they encourage the spread of disease, seem symptomatic of a degraded way of life. Since tastes at this level are little susceptible to change, they act as a real barrier to the possibility of a unified civilisation. The English love of order, neatness and the picturesque are exemplified well in the description of houses outside Madras in the late eighteenth century. In this, as much as social conditions, they are remote from the realities of Indian life: '. . . every house on the plain was illuminated. Each family, with their friends, were in their open porticoes, enjoying the breeze. Such a scene appears more like a tale of enchantment than a reality, to the imagination of a stranger just arrived . . .'[17]

But the enchantment also had its limitations to the majority of the Indians whose own differences of taste were no less well-defined and exclusive:

The fact that we eat one dish – ham and eggs – is alone sufficient to alienate us from both [the Muslims and Hindus]. The Hindu regards the egg of a fowl as defiling; while a Mahomedan's disgust for an eater of pork is too well-known to be a matter of special comment . . .[18]

And it wasn't only a question of what we ate, or how we ate . . . but the constant consumption of alcohol.

The fact that throughout the nineteenth century at least the majority of English and Indians could not eat at each other's houses played a considerable part in confining the contacts between the communities to official business. In particular, the problem of pollution proved an intractable difficulty. Even the casting of a shadow was sufficient to cause a strict Hindu considerable embarrassment in terms of purification. Only when the Mutiny made it a matter of life and death did a magistrate like Mark Thornhill find himself for the first time, after seventeen years, inside a Hindu house. He admits that he was

almost entirely ignorant of how the natives lived and was even
surprised to find that they did not use knives and forks. In the
eighteenth century when social relations between the communities were more relaxed, the rigidities of religious belief
seem in many cases to have been temporarily waived, particularly by those in larger cities. But as other factors began to
estrange the communities in the course of the nineteenth
century, such beliefs could be used as an excuse, and a reason
for the English to remain at a distance. It was easy enough for
a man to argue that he saw no reason to be sociable with
another who would not eat at his table, or introduce him to his
wife. Intolerance when it grew had plenty of food to ripen on.
And in fact the problems of contact with women who had spent
all their life in the *zenana*, even if they had been accessible, were
daunting enough to deter all but the most intrepid - like Fanny
Parkes whom we shall meet again later on. English women,
for their part, resented the fact that they were regarded as
utterly depraved by Indian princes when they went dancing
with men in public. On 10th November, 1837, Emily Eden
wrote of a reception in Dinapore: '. . . there were some rajahs
in splendid dresses; such magnificent jewels, and some of them
had never seen an English ball before. They think the ladies
who dance are utterly good for nothing, but seem rather
pleased to see so much vice . . .'[19] By the end of the nineteenth
century progress was already being made by Indian women
themselves towards a new and larger enfranchisement. They
were starting to be trained as doctors and nurses and teachers;
the problems of the *zenana* itself were attracting the energies
of women like Cornelia Sorabji.* But changes of this sort were
only just beginning to make their impact on the social life of
Anglo-India by the time of the First World War. The Quin-
quennial Report for 1917-22 showed that among Hindu girls in
that year only 0·9% were going to school; and among the
Muslim population 1·1%; of those attending school 40% had
not reached the stage of reading printed books.[20] As has often
been remarked, the enclosed life that many women lived in the

---

* Cornelia Sorabji was among the first Indian women to qualify as a lawyer. In
the early part of the century she devoted herself in particular to the status and
problems of Indian women (see her autobiography, *India Calling*, 1934).

zenana did not prevent them from exercising a great deal of power over their husbands, and consequently on the world outside. But as with the problems of food and drink, caste and pollution, the possibility of any natural social life between the majority of people in either community was ruled out. The nautch* was the most common form of entertainment at which both communities would meet; but that, though it might have been a bridge, did not on the whole prove so![21]

*

None of the problems so far discussed was as universal or as absolute as that of language. It affected every kind of social relation and prescribed limits to almost all forms of contact. To begin with, the majority of Englishmen did their trading on the basis of a kind of pidgin Portuguese. The gradual introduction of more English words turned this into the curious hybrid of Indian English which even the adoption of English as the official language of India in 1835 did little to rob of its self-contained peculiarities. During the period of the British presence the attitude of the English towards the learning of Persian, Urdu, Hindu, as well as the numerous other languages and dialects in the sub-continent varied as much as the talents of particular individuals.† Any discussion of the barriers created by the absence of such linguistic skills can only be usefully carried on in particular instances or contexts. But because of the problem's centrality in the past, and in the present, a few general observations may be useful in suggesting a perspective.

The ability to master and converse in a foreign language is a rare gift; and the number of men, even of good-will and industry, who achieve it will probably always be limited. The analogy between language and music is a close one; words, like notes, convey feeling in themselves, *and* in their sequential relation. When we speak of a man having a good ear for languages, we mean much more than his ability to reproduce a particular sound accurately; we refer also to that inner ear for something approaching a precise equivalence between one

---

* An entertainment with dancing-girls, especially common in the eighteenth century.

† At the beginning of the twentieth century, 179 separate languages and 544 dialects had been established.

language and another. The man who is naturally multi-
lingual will not translate in his mind from one language to
another, but express himself in the idiom of one language or
another according to his situation. At sophisticated levels of
communication, even he may be more adept in one language
than another, for the simple reason that those feelings and
intuitions which make us individuals are not only determined
by environment, and that modes of expression natural to a
particular individual may for complex historical reasons find
their outlet in one language rather than another.

Once these difficulties, not peculiar to Anglo-Indian civilisation, are accepted, then two major facts about language in that
environment begin to settle into perspective: first, the very
remarkable fluency in English achieved by large numbers of
educated Indians from the mid-nineteenth century onwards
(again, the origins of this will be considered in their proper
place); and second, the particular nature of the botch which
existed on both sides at lesser levels of expertise. At no time did
the majority of the English achieve anything more than a
rudimentary knowledge of any native language; and after the
official adoption of English as the language of India in 1835, the
incentive to do even this diminished, except among the more
dedicated members of the Indian Civil Service; among some, in
the period of Empire, it even became part of the attitude of
racial superiority not to learn the language of the 'damned
niggers'. From the earliest times the peculiar nature of the
Anglo-Indian situation had necessitated the partial invention
of a new language, now enshrined in *Hobson-Jobson*, a dictionary of Anglo-Indian terms, and the necessary glossaries to
many works of Anglo-Indian literature. Charles Dickens's
journal, *Household Words*, found this a particularly irritating
aspect of our Empire in the East, especially at the time of the
Mutiny. On 3rd October, 1857, it commented: 'When the
English in a station escape to the cutchery,* it would surely be
desirable to know what sort of a place that may be, and whether
our apprehensions ought to be increased or allayed by the fact
of the said cutchery being pukka.'[22] But the use of new and
'barbaric' terms by the English in India, as part of their

* 'cutchery': usually, a court-house.

response to the uniqueness of their situation, indicates at a superficial level problems of communication not only between them and people at home, but also with those Indians who, for practical or private reasons, had acquired some fluency in English. With them such terms were shared; but much that was natural to them in forms of feeling, and modes of courtesy, found, because they had, no natural equivalent in English. The very first letters written by a Moghul Emperor, Jahangir, to King James I must have caused even that learned Majesty some surprise in their translation from Persian: 'When Your Majestie shall open this letter, let your royall heart be as fresh as a sweet garden; let all people make reverence at your gate ... Let your Majestie be the greatest of all monarches, who may derive their counsell and wisedome from your brest as from a fountayne . . .'[23] In the light of Jahangir's treatment of his ambassador, Sir Thomas Roe (to whom we shall come in the next chapter) King James may have found it a rather notional metaphor that the Great Moghul claimed to fix his eyes upon him, 'as upon a rose in a garden'.[24] The boundary between decorum and insincerity is a subtle one; and in an environment where the English from the start thought the behaviour of the natives in business matters to be characterised by duplicity, the problem of difference in conventions acted severely upon the problem of communication. Floridity and extravagance in speech has rarely appealed to the English temperament; and it did so less in the nineteenth than the seventeenth century – a time when formal and decorous modes of address were still used. Difficulties of this sort applied equally to public and private relations. At one of his durbars, Lord Auckland remarked that he hoped the deputation had not suffered from the rain. They replied that 'the canopy of friendship had interposed such a thick cloud that their tents had remained quite dry.'[25] In fact, the tents had become so soaked that it was necessary for the visiting prince to hire a house. At best the English were irritated by what they considered to be 'flowery nonsense'; at worst it intensified a feeling of mistrust and estrangement. In the happiest circumstances, clever interpreters developed the knack of turning six dozen pearls into one dozen pebbles; but in the everyday relationships between ordinary people such skills were not available to make conversation an easy and natural affair. Inadequacy of mastery on both sides exacerbated the problem of lack of natural equivalents for modes of expression; and all too frequently the English in their position of authority vented their irritation in blows.

But like many of life's serious problems, that of the limits to human communication set by the barriers of language in Anglo-India, can often be seen most clearly in humorous examples. If I were learned in Persian or Hindi, I could parallel them no doubt with comparable mistakes made by Englishmen who acquired some fluency in these languages. But the point I wish to stress is how particular idioms distort the tone of a language, and so, while the meaning is clear enough, communication will inevitably remain an elementary thing. As the letter from Jahangir to King James illustrates, it is not only education that counts, but a comparable education rooted in circumstances of personal and cultural similarity. And these never existed in Anglo-India, although for a short time some Indians lived, wrote and spoke as though they did. The first example is a letter to a collector's wife from the shop-keeper who had supplied her Sunday joint:

Honoured Madam,

Madam's butler says that madam is much displeased with poor butcher, because mutton too much lean and tough. But sheep no grass got, were get fat? When come rain, then good mutton. I kiss your honour's pious feet.

> I have the honour to remain, madam,
>> Yours affectionate butcher,
>>> Mahomed Cassein.[26]

Next, a testimonial to the efficacy of a patent medicine, printed in an English newspaper:

Several of my friends and myself have been using your ——— for over four months for Influenza, Lumbago, Dyspepsia, Syphilis, Rheumatism and Nervous Debility with complete success. There has not been a case in which it failed. I will call it an Ambrosia.[27]

And last, the reply of a student when passing out of the Mahometan College, Ambala, to a question as to what he had derived from it:

When I came here I could not speak English; religion was a mystery to me; I could not even handle a lawn-tennis bat.[28]

In the last, it is not only the mistake which counts; but a tone which is both English and un-English at the same time, for reasons that would not be easy to identify, but involve a different mode of thinking and feeling. At this level, the way in which we talk is often closely related to the existence of feelings of friendship and trust, or their absence.

But communication, of some sort, in shared or half-shared languages, existed for the most part as a twilight on the edge of an extensive night. Among the majority of people outside the larger communities English was unknown; and while a magistrate might conduct his business in the local language, his pleasure and his social life became increasingly in the course of the nineteenth century a version of the way he would have lived in England. In a situation of such limited linguistic and social possibilities, no close rapprochement between the two communities was likely to occur; and the kind of civilisation they shared was inevitably restricted. Again, it would be difficult to assess the degree to which lack of sufficient familiarity with what was being said around them contributed to a common enough dislike of Indian life among the English; but failure to comprehend is never a long way removed from fear:

It certainly is tiresome not being able to speak the language of the country one lives in, but as for attempting to learn their gibberish I can't. I get such horrible fits at times (particularly when I'm driving out) of thinking that we are gone back to an entirely savage state, and are at least three thousand years behind the rest of the world. I take all the naked black creatures squatting at the doors of their houses in such aversion, and what with the paroquets, and the jackals, and the vultures which settle in crowds on the dead bodies that are thrown on the banks of the river, and what with the climate and the strange trees and shrubs, I feel all Robinson Crusoeish. I cannot abide India.[29]

An excess of emotion here serves to highlight a reaction experienced in a modified form by many.

At this point the problems of language must be left until they arise in particular contexts; but as the last paragraph also shows, the absence of a common language for communication precipitated what was perhaps the most recurrent English comment on Indian life: a sense of exile. Whether people actually liked India or not, there were very few indeed to whom it became a home. In the early Company days, men looked forward to the acquisition of a sufficient fortune to enable them to live like gentlemen (or Nabobs) in England; under the Empire they looked forward to their retirement on a pension. With improved means of communication and more frequent furloughs, a sentence of a lifetime's exile was reduced – and the necessity for a sense of belonging to India was diminished. In one respect, it would have been odd if an awareness of exile had not played over the Englishman's life. The longing of Odysseus for his home-land and hearth; of the Seafarer for his companions in the Hall are impulses so deeply rooted in the human consciousness that circumstances, however strong and favourable, are unlikely to overcome them. Much in the circumstances of Anglo-Indian life offered no compensation, or was actively hostile to the Company man or Empire builder. The work could be exacting and monotonous, the climate a challenge which had to be overcome, before the predictable human problems began. The records of those who lived in Calcutta or Madras speak time and again of the indolence and inertia which settled upon them in those climates. And the feelings of the wretched Eleanor in W. B. Hockley's novel *The English in India* (1828) will be appreciated by anyone who has spent even a short time in a hot and humid climate: 'At breakfast, Eleanor sat a silent spectator, appetite was banished, leaving nought but languor and inertness: such is the debilitating influence of the heat over the faculties of both mind and body.'[30] Those who were burdened with too much work could, and all too often did, destroy themselves or their health in a climate to which few adjusted easily. The penalty for living the wrong way was paid by many besides the surgeon of an Indiaman who 'fell dead after eating a hearty dinner of beef', when the thermometer was 98° in the shade.[31] Less drastically, but not less significantly, the climate must take a share of the blame for that proverbial English irritability,* which all too often ended up in a physical abuse

* Proper hot-weather clothing has only been developed in the recent past; the lack of this aggravated the situation.

of the natives. For a sharp insight into the psychological effects of the Indian heat on an isolated hard-working European, I know of none more powerful and horrifying than that in Kipling's, 'At the end of the passage.'

The men flung themselves down, ordering the punkah-coolies by all the power of Hell to pull. Every door and window was shut, for the outside air was that of an oven. The atmosphere within was only 104, as the thermometer bore witness . . . The punkah flagged, almost ceased. The sweat poured from Spurstow's brow. Should he go out and harangue the coolie? It started forward again with a savage jerk, and a pin came out of the towels. When this was replaced, a tom-tom in the coolie lines began to beat with the steady throb of a swollen artery inside some brain-fevered skull. Spurstow turned on his side and swore gently. There was no movement on Hummil's part. The man had composed himself as rigidly as a corpse, his hands clinched at his sides. Spurstow looked at the set-face. The jaws were clinched, and there was a pucker around the quivering eyelids.[32]

Kipling takes to an extreme, for his own artistic ends, the effect of the heat of the plains on a man who suffers from isolation and insomnia. What he incidentally brings out is the exceptional pressures and hardships which Anglo-India involved for many who went there, and the inevitable effect this had on their relationship with the people of India, as well as their attitude to it. It would be unhelpful to try to distinguish between a natural longing for home, and a dislike or unease in the land of one's exile. But certainly those who felt a positive affection for India are the exceptions, even among those who served her best. Sir John Malcolm, among the most remarkable of the Company men, wrote on his way to take up his post as Resident in Mysore in 1803: 'I shall continue to do my utmost till I am a pensioner, which I shall be in 1806 . . . Nor is it in the power of gold to bribe me to longer banishment . . .'[33] A few years later the young Charles Metcalfe, destined to become Governor-General, recorded much the same feeling: 'Here it is a perpetual banishment . . . But if a man is to slave all his life, he had better do it in my opinion, in his own country, where he may enjoy the society of his friends, which I call enjoying life.'[34] Even the good Bishop Heber bore frequent witness to the bitterness for him of being banished from his own land:

> Yet who in Indian bow'r has stood
> But thought on England's 'good green wood?'
> And bless'd, beneath the palmy shade,
> Her hazel and her hawthorn-glade.
> And breath'd a prayer, (how oft in vain!)
> To gaze upon her oaks again?[35]

In addition to the rigours of the Indian climate, the landscape itself often appeared impoverished and dreary. The conventionally romantic view of India as the Taj Mahal, Darjeeling, Simla, or in the valleys of Kashmir bore no resemblance to the physical landscape in which many English people passed their lives; or the drabness they endured. In 1878 the Chief Criminal Court for a district of over 6,000 square miles with more than four million inhabitants looked like this: 'The walls *had* been white, but were now of various hues of black and dirty brown. Ink seemed to have reached everywhere, even to the punkah, which, in this, the cold season, hung motionless and dirty over Darville's head . . .'[36] An alien landscape, an exacting routine, an arduous climate were sufficient in themselves to awaken a longing for home; but another and more sinister companion looked over the exile's shoulder and intensified a desire to escape. That companion was death; and it came, as the quotation from Honoria Lawrence at the start of this chapter illustrates, with a speed and unexpectedness sufficient to unnerve even the robust. Cholera carried off countless victims in a few brief hours; those who died in the morning would be buried before supper. India meant for a great number of English people not a licence to make money, or an opportunity to serve the Queen, but a death-certificate; even among those who survived there were many more whose health was permanently ruined. Anxiety concerning disease left no one untouched; and its effect was intensified by the prolonged absence and parting which Anglo-Indian life meant for many families – especially in the second half of the nineteenth century when it became common to send children home at the age of seven for education. It was no mere nostalgia that made Alfred Lyall write in one of his elegant lyrics:

> Listen and linger – she yet may find me
>   In the last faint flush of the waning light –

> Never a step on the path behind me;
> I must journey alone, to the lonely night.[37]

Kipling put the matter with more masculine optimism:

> The Exiles line brings out the exiles' line
> And ships them homeward when their work is done.[38]

It did, if they were lucky.

The British presence in India was brought about and maintained for economic profit.* Critics of imperialism, like W. S. Blunt, who visited India in 1879, lost no time in pointing out that our presence could only be justified if this meant the profit of India and the Indians. As he observed it didn't. He was oppressed and horrified by the endless squalor which surrounded the worthless ostentation and extravagance in much European life. His response was shared by many others including Ramsay MacDonald, Aldous Huxley, and George Orwell who concluded some sixty years later:

> Once check that stream of dividends that flows from the bodies of Indian coolies to the banking accounts of old ladies in Cheltenham, and the whole sahib-nexus, with its haughty ignorance on one side and envy, and servility on the other, can come to an end.[39]

Of course, as he also knew, it was not as simple as that. Economic factors alone did not account for the ignorance, nor was the sahib-nexus only a matter of dividends. The interest of the Anglo-Indian relationship is not to be reduced to a matter of exploitation. Different ways of life, forms of belief - differences in what men do when they are not working, and what they work at, and in the modes by which they express their inherited traditions - all form part of the interwoven pattern which constitutes and divides a shared civilisation. While not denying the importance of economic factors in determining the quality of that civilisation, this book will not primarily be concerned with them.

* Before the First World War (and in the second half of the nineteenth century) 'the key to Britain's whole payments pattern lay in India, financing as she probably did more than two thirds of Britain's total deficits.' (S. B. Saul: *Studies in British Overseas Trade, 1870–1914*, 1960, p. 62). The ruin of the Indian cotton-spinners, in the earlier part of the nineteenth century, by export of raw cotton to Lancashire is also well-documented.

It is impossible to think of India for long without recalling the swiftness with which almost all human things decay in it. As that wilderness of tombs outside Delhi powerfully reminds the traveller today, it is in the nature of India to assimilate its conquerors, and also destroy them. There is no place in that land for the vanity of belief in the permanence of human greatness; but as clear a summons as anywhere in the world to the necessity for human endeavour.

Chapter 2

The Single Spies

I'll have them fly to India for gold,
Ransack the ocean for orient pearl.
CHRISTOPHER MARLOWE, *Dr Faustus* (1588)

High on a throne of royal state, which far
Out shone the wealth of Ormus and of Ind,
Or where the gorgeous East with richest hand
Showers on her kings barbaric pearl and gold,
Satan exalted sat . . .
JOHN MILTON, *Paradise Lost* (1667)

ON the morning of 5th April, 1584, three Englishmen broke their bail in Portuguese Goa, and made their escape over the River Mandavi into the territories of the Moghul Emperor, Akbar. To avoid the possibility of pursuit and arrest which meant certain death, they left behind their possessions, except for a letter of greeting from Queen Elizabeth of England to the ruler of lands on which no English eyes had previously looked. Without maps or guide they fled into the unknown, convinced only that their fate ahead could be no worse than that which they would ultimately suffer at the hands of the Portuguese Viceroy, who had had them arrested on the correct suspicion that they were spies for the English. Only one of these men was to reach home seven years later, bearing news of a country of 'infinite riches', which Portuguese cunning was keeping concealed.

But the surprise of those three adventurers on that morning in April at what they saw would not have surpassed their astonishment at the course of events which slowly and deviously would result from their escape. As in individual lives, so in the destiny of nations, it is on occasions the chance-encounters from which new rivers start to flow; and if here in the

tiny catalyst, the origin of a vast change involving the lives of
many millions of people can be seen, then it is to the body on
which it worked this change that our attention must first be
directed.

From the start it was the state of India that determined the
nature of the English relation with it, as much as the aims and
ambitions of the English within it. At the moment when the
three Englishmen made their appearance the power of the
Moghuls was rapidly spreading through the northern part of
the continent; that power was in the following century to
waste itself in an attempt to subdue the south. In the decline of
their rule emerged the 'little rift within the lute' through
which another imperial dream came slowly and inevitably to
be born.

In the history of sixteenth-century India three kinds of
people stand out with particular sharpness in their relevance
to the arrival of the English: the Portuguese the Moghuls and
the Jesuits. The discovery of the sea-route to India by Vasco da
Gama in 1498 had enabled the Portuguese to establish a rich
and varied trade with the continent of India. From their port
at Goa they traded both on the Malabar Coast and inland with
the Hindu city of Vijayanagar, for more than two centuries the
ruling power in the south. But in 1565 Vijayanagar was sacked
by Muslim forces in the Deccan; and within two years only
'tigers and wild beasts' dwelt there.* From this time too the
decline in wealth of Portuguese Goa also set in. On a larger
stage the destruction of relatively stable power at Vijayanagar
brought no hope of peace for the people of southern India.
The triumphant Muslims in the Deccan were unable to re-
concile their conflicting interests, and the rulers of individual
states turned from the common Hindu enemy to fight each
other. It was a pattern of political instability upon which
Aurengzebe, the last Great Moghul, was to attempt to impose
his authority, and fail. Such conditions of war and anarchy
were not confined to southern India; but it was to be significant
for the English that the lack of any real control over those
large areas of land caused the Moghul authority to extend and

* The story of the rise and fall of Vijayanagar is well told by Robert Sewell in
A Forgotten Empire, 1924. See, in particular the account of Domingo Paes.

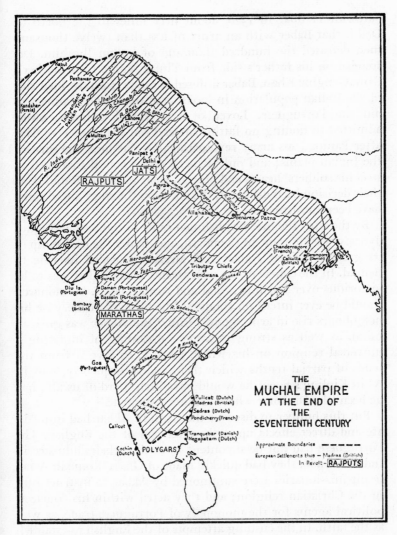

THE
MUGHAL EMPIRE
AT THE END OF
THE
SEVENTEENTH CENTURY

Approximate Boundaries ━ ━ ━ ━ ━
European Settlements thus — Madras (British)
In Revolt — RAJPUTS

expend itself in them. But all that lay some hundred years in the future.

Of more consequence for the English at the time of their arrival was the strength of Moghul authority in the areas where they would first come to trade. Even that possessed a shorter history in India than Portuguese power. It was at the

battle of Panipat in 1526 about fifty miles to the north of
Delhi, that Baber with an army of less than twelve thousand
men defeated the hundred thousand of Sultan Ibrahím. De-
scended on his father's side from Timur, and on his mother's
from Genghiz Khan, Baber differed as much from the majority
of the Indian population in looks, traditions, and manners as
did the Portuguese. Lover of battles and gardens, Baber
admitted to finding no faithful friend but his soul. Five days
after Panipat, his army revolted against the heat and dust of
the Indian plains; and only Baber's direct appeal managed to
steel his soldiers' hearts and prevent their return to Kabul. Had
their decision been different, the effect on the story ahead must
have been incalculable.

By the time the first Englishmen came to India, the Moghul
dynasty was supreme in the north, and, under the leadership of
its greatest prince, Akbar, had already extended its rule to
Bengal. In the course of the next twenty years Akbar was to be
victorious over Kashmir, Sind and Ahmednagar. 'A monarch
should be ever intent on conquest,' he believed, 'otherwise his
neighbours rise in arms against him.'[1] But Akbar was great in
mind, as well as strong in arms - dreaming of imposing a
universal religion on his whole Empire, to save it from the
feuds of partial truths which then, and subsequently, rent it.
As in Kipling's poem he would have been 'Lord of us all', had
he been 'the Dreamer whose dreams come true.'[2]

But this hunger to discover the truth in Akbar had immediate and direct effects upon the reception of the English. The
Portuguese had not been content to confine their influence in
India to trade; they had quickly made of Goa a 'Rome in Asia'.
Jesuit missionaries were summoned by Akbar to instruct him
in the Christian religion; and they acted within his court, as
political agents for the monopoly of Portuguese trade, as well
as the faith. In the ensuing attempts of the English to establish
trade-relations, the presence of the Jesuits was to provide both
Akbar, and his successor Jahangir, with a standard by which to
measure the new Europeans in his land, and a diplomatic excuse
for not coming to terms with them at once. Advantage accrued
to the English in 1612 when the Portuguese fleet was defeated
off the coast of Surat before the eyes of thousands of inhabitants

- a tale which excited the admiration of Jahangir because he had formerly believed them to be invincible at sea, from which he knew he needed protection. In addition, the Portuguese did the English a good turn by seizing a ship belonging to Jahangir's mother, and refusing to restore its cargo. A second naval defeat for them at the hands of the English in January 1615 gained the unusual distinction of being noted in the Emperor's Journal.*

These factors formed the contours of the landscape in which the first Englishmen made their appearance. The early travellers, unlike the majority of their successors, saw India without preconceptions about it - and with few expectations as to what they would find, except in terms of proverbial luxury and wealth. Consequently, there exists in their first impressions evidence of particular interest concerning the problems which might arise when one civilisation met with another in greater numbers, and in more complex relations. The prejudices with which they judged, or some of them judged, what they saw, bore the mark of their Elizabethan or Jacobean upbringing. But both of those had more in common with the attitudes of nineteenth-century Englishmen than with the predominant characteristics of life in India. Before returning to look at these first responses in detail, it is worth recalling one notable difference between this chapter and all that follows. Only here is the setting the Moghul Court. The early Company settlements came to be sited around the coasts, with trading-posts inland. The conditions of life which Company men saw and endured were not those which reflected what was best or highest in Moghul India. Their impressions were formed in places constantly under the threat of war and plunder; and as time went on, with the loss of the stabilising effect of Moghul authority. In the twilight of an important dynasty no nation is likely to show itself at its best, nor to provide invigorating examples of its own native greatness. From the death of Aurengzebe in 1707, until the commencement of the renais-

---

* It is clear from the records of Akbar's and Jahangir's reigns that the embassies from England did not attract much attention. The slight interest in the English for the next 150 years meant that Indian 'attitudes' to the English are not often recorded.

sance in Bengal about 1820 India lived through a dark century. The sack of Delhi in 1739 by Nadir Shah, the Bengal famine of 1769-70 which killed a high percentage of the native aristocracy – to say nothing of the feudal wars within the land itself – meant that the rise of British influence coincided with, though was not directly related to, an increasing 'social and political bankruptcy' in the northern part of the continent.[3] These were not propitious circumstances either for the establishment of good relations between the English and the people of the country itself; or ones likely to impress the English settlers with the civilisation or culture of India. It required the rediscovery of the Indian past, in terms of religion, literature, and architecture, to modify the prevailing view of it as a country that had not yet learned to rise above the level of barbarity. In the Moghul court at least the early travellers had the advantage of seeing a high point of that civilisation which existed around the Emperor, and which made even of the final puppet Emperor, Bahadur Shah, 'a poet and man of culture.' Much of the early and formative attitudes to India might have been different, if the emphasis had been less remotely commercial, and more men had had contact with the traditional culture which existed around the Court at Delhi.

But, in one respect at least the English expectations of India were not disappointed; even before the publication of Ralph Fitch's report on his preliminary reconnaissance, visible proof had been discovered of the wealth to be derived from trade in the East. The capture of the *Madre de Dios*, a massive Portuguese carrack, in 1592 by Sir John Burrough revealed seven stories of Indian cargo. When this was catalogued on 15th September at Leaden Hall, London, it was valued at £150,000. The cargo contained, amongst other things, jewels, spices, drugs, silks, calicoes, quilts, carpets, dyes, elephants' teeth, porcelain vessels, and coco-nuts.[4] The legendary luxuries of India which had formed part of the Western European imagination since they were incorporated into the accounts of classical writers had now become fact. The gorgeous East had shown that she could indeed shower on her kings 'barbaric pearl and gold'; and Fitch's account of his visit to the court at Agra and Fatephur Sikri, although disappointingly lacking in any information about Akbar himself, confirmed the legend about oriental opulence, at the same time as it illustrated a field of endeavour from which the English were as yet excluded. Around his court, Fitch claimed, the King kept a thousand elephants, thirty thousand horses, fourteen hundred tame deer, and eight hundred concubines.[5] That was not a bad start; but the Emperor's court also attracted the merchants of Persia and India who traded in rubies, diamonds, pearls, silks and cloths of all kinds . . . In an age when a new English middle class were looking for fresh fields of economic expansion, the rewards were too large to be resisted for long. On the last day of 1599 the East India Company was granted its first royal charter for trade by Queen Elizabeth I.

But Fitch's account was not confined only to material profit. His journey down the Ganges had been like a trip into the pagan past where the world still retained the monstrous colourfulness and distortion that Christian civilisation had modified. The idols 'are black and have clawes of brasse with long nayles, and some ride upon peacocks and other foules which be evill-favoured with long hauke's bils . . .'[6] Their mouths are 'monstrous, their eares gilded, and full of jewels, their teeth and eyes of gold, silver and glasse, some having one thing in their handes and some another.'[7] The tone of contempt is not hard to detect under the amazement; and in less gilded situations this predominates without concealment. In Patna he sees a 'false prophet' who sits on a horse and pretends to be asleep while the people touch his feet with their hands, and then kiss them. 'They took him for a great man,' Fitch remarks; 'but sure he was a lasie lubber.'[8] His sympathy with religious customs in India is by no means improved by witnessing a Hindu wedding, or the self-immolation of a widow on her husband's funeral pyre (*suttee*). In the latter case, what had been a mixture of irritation and dislike of pagan habits, becomes a moral disgust for the practice of a rite which offends his basic human principles. Until its abolition in 1829 by Lord Bentinck *suttee* remained one of those issues which symbolised a major difference between East and West in ethics and belief.

Among the first of the English agents to arrive in Agra, after the granting of the charter, was Sir John Mildenhall. He got there in 1602 to find the Jesuits at the court implacably opposed to the Emperor's allowing the English to trade. They claimed that the English were a nation of thieves; that Mildenhall was a spy; and that once Akbar had granted the English friendship they would come in great numbers, and seize his ports.[9] The Emperor's own position was sufficiently novel, in the face of these requests for trading rights, to make him want to move with caution, and play one side against the other. Mildenhall claimed that the Jesuits turned Akbar wholly against him, until he himself pointed out that their hostility was depriving Akbar of the princely gifts he would otherwise receive from England. Whether or not Mildenhall did secure some kind of local agreement with Akbar remains in doubt. Mildenhall fell out of favour with the Company; and Akbar died in 1605. It was left to the next emissary of King James, William Hawkins, to start the negotiations again with Jahangir, which he did between 1608 and 1611. Hawkins marks the appearance on the scene of a type who was to become common enough: the adventurer determined to 'feather his nest' as well as 'perform his Worship's service.' Like many of his successors, Hawkins adopted an oriental style of life - and lived with a splendour which would have been inconceivable at home. Trained in the Levant, fluent in Turkish, Hawkins quickly won his way to Jahangir's confidence; and for two and a half years lived in daily contact with him, dressed as a Muslim nobleman, and known popularly (and unpopularly) as the 'English Khan'. Jahangir enjoyed his company and conversation, sharing, with his father, an interest in the life of Europe; he provided Hawkins with an Armenian girl as wife, to prevent him from being poisoned;* and command of four hundred horse, or the equivalent of an income of £3000 a year. Every evening Hawkins drank and talked with Jahangir, while pursuing his real end of the trade agreement he wanted. As might be expected, his behaviour did not meet with the approval of his contemporaries. Roberte Coverte observed with notable guardedness that he seemed 'very willing to do his country good';[10] but John Jourdain thought him as 'fickle in his resolucion as alsoe in his religion for in his house he used

---

* She was in charge of preparing his food.

altogether the customs of the Moores . . .'[11] Hawkins went his own way, not caring a fig for the opinions of such men, or for those in the court, both Muslim and Portuguese, who 'envyed much that a Christian should bee so nigh unto the King'.[12] Jahangir played his game skilfully, protecting his drinking companion from being murdered, forcing Hawkins's political opponents in the court to curb their cheating of him, when it became too blatant, and at the same time constantly shifting his position about the permission to trade. It is to be said for Hawkins's integrity, as well as his business sense, that when he saw he was not going to get this, he decided at once to go home with his wife; and leave these 'faithless infidels' to their own devices. As for many other Englishmen, it was to be a fatal return; the English Khan died off the Irish coast, leaving his wife to the mercies of a land where she was a stranger. What Hawkins wanted from India was particular; in the attempt to achieve it he was quite prepared to go along with native customs. But his adoption of Muslim dress, and his appreciation of Muslim cooking were all part of the role he had chosen to play; like the fancy-dress put on for a ball it disappeared once midnight had struck.

The concern which Hawkins shows in his journal for the murderousness, treachery and corruption in the court reflects differences of a more important sort, which eventually caused him to give up, and developed in his successor, Sir Thomas Roe, an undisguised dislike of Asiatics.[13] Roe was made of sterner stuff than Hawkins; the excesses of an eastern court held no pleasures for him; and his rejection of the gift of a whore was no less vigorous than his assertion that he had come for 'Justice'.[14] Roe was not a man to admit interpretations of his word. Its meaning was no more to be argued about than the preposterous notion that he should sit on the floor. Different customs meant much the same to Roe as barbarism; and he missed the conversation of 'those friends I love and honour',[15] even though Jahangir at nights could be very affable. Otherwise, he found in Jahangir's love of bloody sports, in the prevalence of bribery, and the lawlessness of life within, and outside, the court, the cause for a deep personal estrangement from the land to which he had come as he explains to King

James: '. . . the Government so uncertayne, without written law, without policye, the Customs mingled with barbarisme, religions infinite, the buildings of mudd . . . that eaven this greatness and wealth . . . is here . . . almost contemptible and turnes my eyes . . . with infinite longings to see your Majesties face and happiness'.[16] His quickly formed moral disapproval, and even contempt, for the Oriental character as he saw it, is often paralleled later, and paradoxically among those who in fact achieved most, like Clive, Wellesley, Dalhousie and Curzon. But Roe succeeded where Hawkins had failed. By the time he left in 1619, the English presence was officially accepted; they had been granted permission to hire a house for a factory, and govern themselves according to their own religion and laws. In return, Roe had given a written undertaking that the English at Surat would do no wrong or hurt to any.[17] A fundamental and significant shift had taken place in the relationship between England and India; but not one which carried with it the promise of any easy or close understanding.[18]

The sorrows of Roe's four-year stay were deepened by the death of his English cook;[19] and sufficient lack of comforts, as well as consolations, to make him feel his own standards of conduct threatened. By 1618 he is writing: 'Pray for us that God will be Pleased to keepe us, that among the heathens wee may bee as light in darkness; at least that wee shame not the light . . .'[20] His view of the country as heathen was based not merely on its 'religions infinite' and its idolatry, but upon the relation to them of its moral practice. 'All cunning that the Divell can teach is frequent,' he wrote, 'eaven in the court wher is wanting noe arte nor wicked subtilty to bee or doe evil.'[21] Such feelings were closely related to his slow progress in the negotiations with Jahangir; but that does not conceal the more radical and less easily soluble differences of attitude and belief which caused such a conflict. Respect for one's enemy can go a long way to making the battle with him one that is based on mutual understanding; or perhaps is a precondition of such understanding. But Roe altogether lacked this respect.

His chaplain, Edward Terry, while no more sympathetic than Roe to what he sees as notorious and 'stupid idolatries'[22] is yet able to view them with a detachment that arises from his lack of involvement with Moghul politics. On the one hand, he objects – as many did after him – to the intransigent acceptance of practices inherited by tradition; it is not only too bad that people believe as they do; but worse that they never ruminate on what they maintain, 'like to unclean beasts which chew not the cud.'[23] This did not prevent him from observing and admiring the austerity of religion practised by many Muslims, or from recognising the strength of social practice to which it was united. The Muslim habit of having more than one wife at a time was not likely to be changed by the preaching of an alternative faith; especially when the practice of that faith by most Christians in India was characterised by debauchery. What led the irritable Roe to contemptuous dismissal brought the more reflective Terry to the recognition that the differences between the two civilisations were so acute that while they might be disguised for political ends (for instance, in tactical conversions to Christianity) no easy or swift means existed to change or eradicate them.

Terry, with his unbigoted, if not open, mind became a great admirer of Muslim architecture; like Roe himself, he appreciated much in the Indian landscape. Occasionally, they made excursions to places of interest – for instance, one of the Emperor's pleasure-houses near Ajmere. The house contained a 'handsome little garden with fine fountaynes . . . a place of much melancholy delight and securitye, only being accompanyed with wild peacockes, turtles, foule and munkyes, that inhabitt the rocks hanging every way over yt.'[24] Happy occasions of this sort were, however, rare breaks in a life that was arduous and uncomfortable. The estrangement of feeling which both Roe and Terry experienced in varying degrees proved difficult to overcome. The only personal friendship which Roe formed of any warmth was that with Mir Jamaluddin Hussain, a septuagenarian politician and soldier who had served under Humayun and Akbar. Roe appreciated in him those qualities which he honoured in his own background: courtesy, lack of personal ambition, good manners, hospitality to strangers and straight-forwardness (not especially common in the Moghul entourage). Hussain in his turn helped Roe in the conduct of his negotiations, pointing out his grave disadvantage in relying upon court-interpreters to translate what he said to Jahangir, and urging him to find an Englishman sufficiently learned in tongues to ensure his arguments were not misrepresented.

To Roe's puritan temperament, life in the Moghul Court offered little cause for gladness and delight. Its exotic magnificence and wealth was made to seem the more questionable by the obvious close presence of much that was morally and physically squalid. Like the abandoned city of Fatephur Sikri, what should have been a centre of civilisation appeared as a haunt for 'thieves and wild beasts'.

I have left to the end of this chapter an account of the man who in some respects remains the most unusual and certainly the most spectacular of these early travellers in India: the 'Odcombian Belgo-Gallico leg-stretcher', Tom Coryat. (He came from Odcombe in Somerset, and had made his reputation by his account of a walking-tour round the continent which he had done on one pair of shoes.) Not content with this feat, Coryat had decided to walk to India to see the great Moghul in all his glory, and ride upon an elephant. He took three years to walk there, spending little more than twopence a day; and both his ambitions were fulfilled.

Tom Coryat, friend of Ben Jonson, and himself a 'great and bold carpenter of words' was 'the tongue-major' of every company he found himself in. Language like distance, provided no obstacle to him. He mastered Turkish and Persian before his arrival in India, and soon added Hindi. Like Hawkins - and to the mortification of Roe, with whom Coryat's stay at the court coincided - he insisted on wearing native dress, and showed off his Persian to the Emperor by making him an oration, for which he was thrown down a hundred rupees. Roe with a characteristically strait-laced sense of propriety objected to one of his fellow-countryman presenting 'himselfe in that beggarly and poore fashion to the King, out of an insinuating humor to crave mony of him'.[25] Coryat quite rightly gave Roe a stout and resolute answer, with a temerity that he displayed equally in his dealings with Indians, as the following anecdote bears out. A Mahometan in Mandu was foolish enough to call Coryat an infidel - meaning, of course, that he was a Christian. A common language of Italian having been established,

Coryat treated him to a homily against Mahomet and his accursed religion, which ended up with a very neat demonstration that in fact the Mahometan was an infidel, and Coryat a Musulman or true believer. His castigations of the Mahometan faith in public would have resulted in a lesser man's being roasted on a spit for his views – as Coryat himself observed.

But the very proficiency of Coryat in languages serves to illustrate how much in Indian life remained at a basic level unpalatable, or worse, to European tastes. During the course of his travels, Coryat witnessed the Hindu bathing festival at Hardwar; and his attitude to that was no less incisive than his view of Mahometanism:

This shew doe they make once every yeere, comming thither from places almost a thousand miles off, and honour their river as their God, Creator and Saviour; superstition, and impiety most abominable in the highest degree of these brutish ethnicks, that are aliens from Christ and the commonwealth of Israel.[26]

Throughout his letters he refers frequently to the meaning and significance for him of Christ, and of the holy places of the Christian religion which he had visited on his journey to India. His description of himself in that country as a 'desolate pilgrim' conveys more than a rhetorical flourish – and ironically underlines the speedy end to which his adventures were brought. As his friend Terry put it, he 'overtook Death in the month of December 1617' and was buried on the banks of the Tapti near Surat, 'under a little monument, like one of those are usually made in our church-yards.'[27]

In varying degrees Coryat, Terry and Roe all show how in an age when religious beliefs were strongly held on both sides, they inevitably acted as a cause of estrangement. The recurrent hostility of these first English travellers, both to beliefs which they regarded as heathen, and to the social behaviour which they judged by the standard of Christian ethics (whether or not commonly practised by Europeans) indicates in isolation a tension which the complexities of institutionalised power were often to conceal, but never entirely eradicate. The single spies before the big battalions came had the advantage of seeing India without preconceptions about it; in their accounts, their freshness of vision survives them.

Chapter 3

'A company of base quarrelling people'

Who shall doubt the 'secret hid'
  Under Cheops pyramid
Was that the contractor did
  Cheops out of several millions?
RUDYARD KIPLING, *Departmental Ditties*, 1886

I can say with truth that the Christians who served in
the artillery of the Moghuls retained of Christianity
nothing but the mere name, were worse than the
Mahometans or Hindus, were devoid of the fear of God,
had ten or twelve wives, were constantly drunk, had no
occupation but gambling, and were eager to cheat
whomsoever they could. For these reasons the Farangis
(Europeans) have not in the Moghul country the
estimation they formerly had.
N. MANUCCI, *Memoirs of the Moghul Court, 1653–1708*

All distant power is bad.
SAMUEL JOHNSON

DURING the century and a half between the conclusion of
Roe's embassy in 1619, and Edmund Burke's appeal to the
House of Commons in 1783 that the cries of those whom our
rule in the East oppressed, should not go unheard, the nature
of the English relationship to India both expanded and changed.
Not only did the number of Company servants slowly increase,
but the wars with the French in the 1740s and 50s extended the
size of the Army. The gradual modification of social life which
an increase in the size of the population and securer conditions
brought about will be returned to. But before that, three
changes of the central importance need to be stressed. First, the
power of the Moghuls effectively came to an end in the civil
strife of the years 1759-61.[1] Second, Clive's defeat of French
ambitions under their great leader Dupleix enhanced the

reputation of the English throughout India[2] while the Treaty of
Paris in 1763 reduced French power in India to a level which
left England without any serious European rival. Third, the
grant to Clive of the twenty-four Pergunnahs[3] in 1757, and the
right to collect and administer taxes in Bengal, Behar and
Orissa which was conceded by the Moghul Emperor, Shah
Alam, in 1765, extended British wealth and power to an unprecedented degree. The anachronisms of the situation soon
made themselves felt. The precariously established early settlements had become part of a military and economic network
which, as its power and size extended, gathered into its administrative and moral jurisdiction an increasing number of people
whose civilisation and even language was still largely unknown to the new rulers of the land. In addition the administrative and executive powers required for controlling an
Empire of this sort did not exist until the India Acts of 1773,
1784 and 1793 began to create them.

In the course of the eighteenth century both Madras and
Calcutta had grown in size and importance. Calcutta in particular had been transformed from a few huts on a malaria-
infested swamp to a city of palaces which aroused the admiration of all who saw it. The social life of the English had evolved
from austere beginnings to a mode of existence renowned for
its extravagance and dissipation; the fortunes won and lost
were of legendary, though not fictitious, size, and the Nabob
had become on the boards of the theatre at home a figure
renowned for his vulgar ostentation. In the splendour of his life
in Berkeley Square, Clive confirmed the more dazzling aspect
of the popular image.

But in spite of all these changes in the mode of English life, a
century and a half had passed without any serious questioning
of the nature of the relationship between the two communities,
and lands. The Company was a trading concern, with no political ambitions beyond those which helped to secure its commercial interests. Until Clive startled men with his success in
war against apparently insuperable odds, and Burke started to
fulminate against the exploitation of a 'people for ages civilised
and cultivated', India provoked little interest in those at home.
Likewise the Company's agents confined their attention to the

prosperity of their commercial ventures, quarrelling with those, whether Indian or English, who impeded their progress towards the attainment of a fortune sufficient to enable them to return to their native land, and live in comfort upon it. After Burke, and the impeachment of Hastings, the conscience of all thinking men was at least made aware of the obligation to India which the conduct of the Company's affairs included. The over-all effect of this on Company policy may not have been large; but a new attitude had now become apparent. The time had passed when the Indian problem could be regarded as belonging only to the Moghul, while the Company concentrated on preserving its commercial interests against the increasingly divisive forces at work in India itself. This change improved the quality of British-Indian life and rule; but it also pointed clearly in the direction of Imperialism. The awareness of a changed role, apparent towards the end of the eighteenth century, emerged in a society which had formed not only its own identity, but equally had started to adopt attitudes and prejudices about Indian life, which were in turn reflected in the opinions of the Indians about the English.* It is with the origin and growth of these attitudes that this chapter will be chiefly concerned.

Both inside and outside the Company settlements, life for many was 'nasty, brutish and short'. There was violence in the land where lawlessness and anarchy succeeded to Aurengzebe's declining power. Contesting princes sought to extend their rule and wealth, without reference to the cost in life or well-being of their subjects. Among the Company factors greed for personal gain (the highway to survival through escape) led to unscrupulous behaviour from which the natives themselves soon learned how to profit. The times were not propitious for a man to think too deeply about his situation, or the country he plundered. The 'cormorant pouch of death' swallowed many who had arrived in the hope of a fortune; and while the Company's regulations attempted to place every kind of Christian restraint on its agents, under pain of being sent home, nothing favoured the over-nice. Only those who had

---

* See, for example, the quotations from Mir Kasim and S. G. Hossein Khan on pages 61 and 64 respectively.

Jesuits at the court of a Moghul Prince

(a) Jahangir (1605-1628)

(b) Sir Thomas Roe

(c) Coryat on his elephant

Three common objects of
English hostility:

(a) *Fakir*

(b) *Suttee*

(c) Hook-swinging Festival

Masulipatam, near Madras: a Company trading-station in the later seventeenth century

come out young enough, it was said, not to have developed a taste for English life, were likely to find any happiness in India.[4] Of course specific conditions varied from place to place and year to year; in the early years Surat was a quiet enough trading place, while Bengal rapidly acquired a reputation for licence and violence. But the expansion of the Company's trade occurred in the general context of a precariousness that few wished to prolong, or entertained sanguine hopes of surviving, if they were compelled to.

Surat, the major trading-post and port one hundred and sixty-miles to the north of Bombay, was regarded by John Ovington when he visited it in the later part of the seventeenth century as a good example of a cosmopolitan mart. He noted that as well as the European traders, there were merchants from Persia, Arabia, China; and the incidence of crime very low; none had been put to death for twenty years. He attributed this to the 'inoffensive conversation of the Gentile Indians who are very apt to receive, but seldom to give an abuse.'[5] But the days of Surat's importance were already numbered. In 1664 and 1670 Surat had been sacked by the leader of the Mahrattas, Sivaji; and the merchants lived constantly under the threat of the confiscation of their goods or money by the Emperor or his representative. The acquisition of Bombay from Charles II* in 1668 gave the Company an island which could be more easily defended from the forces of the Moghul and the Mahratta, as well as a natural harbour for trade. But the decision to shift the centre of influence from Surat to Bombay by no means brought a quieter or easier life for the Company's servants. Intrigue and ill-treatment of the militia caused a rebellion in 1684 which added to the already large problems of obtaining food from the mainland, now dominated by the Mahrattas, and the effect of the unhealthy climate which put an end to many a poor sailor and soldier who paid with their lives for the hopes of a livelihood. The life-span of the English was also reduced, according to Ovington, by their luxury, immodesty and dissoluteness. In addition, their avarice, envy and a thousand other black infernal vices also added to the insecurity which resulted from the

---

* Charles II had acquired it as a wedding-gift with Catherine of Braganza in 1661. He leased it to the Company in 1668 for £10 a year.

permanent threat of war. It was scarcely surprising, though of no comfort, that the English cemetery was 'never satisfied with the daily supplies it receives.'⁶

Inland, the frequent revolts and wars made the life of the Indian peasant a matter of fear, poverty and famine. The persecution of the Hindus by Aurengzebe also forced many of them to seek refuge in the English island. But religious toleration was not in itself enough to maintain the livelihood of the community, and throughout the greater part of the eighteenth century the importance of Bombay declined. It was not until the power of the Mahrattas was eclipsed in Wellesley's* and Hastings's† wars at the beginning of the nineteenth century that the fortunes of Bombay under its well-known Governor, Jonathan Duncan‡, began once more to revive. As late as 1825 a minute of the Council recorded: 'For a century and a half Bombay has been of little importance to the Company. A settlement on the coast of Africa could scarcely have been of less consideration.'⁷ But though Bombay remained small and provincial, it was not untypical of the unheroic tenacity which went into the making of the Empire. The man who lived, and often died, in the obscurity that came to Bombay in the eighteenth century represented the firm foundations on which imperial dreams were later built, and like the dreams, the foundations had little more than a geographical connection with India. The situation as J. H. Grose saw it in the mid-eighteenth century indicated no hope of reconciliation between the communities: '. . . There is no such thing as either quarrelling with the Mahrattas to advantage or trusting to them with safety, nor indeed seeing any end of this dilemma.'⁸ It was not until the opening of the Suez Canal in 1869 that Bombay's fortunes fully revived.

The decline of Bombay had been matched by the rise of

---

* Richard Wellesley, 1760–1842, appointed Governor-General in 1797, and established his fame through his victory over Tippoo Sultan at Seringapatam in 1799.

† Hastings, 1st Marquess, 1754–1826, distinguished himself in the American War of Independence. In 1793 he succeeded his father as 2nd Earl of Moira. A close friend of the Prince of Wales, he took an active part in English and Irish politics, before he was appointed Governor-General and Commander-in-Chief of the forces in 1813. He finally put an end to the power of Mahrattas.

‡ Jonathan Duncan, 1756–1811, had made his name while Resident at Benares for his work in helping to suppress infanticide.

Madras and Calcutta. The circumstances, internal and external
to them, did not encourage reliance upon the country where
they were established. The life of the founder of Calcutta, Job
Charnock, is indicative of the attitudes and values which underlay the growth of English society in India. Charnock won a
rare degree of approval from the Company in London; but his
success, if larger than many of his contemporaries, does not
provide obvious material for the English *Æneid*.

Charnock turned up in Bengal in the mid-1650s. How he got
there or why he came remains part of his legend; but some
years later he was admitted to the Company's service. Unlike
Roe, or the early well-known Governors of the Company
factories, Gerald Aungier, Streynsham Master, and Josiah
Child, Charnock was neither well-bred nor educated. A rough
fierce man, he was well-suited to the opening up of Bengal - a
part of the country which Akbar himself had described as a
'hell full of good things'.[9] The hell consisted not only of the
disease-ridden islands and swamps on the Gangetic delta, but
the lawlessness of the country, and the treachery of the local
ruler, the Nawab of Bengal. His perfidy, Charnock soon
realised, was too subtle for any argument except the sword; and
this he was able and willing to use. Fluent in Persian, and
informed about the topography of the country, Charnock
showed a resource in times of war that matched his skill in
local negotiations. Thomas Bowrey, who travelled much in the
last thirty years of the seventeenth century around the Bay of
Bengal paid him this tribute:

The English Chiefe (by name Job Chanock) hath lived here many
years and hath learned the Persian (or Court) language as perfect as
any Persian borne and bred, and hath lived wholy after their customs
(save in his religion), by which he hath obtained vast priviledges and
love of the Grandees that sway the Power of the kingdome, and is
dayly admitted into the Nabob's presence.[10]

Charnock was a man who got what he wanted. The authoritarian vigour with which he ruled his settlements was based
on a crude but effective ruthlessness. When an ignorant native
broke his laws, Charnock would have him whipped - and 'the
execution was generally done when he was at dinner, so near

his dining-room that the groans and cries of the poor delin-
quents served him for music.'[11]

A law unto himself in his punishment of natives, Charnock
also showed no prejudice. For fourteen years he lived happily
with a 'Gentu'* woman, had several children by her, and on her
death built her a tomb, on which, it is popularly related, he
sacrificed a cock each anniversary of her death. Charnock was
from all accounts not a likeable man; but he knew nothing of
that unwillingness to soil his hands with native life that became
a deeper evil in the future. In his view that 'a fort was worth
more than an ambassador'[12] he expressed the truth about life
in Bengal in the later part of the seventeenth century, as he had
personally experienced it in prison and war. It was a place and
time in which the fittest survived. Charnock proved himself one
of them.

Strife just as bitter went on in the Company's factories,
reflecting in internal dissent the tone of life in the Company's
relations with India. Sir Streynsham Master, Governor of
Madras from 1675-80, recorded how the Company's servants
vied with each other in lining their own pockets, and made
charges of peculation against one another when they appeared
to be failing. To make things worse both the local government,
and the Company's servants were quite willing to take advantage of any circumstances that occurred for 'personal gain or
private revenge'. Alexander Hamilton in his *New Account of the
East Indies* (1727) regarded the corruption, bribery and treachery
among the English as part of a pattern of behaviour shared by
all the traders in India, whether Portuguese, Dutch or native.
Zeal in trade, intensified by a desire to leave the country with a
competent fortune, inspired the Agents of the Company with
a competitiveness among each other that left little time for
the consideration of any large problems concerning their
presence in India, or their effect upon the native population.
A governor and superintendent of the Bay, like William
Hedges, in the early sixteen-eighties, had his hands more than
full in dealing, or trying to deal, with the growing exactions of
the native rulers, with the interlopers who attempted to break

---

* 'Gentu': a 'gentile' or heathen which was used of the Hindus as distinct from the
Moors or Mahometans.

the Company's monopoly in trade (which survived until 1813) and in combating the indiscipline and unfaithfulness of the Company's servants. Hedges left India in 1684 with a relief in which he was not alone:

I blesse my God, the Creator of Heaven and Earth, who has been graciously pleased to carry me through so many troubles and afflictions of diverse kinds, to see this joyfull day; maugre all the plots and contrivances of my implacable enemies, President Gyfford, Agent Beard, Mr Charnock, and the rest of that wicked confederacy, out of whose hands he hath been pleased to give me deliverance.[13]

Like Charnock, Thomas Pitt - the grandfather of the Earl of Chatham - was another man of haughty and daring temper, who by force and ability rose to a position of prominence as Governor of Madras in the early years of the eighteenth century. He publicly declared his distrust of the Moghul Government whom he suspected of wanting to make war; and advocated a policy of keeping order by force: 'I hear in Bengall that they chawbuck* Englishmen in their public durbars, which formerly they never presumed to doe, and the Junka-neers† all over the country - are very insolent, only those within our reach I keep in pretty good order, by now and then giving 'em a pretty good banging'.[14] Pitt's concern with India, like those of his contemporaries, was restricted to Company and personal affairs. He was a man of sufficient energy and vision to recognise the adversity of the circumstances which faced the Company, and to do all in his power to improve them. Unlike many of the Company's other servants Pitt possessed great ability at running their business, and making money for himself. The story of his acquisition of the Pitt diamond which was subsequently to make its way into the Crown jewels of France remains one of the more romantic tales of the period. A practical man of affairs Pitt had no time or concern for the country he was in. He held as low an opinion of the Brahmins as he did of the Moghul Government: 'They are rogues enough and study nothing else but cheating'.[15]

This contempt for the natives left little incentive for explor-ing the culture to which they belonged. Life in the interior was still largely unknown to the Company's servants; and the

* Chawbuck: whip.   † Junkaneer: a collector of transit duties.

communities which they inhabited were ones in which the
natives had every enticement to duplicity. Even those, like
Alexander Hamilton, who did manage to travel more widely
saw little to impress them. A lack of civil order, the ubiquity of
robbers on the road, the prevalence of theft and murder – all
bore witness to a civilisation and nation in a state of decline.
At Gujerat, Hamilton commented on the old religion of
paganism – and the old trade of thieving and pirating, for 'they
plunder all whom they can overcome'.[16] Rule by the sword was
the norm of the day; and all were trained in the art of killing.
If the men were defeated in a skirmish, their wives wouldn't
cohabit with them until their honour was regained. It was a
situation which must have caused honour frequently to oblige.
The hostility that often led to bloodshed between the Muslims
and the Hindus was also apparent to him. Furthermore at Goa,
which was still the centre of Catholic civilisation, he saw the
corruption of the values for which Europe was meant to stand
in the East. The church acted as a sanctuary for thieves and
murderers, while the Church Vermin, whom he numbered at
30,000, lived idly and luxuriously on the labour and sweat of
the miserable laity.[17] Among that laity the most violent crimes
were condoned, if material gain was achieved by them. Wars
and feuds between local rulers, pillage by Mahratta freebooters,
paganism and superstition of all sorts built up a picture which
if it did nothing to excuse the behaviour of the English in a
wild and uncivilised land at least explained the circumscription
of their horizons.

Feud, faction and treachery, then, were part of the daily lives
of the Company's servants both within and outside their
factories. The rules which controlled them were strict in relation to personal behaviour – such as drunkenness, blasphemy,
fornication, abuse of natives – but difficult to administer in
relation to matters of trade, with the Board of Directors a year's
correspondence away in London. The problems of trade too
were exacerbated by the changing attitudes of native princes,
which became more volatile with the decline of Moghul power;
and the threat under which all the Company settlements lived
of war and destruction. The incident of the Black Hole of
Calcutta (1757) exemplifies the instability and insecurity that

persistently threatened the lives of the Company's servants, and those of their wives and children. Bengal was renowned for its violence and dissoluteness; but Madras suffered too. In 1769 and 1780 the houses which the English had built for themselves on Choultry Plain outside Madras were ransacked by the forces of Hyder Ali, just as Calcutta had been plundered a few years earlier by Suraj-ud-Daula. The English responded often enough with behaviour no less notorious, as Mir Kasim pointed out to the Governor of Bengal in 1762:

And this is the way your Gentlemen behave; they make a disturbance all over my country, plunder the people, injure and disgrace my servants . . . Setting up the colours and showing the passes of the Company, they use their utmost endeavours to oppress the peasants, merchants and other people of the country . . . They forcibly take away the goods and commodities of the peasants, merchants, etc., for a fourth part of their value, and by ways of violence and oppressions they oblige the peasants to give five rupees for goods which are worth but one rupee.[18]

Such were the conditions of lawlessness, together with death by disease, under which the presence of the English in India was established. There was much truth in the metaphor which Clive used of the Augean stable that needed to be cleansed; and this had to involve the restraint of the Company's servants in their own private trade, by paying them adequately for their services, as well as the maintenance of order by a strong military force.

But while neither the conditions under which the Company servants worked, nor the anarchy within India itself favoured the growth of mutual respect between the communities, a number of other factors made it conceivable that a closer rapprochement could occur, and larger understanding grow, once the problems of distant and dissolute power had been resolved. The attitudes that favour the growth of sympathetic appreciation of differences were apparent at least in the early days of the Company. The communities lived for the most part separately (for reasons which were given in Chapter 1) but this did not as yet imply an assertion of racial superiority; and the English had not as yet developed any prejudice against much in the Indian way of life. The Englishman smoked his hookah, wore Indian clothes, and often enough had a *zenana*. And although the problems of caste made social contact with the Parsees or the Muslims easier than with the Hindus, little serious hostility seems to have arisen from this. Local princes gave public breakfasts, dinners and nautches, to which they would invite their English neighbours. John Fryer records how the Muslims would drink no wine publicly, but 'privately will be good fellows'.[19] They were even not above eating ham. The English for their part would go out to eat with them, and enjoy their 'pilaos and biraunis'. Even more important than these social contacts was the existence of a basic respect for customs or beliefs which the English did not happen to share. At Surat, Ovington noted that the chapel in the factory contained no sculpture of any living creature so as not to give offence to the Muslims.[20] An Englishman who wanted a drink on the road from a high-caste Brahmin would consent to lie down on his back while the water was poured into his mouth, so that he did not defile the vessel by the touch of his hands or his lips.[21] A magistrate touring his district in the 1770s might be compelled to sleep in a cow-house so as to avoid contaminating the human accommodation. It does not seem to have worried him greatly, provided he and his office were treated with dignity and respect.[22] And although the English were not to be deterred from their hunting, the Hindus at Surat at least felt able to offer them money not to take pot-shots at the pigeons.[23] A rough kind of mutual toleration existed then which was later to be buried by far more rigid racial attitudes.

In clashes with authority the native might expect a rougher kind of justice than the European. The Magistrate at the Black Town in Madras was in the habit of flogging, imprisoning or fining the natives at his own discretion while the Europeans were entitled to trial by judge and jury.[24] At the same time, the European who assaulted an Indian was liable to be fined £5 and set in the stocks all day. The good behaviour that was expected of the Englishman on pain of being sent home reflected the Company's awareness that they were only in India under sufferance. By the last quarter of the nineteenth century, the situation had been almost reversed. The death of an old man from injuries received after being assaulted by two Europeans because he happened to be riding a horse when they were standing could go unpunished.[25]

But these examples of limited social contact and mutual tolerance need to be set against forms of behaviour that were to bear more sinister fruit. The determination of the Company that their servants should uphold the good name of Christendom in heathen lands made them insist upon the observance of Sundays, and that they should maintain the right public image when they left the factory. Whenever any of the Council did, they went well-attended, with servants on their coach. This creates, Ovington observes, 'a respect from the natives . . . and makes them value our friendship and place an Honour in our intimacy and acquaintance.'[26] The desire for friendships was not one which many were to share at a later more complex stage of the relationship. But in each of the presidency towns the pomp that surrounded the Governor's appearance became part of the ritual of Company life. Charles Lockyer in his *Account of the Trade in India* (1711) describes the Governor's entourage in Madras flamboyantly:

The Governor seldom goes abroad with less than three or four score Peons arm'd, besides the English guards to attend him, he has two union flags carry'd before him . . . he is a man of great parts, respected as a Prince by the Rajahs of the country, and is in every respect as great: save, those are for themselves, this has masters . . .[27]

With the gradual increase in English power, magnificence came to be regarded as a fitting emblem of the conquering race.

Prolonged contact also did not help to diminish the dislike which many Englishmen felt towards habits and customs that were alien to them. Edward Ives cites the chewing of betel which 'occasions them to be continually spitting', the length of their nails, and the blackness of their teeth as especially 'disgustful' to the European.[28] According to the natives, he comments, 'white teeth are only fit for dogs and monkeys, and long nails shew they have not been accustomed to do servile offices.'[29] Two other factors, though, were undoubtedly of more significance than differences of this sort. First, the apparent discrepancies in moral standards. As we have already seen, there was something anomalous in English attitudes here in that while they were driven to sharp practices by the conditions of their employment, they nevertheless regarded their own moral standards as beyond reproach, while the Hindu traders were persistently regarded as an absolute 'map of sordidness'. In part, the English dislike of Indian trading habits stemmed from the prevalence of bribery. This custom affected every kind of negotiation from an audience with the Emperor to securing the neutrality of a local prince in the wars against the French. But this was only one factor in a general evaluation of the natives as untrustworthy. 'It would be too mean to descend to indirect ways,' writes Fryer, 'which are chiefly managed by the Banians,* the fittest fools for any deceitful undertaking.'[30] Grose comments on the impossibility of trusting the Gentus† from day to day. Verelst complains of the Bengalis that they scarcely require the use of the English name to 'prompt them to every villainy',[31] while Macaulay's celebrated indictment of Nuncumar becomes, as only Macaulay could make it, the damnation of a people: '. . . Large promises, smooth excuses, elaborate tissues of circumstantial falsehood, chicanery, perjury, forgery, are the weapons, offensive and defensive, of the people of the lower Ganges . . . In Nuncumar, the national character was strongly and with exaggeration personified.'[32] The indictment of a people through the example of an individual showed Macaulay's historical method at its least sympathetic. Neither the English traders nor the native had much to congratulate themselves on in terms of the morality of public life. The English were described by one native as men who would eat and fight everything. This low opinion of the English was corroborated by S. G. Hossein Khan, the author of the *Seir Mutaqherin* (c. 1786), as well as the more honest company servants and travellers. After conceding that the English might alleviate the sufferings of the people of this land, S. G. Hossein Khan went on:

They are come at last to undervalue the Hindustanees, and to make no account of the natives from the highest to the lowest; and they carry their contempt so far, as to employ none but their own selves

---

* Banians: a Hindu trader; sometimes used of Hindus generally.
† Gentus: see p. 58.

in any department and in every article of business, esteeming themselves better than all others put together.[33]

This contempt was coupled in his view with an aversion for the
society of Indians, and a disdain against conversing with them,
so that both parties remained ignorant of each other's state
and circumstances. As early as 1780 this aloofness was making
it difficult for 'even the most illustrious' Indians to approach
the Governor, and causing the decisions of the English to be
made without any real knowledge of the concerns of the people.
The dangers of such a trend were exacerbated by the short
length of time which many Englishmen stayed in the country,
and their lack of affection for it. Even the fortunes which they
made were spirited away to England as soon as possible so that
they did no good to the country where they were earned.

These criticisms by the author of the *Seir Mutaqherin*, which
are of special interest for the paucity of detailed Indian comment upon the English, were soon to find monumental expression in the oratory of Burke.* But the author of the *Seir* speaks
also of what Burke could never know in England – the degree to
which the isolation of the English community was causing a
break-down in normal human relations, and obstructing that
harmonious partnership which might have made Anglo-India
a civilisation of a different order. William Mackintosh, who
was in India in the 1780s, recognised the damage which the
English were doing to themselves:

If the British nation would derive all the advantages from the soul
of Hindustan, and the ingenuity of the natives, which they were
capable of yielding, they must resolve to treat the Hindus, not as
slaves or inferior animals, but as fellow-men, entitled to protection,
liberty and justice.[34]

Lack of trust in the natives formed one aspect only of a
generally unfavourable opinion of them, which was commonly
found in the seventeenth and eighteenth centuries, whether the
subject was a prince or a trader. A contemporary description
of Sivaji, the Mahratta leader, in 1664 typifies the conventional

* Growing public concern in England over the behaviour of fellow-citizens in the
East is reflected in the fact that the translation of the Abbé Raynal's critical *Histoire
philosophique et politique des Etablissements et du Commerce des Européens dans les deux
Indes* went through twelve editions between 1776 and 1794.

attitude: 'He is distrustfull, seacret, subtile, cruell, perfidious, insulting over whomsoever he getts into his power.'[35] Habits, as well as personalities, elicited the contempt of the English for 'semi-savages and mere idolators'.[36] The hook-swinging festival, corruption among the *fakirs*, the hospital for fleas (which were given free medicine in the form of beggars) as well as *suttee* itself exacerbated feelings of dislike which became particularly virulent in relation to the treatment of the sick. The sick person was carried down to the Ganges, where his head was lifted back and river water poured down his throat until his belly swelled. Sometimes mud was clapped over his mouth . . . while his family sat round howling. Practices of this sort did not endear India or its people to the European; but it took that shrewd Scot, Alexander Hamilton to recognise the central significance of a common language in the establishment of good relations. 'One great misfortune that attends us European travellers in India, is, the want of knowledge of their languages, and they being so numerous, that "one intire century could be too short a time to learn them all". '[37] Among the Indians he could not find one in ten thousand who could speak intelligible English.

The Company itself had recognised the importance of its Agents' competence in native languages; but its policy of additional emoluments for those who proved their proficiency had only met with mild success. The Hindu traders themselves did not encourage it as they recognised that a man who could speak their language was as good as a spy. They revealed quite quickly an aptitude for poisoning those who pried too closely into their affairs; and an able linguist was inevitably suspect.[38] In spite of the Company's offer of additional pay, most preferred safety to conversation. Other less sensational reasons existed as well. The Company's agents were men in a hurry. Their energies were directed towards the acquisition of a fortune large enough for retirement. And though the really successful were far less common than the dead, the degree of success could be exceptional. One Mr Farrer, for instance made £80,000 as a barrister in three years.[39] Thomas Pitt's acquisition of the Pitt diamond established the family fortune for generations to come: and in the English shires the larger country houses often showed the rewards of a brief but energetic Indian career. It was neither a country nor a climate in which the tortoise was likely to win. It was on the whole quicker, easier and safer to acquiesce in the pidgin language which the merchants employed, than waste energy in the acquisition of a language or languages which would not bring the goal of escape appreciably closer. The degree to which inertia and indifference also affected this issue can be seen in the fact that in the year 1776 when the Company was engaged in negotiations with the Moghul at Delhi it could find no one capable of translating Persian documents. All this was to change in the course of the next thirty years; but still it remained the case that for the first two hundred years of the English presence in India communication through a common and sophisticated language remained confined to a very few people indeed.

What followed from the inability of most English people to converse fluently in any native language was the separation of business life from social pleasures; and this in turn was intensified by the religious taboos on the Indian side. But also a matter of economics was involved. From the earliest days of the Company settlements travellers had remarked on the good eating and drinking which went on in the factories: often too good for the climate. At Surat, in the 1680s Ovington describes the pleasures of the table like this: 'And that nothing may be wanting to please the curiosity of every palate at the times of eating, an English, Portuguese, and an Indian cook are all entertained to dress the meats in different ways for the gratification of every stomach.'[40] At home the factors often ate English style, but followed their guests' tastes when they went out. In Bengal in the early part of the eighteenth century, Hamilton observed that most gentlemen and ladies lived both splendidly and pleasantly. In Madras some fifty years later Ives remarked that 'many of our countrymen residing there, to maintain their dignity among the natives, live in all the magnificence of the east.'[41] But already it is possible to detect a difference between the dignity which the early Governors wished to show as Christian gentlemen in a heathen land and a more purely social ostentation that reflected a growing social and economic inequality. Ives implicitly recognises this in his contrast between the houses of the English and the natives in Madras. 'The buildings where the English only reside are handsome, and built in the modern European style; but the homes of the Black Town are very low and flat-roofed.'[42] The miserable conditions under which the poor lived were overpopulated and uncomfortable. When Charnock first established his small band of followers in the three villages that were to become Calcutta, the English lived in huts that were probably little better than those of the natives, which one traveller referred to as 'hog-styes'. But the immense rewards of successful trade had rapidly changed the original austerity of factory life, and in various forms marked the change in European circumstance. By the mid-eighteenth century almost all the Europeans resident in India kept their own palanquin;* and were surrounded by numbers of servants.[43] The Indians, by division of labour, made it necessary for the European to employ as many of them as possible. Even when living by himself William Hickey kept as many as sixty-three servants and Philip Francis cites an occasion when there were 110 servants to wait on four people. Hickey himself found it agreeable to have 'every wish . . . in a great measure anticipated by being gratified before announced.'[44] But others thought it a mixed blessing. Mackrabie, secretary to Philip Francis, laid the blame on the natives themselves:

The cursed examples of parade and extravagance they are holding up for ever to us. 'Master must have this. Master must do that.' A councillor never appears in the street with a train of less than twenty fellows, nor walks from one room to another in his house, unless preceded by four silver staves . . . What improvement India may make in my affairs I know not, but it has already ruined my temper.[45]

In Calcutta, in particular, the grandeur and scale of living ruined many men for life almost as soon as they stepped on shore, and accumulated large debts at exorbitant rates of interest. The outward picturesqueness of the city of palaces was undoubtedly a seductive façade; but like the *Lorelei* its song lured many to their destruction. Hickey's friend, Bob Pott, who was fortunate enough to get the lucrative post of Resident

---

* palanquin: 'a box-litter for travelling in, with a pole projecting before and behind, borne on the shoulders of 4 or 6 men.'

at Murshidabad, exceeded even the usual Calcutta extravagance.
As he went out every morning, he would have the grand staircase lined on both sides with salaaming servants, and a party of
light horse waiting to accompany him to Berhampore.[46] It
wasn't long before he went bust.

Such style and splendour of existence could scarcely be more
different from that in the early factories, where attendance at
divine service, celibacy, restraint from drunkenness were demanded as conditions of continued service. No one was even
allowed to live outside the factory without permission.[47] In
many respects the way of life of the early factors at its best
resembled that within a monastery. Few traces of that austerity
remained in the lives of Englishmen towards the end of the
eighteenth century:

About the hour of seven in the morning, his durwan (door-keeper)
opens the gate and the viranda (gallery) is free to his circars, peons
(footmen), hurcarrahs (messengers or spies) chubdars (a kind of
constable) houccaburdars and consumahs (stewards and butlers)
writers and solicitors. The head-bearer and jemmander enter the
hall and his bedroom at eight o'clock. A lady quits his side and is
conducted by a private staircase, or out of the yard ...[48]

Things had changed since the early days at Surat when on
Friday nights the agents had met together after prayers to
drink a health to their wives. But in fact women had remained a
problem; and several expedients had been tried. In 1640 in
Madras a policy of inducing soldiers to marry native women
had been adopted.[49] In 1662 Gerald Aungier, the Governor of
Bombay, had 'sent home for English wives for factors and
others'.[50] But throughout the period of this book supply continued to fall far short of demand; and particularly in the early
period the women who were prepared to come out were often
those who had been unable to find a husband at home, or enjoyed a freedom which was not at all what the more puritanical
Company servants had in mind. Sir Edward Lyttleton, president
of the Company at Hughli in 1700, was appalled by the low
behaviour of Englishwomen in the country.[51] It came to be
common for the authorities to object to what they considered
unsuitable marriages, but to accept the practice of the factors

keeping Indian mistresses, sometimes individually or else in some numbers. Of course there were those like Mr Hervey in Bengal in the 1680s who allowed pleasure to distract him from business, and thought of nothing but enjoying his little seraglio of six strumpets, and living at ease upon the Company's expense.[52] And at Barnagul near Calcutta there existed what Hamilton described as a seminary of female lewdness, where 'numbers of girls are trained up for the destruction of unwary youths.'[53] But little or no racial feeling existed about sexual relationships between Englishmen and Indian women, as was to be the case in the nineteenth century. Plenty of evidence exists for the happiness which such relationships brought, as in the case of Charnock or William Hickey, a century later, with his charming Jemdanee:

I had often admired a lovely Hindustanee girl who sometimes visited Carter at my house, who was very lively and clever. Upon Carter's leaving Bengal, I invited her to become an inmate with me, which she consented to do, and from that time to the day of her death, Jemdanee, which was her name, lived with me, respected and admired by all my friends by her extraordinary sprightliness and good humour.[54]

How different this is to the ominous opening of Kipling's tale, 'Beyond the Pale':

A man should, whatever happens, keep to his own caste, race, and breed. Let the White go to the White and the Black to the Black. Then, whatever trouble falls is in the ordinary course of things – neither sudden, nor alien nor unexpected.[55]

But although sexual relationships between the races were common, and accepted, the number of English women in India continued to increase and to modify the organisation of social life. The economic possibility of living in India in a style far grander than could have been achieved in England – together with the freedom which a profusion of servants permitted – cast the inhabitants of a city like Calcutta back on their own resources for keeping amused, to an unusual degree. In the mid-eighteenth century it was the custom for Indians to give nautches* for the entertainment of their European friends;

* Although the nautch was more common in the eighteenth than the nineteenth

Murshidabad, c. 1770 with Company boats in the foreground. When William Hickey stayed there, he enjoyed all the luxuries of the East, and described his friend, Bob Pott, as living in princely magnificence

Calcutta Cotillion, c. 1775
'. . . most people got drunk
at dinner; supper,' and what
followed 'was equally
hilarious . . .'

(a) smoking a hookah

(b) family life

(c) an exile's friends

The Old Court-House and Writers' Buildings, Calcutta, 1786

but problems of language, as well as differences of custom
tended to keep each community confined to its own amusements; and to encourage separate, if not unfriendly, ways of
life. Furthermore, the forms of entertainment which the
majority of English people selected were not those likely to
appeal to their Indian associates. In some respects this had been
the case since the earliest Company days: the favourite sports of
the factors had been drinking, hunting, hawking and cock-
fighting. In eighteenth-century Calcutta, the drinking had
remained at the top of the list which now also included gambling, dancing, and driving on the course in the cool of the
evening. In all these activities, the women participated: a form
of behaviour which was as disgusting to the strict Hindu and
Muslim, as it was inconceivable that their own wives could live
in a similar way. One example will suffice to indicate just how
wide the gulf between the communities had become at the level
of social behaviour. 'If most people got drunk at dinner, supper
was equally hilarious. At a party on November 3, 1775, at
the Claverings all the ladies drunk themselves silly on cherry
brandy, and pelted each other with bread pellets.'[56] This habit
of throwing bread pellets was a favourite pastime until one
Colonel Morrison in a fit of ill-temper at this sport flung a leg
of mutton instead, and brained his antagonist. By no means all
of the English enjoyed the normal modes of social entertainment, but few made any attempt to resist their triviality or
hectic gaiety. The pages of William Hickey are filled with a zest
for existence that half-conceals the lack of any real curiosity
about the country. When India intrudes, after the day's business
is over at lunch-time, it does so only as an irritant at the inter-
ruption of enjoyable pastimes. Hickey's *Journal* conveys with
unreflective gaiety a tempo and extravagance of life that would
have been economically unattainable, and morally displeasing

---

century as an entertainment, its continued existence and limitation was still apparent
at the time of the Delhi Durbar in 1903: 'During the Durbar wealthy natives kept
high holiday, and nautch dancers were in great requisition, this form of entertainment being to them irresistible, though quite monotonous to Europeans . . . The
music is supplied by cymbals, tom-toms, and peculiar stringed instruments which
create a tumultuous discord.' [Official Photographic Record of the Coronation
Durbar, London, 1963].

to the majority of Indians. As President of the All-Male Catch-Club he scores a big hit by introducing a new custom, which goes down very well. At two o'clock in the morning (the wining and dining having started at ten) he ordered the master of the house to produce some kettles of burnt champagne. This measure was 'highly applauded by all, particularly by Mr Platel, who declared it was a glorious thought, and that I deserved to have my name recorded in letters of gold.'[57] The custom kept the club drinking until an hour after sunrise. When Hickey wasn't drinking (and that wasn't often) he preferred conversation to the other normal pursuits of dancing or playing cards. Stakes were high, and fortunes regularly lost in an evening. This kind of extravagance was matched by the lavishness of entertainments. On one occasion, Commodore Richardson gave a splendid fête on board his ship the *Britannia* to the whole gentry of Calcutta. When the meal was over, the ladies adjourned to the quarter-deck for coffee and tea, until the dancing commenced under an awning brilliantly illuminated by many hundred coloured lamps; the men who did not want to dance remained below swilling burgundy, champagne and claret.[58] But beneath the geniality and lavishness Hickey time and again gives glimpses of the triviality, the inward-looking concern for personal scandals, and the boredom which underlay the laughter. Even more surprising perhaps is the degree to which the distance between the lives of the Indian and English communities had started to create two different standards of judgment. One year during the Mohurram festival the natives attack the court under the influence of an intoxicating drug called Bang. They are regarded as being in a state of absolute madness, although to the Indians the English must have appeared in this state most nights of the year. If the natives were incited to attack the seat of English justice, that same place was noticeably indifferent to the Englishmen who regularly ran down natives in their carriages or whipped them in the streets. The dual standard of judgment for civilised Englishmen and vagabond natives had existed for a long time in some form; but the separate ways which the two communities were now increasingly going made it harder for the English to see the reflection of their own behaviour in the clouded mirror which faced them.

The process of change in tone and attitude was neither sudden nor dramatic. It arose from the gradual expansion and ramification of Company life. More people meant less contact with anyone outside the community; and brevity of stay or death ensured a rapid-turnover in population. With little knowledge of languages and no incentive to learn them, the Englishman's view of India was restricted by the expatriate community in which he lived; and that community was more than ever likely to be one in which interests were so ingrown as to inhibit any wider curiosity about the Indian scene, even if time and methods of transport had permitted it. The records of that way of life allude all too frequently to its inadequacies:

Most gentlemen and ladies in Bengal live both splendidly and pleasantly, the forenoon being dedicated to business, and after dinner to rest . . . On the river sometimes there is the diversion of fishing or fowling or both; and before night they make friendly visits to one another when pride or contention do not spoil society which too often they do among the ladies, as discord and faction do among the men.[59]

Wrapt in itself and in its commercial ambitions, this society remained indifferent to the alien or strange.

With the conquests of Clive, and among the men who surrounded him, however, there started to grow up a new kind of awareness and responsibility towards India. India itself became a subject of debate and concern. Roughly speaking during the first one hundred and sixty years of the Company's existence this was not the case. The troubles and factions within the Company, as well as its uneasy relationship both to the court at home and the local rulers with their variable demands, had mainly confined the attention even of exceptional men to their own particular province of trade. Outside the Company territories the accelerating degeneracy of the Moghul Empire had left both the problems of central power and local authority to the direction of forces far beyond the Company's control but which nevertheless directly or indirectly affected their affairs. The depredations of the Mahrattas in Bengal in the

1740s and 1750s had reduced the land to a state of waste and pillage which could only serve to make the Company servants more aware of the insecurity of their position. But while the nature of the original trading agreements, and conditions under which the English were tolerated in India made it a matter of good sense, as well as policy, not to become involved with the affairs of a sovereign state, the growth of English life, and its inevitable contacts (or lack of them) with the native population drew men's minds to what England was giving to India as well as what she was deriving from it. To the unscrupulous, like the infamous Bolts,[60] the poverty and lawlessness of the land meant a free hand in excessive exploitation; but to men of more serious intention like Henry Vansittart and Verelst and Shore, it meant an enlarged responsibility which even without any thought of Empire could not be shirked. Until the time of the conquests of Clive, it had been true that while good men as always tried to do good, according to their lights, and bad were content to do bad, policy in India was controlled by a cross-fire between Leadenhall Street and Company agents in India (conducted over long periods of time) while the Englishmen in their several factories prosecuted Company business, and their own private trade, in whatever way local circumstances permitted. It was, to say the least, a haphazard method of control, determined by profit, and uninvolved with the administration of the country which still remained the responsibility of the Moghul. Even when Clive was appointed the Revenue Minister for Bengal, Behar and Orissa he preferred to leave British power concealed by the shadow of the Nawab's name.

But Clive also saw that in the increasingly chaotic state of Indian affairs the Company's business needed to be controlled by a powerful and efficient administration. He shared the view of many of his predecessors that Muslims and Hindus were 'equally indolent, luxurious, ignorant and cowardly';[61] and he was determined that Englishmen should not be allowed to sink to their level. Sympathetic to the victims of bad government of whatever race or religion, he believed in a properly constituted and administered authority to improve existing abuses, and prevent the worst forms of exploitation. But his contempt for the Indians, and his own love of wealth, did not in themselves promise any radical or deep change in the nature of the relationship, except as this had inevitably been altered by conquest. After his military victories over the French, the Dutch, and Suraj-ud-Daula, Clive left for England in 1760. Famous, rich, and ambitious, he looked forward to a great political future in his own country. But within four years, the precarious state of Company affairs, which resulted to a large extent from lack of control over their own agents, led to the return of Clive for the purpose of 'cleansing the Augean stable', and creating suitable conditions among the English for the pursuit of trade. He aimed to enable the two communities to pursue their own way of life independently, and without mutual contamination. Clive brought to his work as administrator the same lucidity, decisiveness and fearlessness which had characterised him as a military commander. He purged his council of those members whom he found to be corrupt, and he initiated a policy which led to the restraint of private trade by the Company's agents, and the provision of an adequate salary for them. As a man who had himself made an enormous fortune out of his Indian career, this did not endear him to those less well endowed with outstanding gifts and ability. But Clive, like other men of commanding temperament, lacked sympathy with those who did not measure up to his formidable standards.

When called to account for his period of Indian rule before the House of Commons in 1772, Clive claimed that trade was not his profession. His line was military and political . . . 'his intention to see if trade could be regulated for the advantage of the Company, and also for the Company's servants, without oppressing the natives . . .'[62] But Macaulay was right when he observed that the great difference between Asiatic and European morality was constantly in his thoughts. Clive never learned to express himself with any facility in any Indian language; and when he spoke of the natives it was with suspicion or contempt. The inhabitants of Bengal in inferior stations are 'servile, mean, submissive and humble. In superior stations, they are luxurious, effeminate, tyrannical, treacherous, venal and cruel.'[63] From this viewpoint the best that could be hoped for was a civil and military authority strong enough to control the worst abuses; and the appointment of Indian rulers who would in fact act under the instructions of the British.

Clive showed an equal severity towards the behaviour of many of the English; his criticism there, though, was levelled not at a race or nation, but at individuals. He strongly opposed the situation in which young writers to the Company could be so sure of making a fortune that they could fix upon a period for their return before their arrival; and he recognised that the shortcomings of the English in India often resulted from their being placed in 'situations, subject to little or no control'.[64] Clive, no less by his brilliance as an administrator, than by his decisiveness and tenacity as a soldier was able to restrain the excesses of his countrymen. Few have achieved as much as he did in so short a time; but it was not the warmth of human affection for the country which inspired him. He had no desire to prolong his time there; and while, no doubt, the extra-ordinary combination of his talents in bringing some kind of order to Bengal could only have been achieved by a man whose pride and aloofness gave him the freedom to wield the sword alone, the memory of him stands out with a grandeur that inspires little affection. The return to anarchy and chaos which followed Clive's departure in 1767 is perhaps partly the measure of his limitation; his authority whilst present was sufficient in itself to maintain a balance of forces; but once it was removed there remained no bondage to make the centre hold.

It was in the generation after Clive that for the first time an awareness began to be born of the distance which had to be travelled, and the ground which had to be crossed before any real kind of understanding could exist between the peoples of East and West. Then, an affection and liking for India enabled men to see how old was her culture, how strong her traditions, and how different (but not necessarily inferior) to our own her customs. India itself, its past, its geography, its variety of peoples started to become a source of inquiry. Knowledge of the country began to assert itself as a condition of Company service; and this in itself was a crucial change from the despairing attitude of Hickey's father on getting his already debauched son a cadetship in the Honourable East India

Company: 'As I find you cannot settle yourself to anything in your native land, we must try another line and another country for you . . . God grant that you may do better in future than you have hitherto.'[65]

But before coming to the time when India became a source of intellectual interest, and the English responsibility towards it, became a matter of public debate, I want to illustrate how the assumption of administrative powers by the Company inevitably brought about an increasing awareness of the complex difficulties that an encounter between the two cultures involved. In the past it had not mattered much if merchants objected in principle to Indian habits, or regarded their religion as pagan. But as the merchants became administrators of land and tax and law it became increasingly difficult for them to remain indifferent when a clash with their own convictions was involved.

It was Verelst, Clive's successor as Governor of Bengal, who devised the system of Supervisors, later to become District Officers, responsible in each province for a wide variety of duties. As well as protecting the peasant from oppression, and teaching him an affection for the humane government of the English, the supervisor was, through his knowledge of the people's language, to judge for himself how the province was to be administered. This new kind of involvement is well illustrated in the memoirs of James Forbes who reveals himself as a man attempting to envisage a common civilisation that would make it possible for the Indians and the English to participate in a shared community.

Forbes was appointed a writer in the East India Company at the age of sixteen; and shortly afterwards went to Bombay where he arrived in 1766. During his seventeen-year stay in India, the greater part of which was spent in considerable isolation, Forbes retained his own personal convictions without allowing them to harden into prejudices against those who did not share them. At the same time this did not prevent him from regarding as abuses those elements of caste which he saw as estranging man from man, or regretting how the absence of education, coupled with strong and inherited beliefs, posed a real barrier to the kind of humanitarian improvements which would have brought about a closer association between the two peoples. 'Among the inferior castes, whose minds are uncultivated, and who have no communication with the rest of the world,' he remarked, 'I found it next to an impossibility to introduce a single improvement in agriculture, building, or any useful art or science.'[66] He saw too without acrimony or moral prejudice the difficulty of changing the religious basis of life upon which many sanctions, as much as superstition, were based. 'Yet it ever was, and ever must be difficult, for either Christians or Mahommedans to convert a Hindoo; for with them theology is so blended with the whole moral and civil obligations of life, that it enters into every habit, and sanctions almost every action . . .'[67] This did not prevent him from feeling a deep-rooted aversion to the barbarism of some superstitions, such as trial by ordeal, or the commonly accepted treatment of the untouchables. Forbes, like many men inspired by the rational enlightenment of the eighteenth century, was deeply concerned with the quality of human life, and the relationship of education and religion to individual human happiness and the organisation of society. It was strong personal feeling that led him to write of the Mahomedans in old age:

With minds untaught by learning and experience, unstored by science and literature, and uncheered by a warm and benevolent religion, they have no relish for those calm delights which soften the declining path of the pious Christian, and gild the rays of his setting sun.[68]

His concern for religious consolation was paralleled by a desire for the improvement of justice and humanitarian standards which he felt to be lacking in the administration of most oriental princes. 'Far from aspiring after the happy title of the "father of his people", an Asiatic despot studies every mode of oppression which avarice can suggest, or intrigue and craftiness carry into execution.'[69] It was the amelioration of this situation which he set as his goal in his service of the Company.

After his return from furlough in 1777 Forbes was appointed to Dhuboy, where his most important work as magistrate was done. While believing in the advantages of English justice for the people of his district, he was acutely aware of the difficulties involved in administering it. It was not only that the logic and reason on which the English system was based did not have any meaning for men brought up in a different cultural context; but also that punishments appropriate in England could not be applied in India. He cites in particular the instance of a Brahmin who even if acquitted would not survive the 'ignominy of having been confined with European culprits, and criminals of the lowest castes.'[70] Caste, as already mentioned, had always been abhorrent to Forbes, on account of the human estrangement it caused; and it was here that he believed in the possible contribution of Christianity to Indian civilisation. He saw the Hindu religion, as it was practised, as being proud and uncharitable; and he regarded a religion which had resulted in the primitive and barbaric customs he witnessed as not possibly having proceeded from a pure and holy God. With this he contrasted the love and charity of Christianity; and the joy which he found in his own belief. The anomaly of his attitude is of course obvious: he contrasted Christianity as it ideally was, with Hinduism as it was practised. Had he considered, for instance, the evidence which the majority of his fellow-countrymen provided for being the beneficiaries of a religion proceeding from a pure and holy God, he might have felt his argument for converting the Hindus to be less strong. To do him justice Forbes himself was partly aware of this problem, as he records the wonder of the Brahmins that the spirit of Christianity was not the actuating principle of European society in India. What impresses about Forbes, is his concern to find a compatible scale of values, and not merely one which dismisses the other out of ignorance or prejudice.

At the same time, he ascribes a specific and practical role to the British in their activities that extends far beyond commercial gain. 'We must by our national character for justice, clemency and generosity gradually secure the gratitude and affection of the natives,'[71] and through good administration, as well as education, put an end to Asiatic despotism, venality and corruption. During his stay at Dhuboy, Forbes was undoubtedly responsible for an improvement in the poverty and wretchedness which had been caused by the recent Mahratta wars. He looked forward to a revival of science, learning and true philosophy on the banks of the Ganges. In the ruins of the Moghul empire he saw how great was the need for reconstruction, and for our commitment to the advancement of the Indian people in useful knowledge, as well as religious and moral improvement. But it is characteristic of the lack of bigotry in his mind that, in spite of his criticism of Hinduism in many respects, he asks for a piece of Hindu sculpture on his departure from Dhuboy, and with obvious sincerity recalls at a later stage the 'heartfelt delight' of his time in India. Forbes's aims were inspired by Christian convictions, and humanitarian ends: to relieve the poor ryots* from the tyranny of religious opinions, prejudices of caste and habits of oppression . . . While he thought British administration capable of achieving much in relation to the last, and regarded the first two ends as great and noble, he had no illusions about the magnitude of the task.

But it is in the larger concern with the relation of the values of one civilisation to another, and their possible beneficial effect on one another, that Forbes stands close to the vanguard of a new kind of thinking about Anglo-Indian relations. He represents a new self-consciousness about the complexity and responsibility which is involved. As yet in Forbes this is not linked to any deep feelings about the age and importance of Indian civilisation. But in the year when Forbes left India, William Jones, destined to become in the next decade the greatest of the early Orientalists, arrived in Calcutta. Forbes, in his isolation, stands out as an interesting transitional figure in the period just before the great debate over the relative merits of Eastern and Western cultures began. It was also in the year when Forbes returned home that Burke aroused the nation to the 'enormity of crimes' committed in their name. From then on, and for other reasons as well, the moderate and kindly forbearance of James Forbes was to be replaced by attitudes both more extreme and dangerous.

---

* 'ryot': a farmer, or cultivator, particularly used as here of 'poor' peasants.

Chapter 4

An Age of Enlightenment

... part of a system which I long since laid down and
supported, for reconciling the people of England to the
natives of Hindustan.
w. HASTINGS, 'Notes' on the *Gita*

... India, where gold is won by steel; where a brave
man cannot pitch his desire of fame and wealth so high
but that he may realise it, if he have fortune to his
friend ...
SIR WALTER SCOTT, *The Surgeon's Daughter*, 1827

Hast thou, though suckled at fair freedom's breast,
Exported slavery to the conquered East ...
... With Asiatic vices stor'd thy mind,
But left their virtues and thine owne behind ... ?
w. COWPER, *Expostulation*, 1782

IN the last forty years of the eighteenth century attitudes to
India among the English community began to be formed not
merely on subjective impressions and prejudice; but on a
foundation of fact that was itself the result of sustained and
serious inquiry. Increase in knowledge about India's past greatness placed its present decline in a new perspective; and at the
same time caused men to consider the nature of the English
responsibility to the country from which their wealth was
being derived. It was the dawn of a new age of enlightenment
in which the question of values as they exist in the relation of
one culture to another was raised from the personal to the
national level. This did not mean either that the attitudes of
exceptional individuals counted for less, or that, as some have
argued, comprehensive theories provided a neat framework for
individual attitudes; but it did mean that India ceased to be
merely a place for making fortunes and became a theatre of
debate about the relative values of two distinct civilisations,

and the nature of the contribution that one might make to the other. Of course, the number of people who made an articulate contribution to this debate was small; the commercial fortunes of the Company and its servants remained the predominant concern of the majority. But both of these came now to be seen in the context of larger humanitarian interests. In this chapter I intend to concentrate on two new kinds of awareness which were fostered, on the one side, by Warren Hastings, and, on the other, by Edmund Burke, with the effect of permanently altering attitudes to British India, both among those at home and abroad.

The administration of Warren Hastings in Bengal from 1772 to 1785, first as Governor and then as Governor-General, was remarkable enough for its foundation of the civil service; and the establishment of civil and criminal courts; but it is with another aspect of his achievement that I am concerned here. Proficient himself in Bengali, Urdu and Persian he regarded a knowledge of Indian culture as the proper basis for sound Indian administration. Discontent with the old type of Company servant who was as ignorant about India as he was avaricious of its wealth, Hastings started to gather around himself a group of men whose interests and ambitions extended to the accumulation of knowledge derived from 'social communication with people over whom we exercise a dominion,' which he believed would prove 'a gain to humanity.'[1]

To get the measure of the change in tone which Hastings brought about, it is helpful for a moment to contrast his personality with that of Clive. The painter of Clive would require to capture his vehemence and robustness, his tactical brilliance and dash; the painter of Hastings would need an altogether finer hand and eye. Hastings's talents derived from a comprehensive and imaginative grasp of the complex issues which confronted him, and a subtle but unyielding energy in his will to solve them. Clive's victories at Kaveripak, Samiaveram and Plassey were all won by a coolness in situations which lesser men would have given up as hopeless, and by a quickness of thought that enabled him to take advantage of the least weakness in his enemy's position. This talent, com-

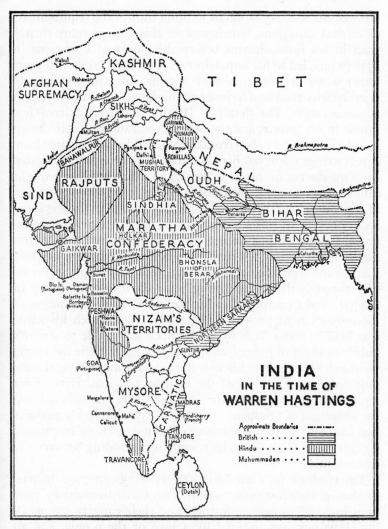

India in the time of Warren Hastings

Approximate Boundaries
British . . . .
Hindu . . . .
Muhummadan . . . .

bined with relentless determination and vigour, made him indisputably, if sometimes crudely, master of his situation. Hastings, however, often appears at his weakest when he attempts to act with the ruthlessness of Clive, as in the execution of Nuncumar or the imprisonment of Chait Singh. Lacking Clive's flair for the boldest of gestures, he also at times allowed his mastery of detail to blind him to the requirements of critical situations. Nowhere does this emerge more clearly than in his impeachment before the House of Commons in 1786 (which led to his impeachment before the Lords two years later) when defending himself against the charges, largely conceived by Burke, of 'crime and misdemeanour' in his Indian administration. The detail of Hastings's defence stirred few minds in his favour; and the details when subsequently shown in certain respects to be erroneous worked heavily against him. But Hastings displayed here an attitude that he had cultivated since the start of his career in India, and which had first brought him to the notice of Robert Clive: a belief in detailed knowledge of the country where he worked, which he used in the service of an improvement in its affairs. In the days of ignorant adventurers this gave him a stature which few possessed. If it did not finally leave him, in the superabundant confusion of Company life, beyond reproach, it gave him an authority which sustained him through the thirteen long years of his Governorship in Bengal. And a century after his acquittal on all the charges of his impeachment preserved the respect with which his name was held in India. It is by no means a safe guide to a man's public conduct to judge him by his private life; but the letters written by Hastings to his wife during his time in Bengal serve only to confirm a view of the fineness and sensitivity of his nature which survived (as for example Philip Francis's did not) the bitterness of Company strife. Not least among his qualities was his belief in the importance of a knowledge of languages, and his use of them for an increased understanding between the communities.

The contrast between Clive and Hastings emerges in particular in their attitude to India. To Clive the natives were luxurious, effeminate, cowardly; and their country unappealing. Hastings was inspired by a love of the people, and an affection for the country. This did not in any way diminish his pleasure in English things, or the delight with which he would order honey-suckle and sweet-briar for his garden – but it won him the friendship and loyalty of many Indians. Even the author of the *Seir Mutaqherin*, whose criticisms of the English have already been quoted, made an exception of Hastings in his notable liking for India. His affection for his friends was not distorted by distinctions of race. A century later, easy and unselfconscious friendships between the English and the Indians had almost ceased to exist.

But Hastings's attitude to India was expressed in what he did as much as by what he felt. In 1773 he attempted to get a Chair of Persian established at the University of Oxford to give such studies the prestige and respect he believed they deserved;[2] and he urged that young men coming out to India should be given a grounding in Oriental languages. Of importance too was the balanced perspective with which he viewed the relationship between the communities. To Hastings the faults were by no means all on one side: the cupidity, the violence and fierceness of the English, particularly of the lower sort, was 'incompatible with the gentle temper of the Bengali.'[3] It took an exceptional man not to adopt the attitude of Philip Francis, which had been expressed in similar terms by many before him, that 'the baseness of the Bengali was proverbial', and leave it at that.[4] Above all, Hastings recognised that the present condition, both moral and political of India, was caused by its exhaustion from long oppression. There was an obligation on the part of the English to rule India for the Indians:[5] this meant to rule them with ease and moderation, and to leave them 'what time and religion had rendered familiar to their understandings, and sacred to their affections.'[6] He believed that an attempt to impose British law would be a 'wanton tyranny'; the authority of the British government in Bengal must be formed 'on its ancient laws.'[7]

Inspired by an unprejudiced affection, Hastings helped to foster the first generation of Englishmen who were interested in India for its own sake: Charles Wilkins, Nathaniel Halhed, Jonathan Duncan, William Jones. His encouragement of interest in the Indian past, and the acquisition of skill in languages, extended the range of contacts between the communities; and Hastings believed that it could and should affect the attitude of the English to the country in which they served:

It is not very long since the inhabitants of India were considered by many, as creatures scarce elevated above the degree of savage life; nor, I fear, is that prejudice yet wholly eradicated, though surely abated. Every instance which brings their real character home to observation will impress us with more generous feeling for natural rights . . .[8]

He recognised too that among the Indians there were men equal in intellect and integrity to any in England.

Such perceptions, uncommon as they were at the time, reveal with clarity and force the civilisation of Hastings's own mind; and his recognition of the degree to which ignorance caused prejudice and dismissal. But the bent of Hastings's mind was practical; and the encouragement and support he gave to diminish such prejudice resulted in reforms. Men who trained themselves to translate Company regulations into native languages, and render native laws into English were handsomely paid. Most important of all he encouraged the establishment of the first printing-press in Northern India. By 1778 Charles Wilkins and Nicholas Halhed had set the press up, and made the first Bengali fount. Halhed's own *Grammar of the Bengali Language*, which remained for a long time the standard introduction to the language, was an early issue. Company papers could now be circulated; and the first English newspaper appeared.

As well as inducing Company servants to learn native languages, Hastings encouraged Indian scholars to translate Indian poems and mythology from Sanskrit into languages more widely known. Out of his own money he founded the Madrasa in Calcutta for the pursuit of Indian studies. Halhed in his preface to 'A Code of Gentoo Laws' expressed his intention in a form that Hastings would have approved. He argued that nothing could serve so well to 'conciliate the affection of the natives', and 'ensure stability in the country' as 'a well-timed toleration in matters of religion, and an adoption of such original institutes of the country, as do not immediately clash with the laws or interests of the conquerors . . .'[9] In matters of religion, Hastings also encouraged Wilkins in his translation of the *Bhagavad Gita*; and in a letter to Nathaniel Smith about the *Gita* expressed the view that Hindu literature would 'survive when the British dominion in India shall have long since ceased to exist, and when the sources which it once yielded of wealth and power are lost to remembrance.'[10] What

above (a) Warren Hastings; (b) Edmund Burke
below (c) William Jones; (d) Wellesley

Thomas Daniell: The Ghats at Benares, 1788. This painting, like the following two illustrations by English artists, depicts the reawakening of interest in the Indian past, and its legacy of belief, as well as art

(a) *left*, Samuel Davis: Muslim Tombs, Jaunpur, 1798

(b) *right*, Henry Salt: Excavations at Karle (Bombay), 1807

Cornwallis's Levee: Cornwallis is standing on the right by the door. 'Able Indians were excluded not only from work which used their talents; but from any working relationship with their English overlords'.

matters of course is not the prophecy but the changed attitude to the Hindu past, and to the present inheritors of that tradition.

In the year 1772 when Hastings was appointed Governor of Bengal,* Alexander Dow had completed publication of his *History of Hindoostan*. He had not spared the English in his criticism of their attitudes:

Posterity will perhaps find fault with the British for not investigating the learning and religious opinions, which prevail in those countries in Asia into which either their commerce or their arms have penetrated. The Brahmins of the East possessed in antient times some reputation for knowledge, but we have never had the curiosity to examine whether there was any truth in the reports of antiquity upon that head . . . Literary inquiries are by no means a capital object to many of our adventurers in Asia.[11]

Like Dow, his contemporary J. Z. Holwell (one of the survivors from the Black Hole of Calcutta) chastised the English on the grounds that 'ignorance, superstition and partiality to ourselves, are too commonly the cause of presumption and contempt of others'.[12] It amazed him that 'we should so readily believe the people of Hindustan a race of stupid idolaters.'[13] As in the case of Dow and Holwell, Hastings's conviction of the importance of oriental learning for the well-being of the Anglo-Indian community was by no means confined to literary ends; nor did those closest to him only use their knowledge for scholarly purposes. Jonathan Duncan (later to become Governor of Bombay) was able to prove to the Rajkumars that their practice of female infanticide contravened the Hindu scriptures; this led in the end to their abandoning the practice. The men who surrounded Hastings recognised in learning a method of social progress; but they did not suffer from the dogmatic assertion of Western superiority which later afflicted the generation of Macaulay. 'Their learning was of the inclusive and comprehensive kind' which characterised the pursuit of knowledge in the eighteenth century. Duncan himself, when Resident at Benares, proposed the establishment of a Hindu college for the preservation and cultivation of their laws,

* Hastings had returned to England in 1765, and after four years, was reappointed to serve in Madras where he remained until he went as Governor to Bengal.

literature and religion, which would also prove 'a Nursery of future Doctors and Expounders of the law.'[14]

Although this new spirit of inquiry about the Indian past, and desire to understand contemporary practice, was confined to a small minority, the challenge of ignorance began to be taken up on many fronts. It was Hastings again who encouraged James Rennell in his scientific surveys which led in 1788 to his production of the *Memoir of a Map of Hindoostan* – the first comprehensive geographical survey of the country, which formed the basis for the triangulation of the continent carried out by George Everest in the 1840s. Rennell in his introduction confirms the changing attitude to India: 'As almost every particular relating to Hindoostan is become an object of popular curiosity, it can hardly be esteemed superfluous to lay before the public an improved system of its geography.'[15] Rennell was perhaps over-emphatic about the extent of popular curiosity; ignorance about India continued to be a repeated criticism of the English. But from the 1760s an increasing amount of knowledge about the history of Hindustan, and the British connection with it became available: for example, Orme's *History of the Military Transactions of the British Nation in Hindustan* (1763); Malcolm's *Central India* (1823); James Tod's *Annals and Antiquities of Rajasthan* (1829–1832); Mountstuart Elphinstone's *History of India* (1841). Tod and Elphinstone both acknowledge a direct debt to the greatest of all the early Orientalists, William Jones, who shared with Hastings that love and affection for the people and country where they spent the most fruitful years of their lives.

Jones's excitement and interest in Asia was already well-formed before he even arrived there.* He wrote on his voyage:

It gave me inexpressible pleasure to find myself . . . almost encircled by the vast regions of Asia, which has ever been esteemed the nurse of science, the inventress of delightful and useful arts, the scene of glorious actions, fertile in the production of human genius . . . abounding in natural wonders, and infinitely diversified in the forms

* William Jones, 1746–94, established his reputation as an Oriental scholar when tutor to Lord Allthorp, only son of the 1st Earl Spencer. He mastered Arabic and Persian, and in 1772 published *Poems, consisting chiefly of translations from the Arabic languages*. Not being able to earn a living as an Orientalist, he was called to the bar in 1774, and nine years later was appointed Judge of the High Court in Calcutta.

of religion and government, in the laws, manners, customs and languages, as well as in the features and complexions of men.[16]

Jones, unlike many other travellers to the East, was not disappointed by the reality, and more than any other of his contemporaries he succeeded in touching a wide audience in Europe, as well as India, with his zest for the learning of the East. Both in England and on the continent he made people aware through his scholarship of the richness of Hindu culture; and in his translation of Kalidasa's *Sacontala* (1790) introduced to Europe a literary masterpiece which had its influence upon the poetic development of Goethe. Of more practical importance his *Digest of Hindu and Muslim laws* (completed after Jones's death by Henry Colebrooke) provided a solid basis for the understanding of the differences between English codes and their own.

Jones was inspired by a boundless curiosity, directed in his case towards a fuller appreciation of the civilisation in which he was living. As a Judge of the High Court in Calcutta, he combined a conscientious public life with an untiring devotion to learning. He recognised too that justice was inseparable from an understanding of the problems and attitudes which belonged to the judged, so that his research also served to deepen his authority on the bench.

Before he had gained proper mastery of Persian he found himself at the mercy of pundits who dealt out the law as they pleased; and this Jones, as a judge of integrity, found intolerable. In the course of his studies, Jones made many close friends among the educated Indian community, who helped him in his appreciation of Sanskrit literature. It was his desire – and a desire by all evidence carried out – 'to discharge my public duties with unremitted attention, and to recreate myself at leisure with the literature of this interesting country'.[17] There were many in India – one thinks of Jones's contemporary, John Shore, who performed their public duties with zeal; but few who shared Jones's wider humanitarian interests. It was these which helped him to make friends among the Indians, and gave him an affection for the country as necessary as it was rare. How many, during the whole period of British influence in India, would have joined Jones in saying: 'I should rather spend the rest of my life in exile at Crishna-nagar than live in my my own country without perfect independence.'[18]

Jones was in that happy, and not always common position, of finding that the studies which gave him pleasure went hand in hand with what his job required him to do. His increasing fluency in Arabic, Sanskrit, and Persian made him master of his position in court; and when the heat of the Calcutta summer became fierce he was able to retire to his villa by the river where, he admits, apart from the precarious health of his wife, he considered himself to be the happiest man alive, and Bengal a paradise of regions. A day to Jones was lost if he had not acquired in it some new knowledge of man or nature; and this increasing knowledge brought with it an increasing respect for much in ways of life and thought which otherwise he would not have appreciated. 'I am no Hindu', he says, 'but I hold the doctrine of the Hindus concerning a future state to be incomparably more rational, more pious, and more likely to deter men from vice than the horrid opinions inculcated by Christians on punishments *without end*.'[19] On matters of faith he had frequent conversations with the Brahmins whose university was close to his villa at Crishna-nagar, and with whom he was able to converse in Sanskrit.

Like Burke, Jones regarded the insecurity of the Indian people in matters of property as being a primary cause of instability in their society; and his desire both as lawyer and man was to give some degree of security and comfort to the twenty million subjects of the English in India. He regarded his *Digest of Indian Law* as his major contribution to this end, and, after the publication of *Sacontala* in 1790 refused to undertake any further translation of plays, which he regarded as a distraction from his proper work. This was dedicated to a country in which for all his dislike of some practices, he appreciated a freedom from the established authority of Crown, Lords and Church. The critic of privilege in England, Jones in India became equally the critic of the widespread attitude among his fellow-countrymen that wealth was the only pursuit for rational beings.

But not the least of Jones's claims upon our attention rests in his founding, with Hastings, of the Bengal Asiatic Society which met for the first time on 15th January, 1784, and was addressed by him. Jones regarded Asian studies as contributing to a new and important branch of human learning which until that time had been largely unknown in the West. The profit that the West might derive from contact with the culture of India contrasted sharply with the common European view of India as semi-barbaric. Furthermore Jones's own scholarship encouraged a professional specialised interest in Asiatic Studies, not least important in its recognition that language was only one method of making a comparative study of the human race.

The contributions of members to the Society were later published in a journal called *Asiatick Researches*, which first came out in 1789. Five volumes had appeared before the end of the century, containing papers on widely different topics, ranging from contemporary problems like the remarriage of widows to the history of pre-Muslim Bengal.

In a recent and fine study of Jones, S. N. Mukherjee discussed the importance of Jones and his colleagues in evolving a methodology for the early period of Indian history which, if later improved on, still rested on firm foundations. The support which Jones and the other Orientalists received during their life-time was restricted but not negligible. The membership of the Asiatic Society was thirty in 1784, and 110 in 1792. But it survived John Shore's lugubrious observation that when Jones left, the Asiatic Society would become a *caput mortuum*. It not only survived, but in 1829 opened its doors to members of the Bengali intelligentsia who had gathered in Calcutta around Fort William College – an inspiration of Lord Wellesley's which will be discussed in the following chapter. Among the first Indian members of the society was Dwarkanath Tagore, the grandfather of the poet. In the awakening consciousness of the splendour of the Indian past, there was also nurtured the seed of future nationalism.

But nationalism itself grew in strength for quite different reasons; and its presence in a later period must not be allowed to conceal or overshadow Jones's achievement in the field of human relations. Jones 'left behind him an attitude of mind, a profound reverence for men irrespective of their race and their different cultural backgrounds'.[20] This expressed itself not only in his published works, but in his friendships and in the pride and pleasure which he derived from being able to talk to Indians in their own languages. He remains a good example of a man in whom unprejudiced curiosity and constant application proved the reciprocal advantage which each culture might derive from the other. That nationalism took the virulent form it did comments sadly on the inability of the majority of the English to follow in Jones's footsteps.

Edmund Burke stands out as the first of two thinkers who deeply influenced attitudes to India without ever visiting the country; the second was James Mill. Burke placed the English responsibility for India on the map of national conscience; Mill threw his disastrous authority into the campaign to denigrate Hindu culture and glorify his own. We shall return to him later.

Burke entered Parliament in 1759 at a time when English political life was distorted by faction, and the struggle for power between George III and his ministers. Burke was a man of principle and causes, which he pursued from a deep emotional as well as intellectual conviction, and his public life whether on behalf of the people in India or against the revolution in France reflects his dedication to what he saw as great, just and honourable. In particular, his speeches on Fox's East India Bill, the Nabob of Arcot's debts, and the impeachment of Warren Hastings remain classic examples of an appeal to principle through a massive mastery of fact. But it would be wrong to give the impression that Burke's oratory burst like a bombshell in a cloudless English sky. A growing unease about the Company's conduct of its affairs had been apparent throughout the 1770s which manifested itself in Clive's defence before the House of Commons in 1772, and in plays and pamphlets that reflected the prevailing dislike of the returning Nabobs. In 1773 Samuel Foote's play, *The Nabob*, was produced at the Theatre Royal, Dublin. A poor piece of work as drama, its historical interest consists in the attention which it focuses on the activities and morals of Englishmen in the East, which a couple of decades previously would not have attracted the least attention at home. The Nabob, Sir Matthew Mite, is described by Lady Oldham like this: '... preceded by all the pomp of Asia,

Sir Matthew Mite, came thundering amongst us; and, pro-
fusely scattering the spoils of ruined provinces, corrupted the
virtue and alienated the affections of all the old friends to the
family.'[21] Understandably she has some misgivings about the
effect of his past activities on his present character. 'Will he
listen,' she wonders, 'to a private complaint, who has been deaf
to the cries of a people? Or drop a tear for particular distress
who owes his rise to the ruin of thousands?'[22] The play justifies
Lady Oldham's fears both as to his unscrupulousness, and his
solvency. And it is only the good nature of her husband's
brother that saves the family from falling into his clutches.
A striking similarity exists between the depiction of the
English character in India, and contemporary Indian attitudes
to the English, in such evidence as exists like that of the *Seir
Mutaqherin*. Young Touchit remarks: 'We cunningly encroach,
and fortify little by little, till at length we, growing too strong
for the natives, turn them out of their lands, and take possession
of their money and jewels.'[23] Like Foote, the essayist Henry
Mackenzie drew attention to the disrupting effect of the
returning Nabob on English social life. His love of extravagance
puts up the prices in the neighbourhood where he chooses to
settle; and the pretensions of his life - to say nothing of the
behaviour of his lay-about servants - disturb the solid virtues
of English country life. But while writers like Foote and
Mackenzie expressed a prevailing unease about the ways in
which the English were making their fortunes, it took the mind
and mastery of Burke to bring the full degree of the tragedy
before the eyes of the English public. Burke was not only a man
stirred by a powerful conscience but a man who had long before
his great speeches on Indian affairs, interested himself in that
country, and made himself master of all that he learned. Always
the champion of the control of politics by moral considerations
Burke found in the Indian question an issue which harnessed
the restless stream of his mind, and enabled him to voice the
conscience of England over an issue that could no longer be
ignored. It was only a bitter and ultimate irony that Burke in
attacking Warren Hastings picked on the one man who - while
bearing as Governor-General the responsibility for British
rule - was more dedicated to India than almost all who served

there. It would be untrue to claim that Hastings's administration did not have its blemishes, in the trial of Nuncumar, the treatment of Chait Singh and the Begums of Oudh. In these respects he seems part of that old Company world, which political action and reform were now bringing swiftly to an end; but in his attitude to India and its people, in his encouragement of an informed dedication from Company servants, he looks to a brighter future. But Burke saw in him only the tyrant responsible for the pitiless oppression of a helpless people.

Burke's effectiveness and influence may be seen to rest on two things: an appeal to principle at a time when principle was required to set the Indian question in perspective, and an immense detailed knowledge of the causes and issues he chose to debate. Burke recognised the peculiar circumstances in which the East India Company's power had arisen; and saw that it was these conditions themselves which imposed an obligation to consider the plight of those less able, economically, socially, and militarily, to defend themselves, and to ensure that they were not exploited through the weakness of their position, or the rapacity of the Company's servants. The East India Company was not merely a trading company but a 'delegation of the whole power and sovereignty of this kingdom sent into the East,'[24] and as such its affairs must be controlled by those moral and humanitarian considerations which proceeded for Burke from a divine dispensation.

On 1st December, 1783 - fourteen months before the end of Hastings's Governor-Generalship - Burke rose in the House of Commons to make his speech on Mr Fox's East India Bill. The Bill, he informed the House, was intended by those connected with it to form the *Magna Charta* of Hindustan.* Conversely, his attack was directed against those who opposed the Bill because they were more concerned with the revenue and commerce in India than with the well-being of its people. As with many who followed him in attacking the Empire, it was the humanitarian callousness of those who exploited the local population for

---

* Although the Bill was defeated, Pitt's India Act of the following year embodied many of its provisions: most important it established a Board of Control for his Company, responsible directly to Parliament.

their own ends that formed the core of Burke's thought. But
he was also aware, like Hastings and Jones, that the plunder of
India was not that of a nation of savages; but of a 'people for
ages civilised and cultivated; cultivated by all the arts of
polished life, whilst we were yet in the woods.'[25] Worse still, the
ruin and degradation of the present population was being
brought about by men who had neither the wisdom of years,
nor the sympathy of the well-informed mind. 'The natives
scarcely know what it is to see the grey head of an Englishman.
Young men (boys almost) govern there, without society and
without sympathy for the natives. They have no more social
habits with the people than if they still resided in England -
nor, indeed, any species of intercourse, but that which is
necessary to making a sudden fortune, with a view to a remote
settlement.'[26]

Burke took it upon himself to make his fellow-countrymen
hear the cries so long neglected of that land whose booty was
lodged in England. He argued the need for a 'protecting and
stable' administration in England which would be capable of
putting an end to the present state of misery and confusion for
the natives. In its present form the Government of the East
India Company was absolutely incorrigible. But his appeal was
always to the universal and general as well as to the political:
he saw himself as participating in the destruction of a tyranny
that existed to the disgrace of the nation, and the harm of a
large part of the human species.

In 1785 in his speech on the Nabob of Arcot's debts, he dwelt
again not only on the ruin which Englishmen wrought in
India, but on the positive obligation which they had to create a
civilisation of common benefit. 'What are the articles of commerce, or the branches of manufacture, which those gentlemen have carried hence to enrich India? What are the sciences
they beamed out to enlighten it? What are the arts they introduced to cheer and adorn it? What are the religions, what the
moral institutions, they have taught among the people as
a guide to life, or as a consolation when life is to be no more?'
And he answered his own questions in terms of a 'debt of
millions, in favour of a set of men, whose names, with few exceptions, are either buried in the obscurity of their origin

and talents, or dragged into light by the enormity of their crimes.'[27]

Burke's claims both for the respect due to the people and civilisation of India, and our obligation to contribute to their future well-being with what was best in the civilisation of Europe, created a new idea of what Anglo-India might be. In attacking the desolating effects of uncontrollable and arbitrary power which he came to identify with the person of Warren Hastings, he argued for a form of government that would leave India enriched by the presence of the English. If the English were to be driven out now, he said, nothing would remain to tell that it had been possessed by anything better than the orang-outang or tiger. The palaces, hospitals, schools, bridges, high-roads, canals, reservoirs which ought to have been built just did not exist. It was not as the champion of technology that he spoke; but of a strong and humanitarian administration, made possible by moral purposefulness and the integrity of those who governed. 'I confess, I wish that some more feeling than I have yet observed for the sufferings of our fellow-creatures and fellow-subjects in that oppressed part of the world had manifested itself in any one quarter of the kingdom, or in any one large description of men.'[28] His plea was that the evil which had been done in India should now be redressed; and his support was pledged to those who would attempt to reform the present and oppressive system of government.

Burke was to waste a good deal of his time and energy in his later years on the impeachment of Hastings. He came to see in him a personification of corruption in human nature. After Burke had finished with Hastings's character, it was impossible to imagine him innocent of his crimes. The sublimity of Burke's rhetoric and his mastery of language became here the ridiculous instrument of his argument and his attack. Making use of widespread ignorance of India and Company affairs, Burke was able to create fantasies about Hastings's behaviour as a young man and dye him deep with crimes which would 'work upon the popular sense'. It was this unreliable instrument which Burke used as his standard of argument; he had reached the point of believing Hastings capable of any crime; and from believing him capable there was but a short leap to accusing him of them. His obsession with the evil in Hastings's nature engaged him in the nine long years of the impeachment – caused him to flog that horse to its sorry (but triumphant) end – and pursued Burke himself to his death in 1797. Hastings was acquitted and vindicated; and the legacy of Burke was to be found not in his fanaticism against Hastings, but in the permanent change of attitude, which he had been primarily responsible for bringing about, as to the size and importance of English commitment in India. The affairs of the Company were no longer a private matter, but of public and moral concern.

Pitt's India Act of 1784 had established a Board of Control responsible to Parliament for the conduct of East Indian affairs; and these in turn were increasingly to be handled in India by civil servants, not commercial entrepreneurs. In the next half-century the Company was to produce its most able administrators – a race of men informed about the splendours of the Indian past and dedicated to its future. In India too a renaissance would begin which would result in a new flowering of national and cultural life. For a time it looked as though the best of both worlds might meet; and, without any threat to the 'familiar' or the 'sacred', reciprocal benefit might derive from the resulting enlargement of understanding and knowledge. If this had come about, Hastings and Burke would have appeared to posterity on the same side as two of its principal begetters.

Chapter 5

The Awakening of Giants

If civilisation is to become an article of trade between
the two countries I am convinced that this country will
gain by the import cargo.
THOMAS MUNRO, 'Statement to the House of Commons',
1813

The Hindu appears a being nearly limited to mere
animal functions, and even in them indifferent. Their
proficiency and skill in the several lines of occupation
to which they are restricted, are little more than the
dexterity which any animal with similar conformation
but with no higher intellect than a dog, an elephant,
or a monkey might be supposed to be capable of
attaining. It is enough to see this in order to have full
conviction that such a people can at no period have
been more advanced in civil polity.
LORD HASTINGS, *Private Journal*, 1818

I N British India of the late eighteenth century it was scarcely
conceivable that Sir William Jones's interests in history and
language should have been shared by many. The majority of
the Company's servants were practical, not scholarly men. But
the significance of the revival of interest in the Indian past
cannot be judged either in academic or numerical terms. It
marks in fact the beginning of a 'debate', carried on at many
levels and in various circumstances about the nature of the
contribution which Indian and English civilisation were
mutually capable of making to each other. In the period between
1790 and 1835 the debate manifested itself in relation to education and religion, to social behaviour and in the end to vital
matters of policy like conquest. At root, little appeared to
change: the same sympathies and antipathies to India and the
Indians still prevailed. But nevertheless the issue between the
two civilisations was beginning to be raised in forms that

affected political decisions (for example, the amount of money to be spent on Sanskrit education, or the force to be used if necessary in the suppression of *suttee*). Questions of rule were involved; and these in turn meant a confrontation between the communities that involved the individual. By the end of the period, the result of the debate was announced in unequivocal terms for the anglicisation of India, to the extent of making English its official language. Even if all the funds appropriated for the purposes of education were employed on English education alone, and it was spent on training intermediaries between the English Government and those they ruled, the magnitude of the task in relation to a largely illiterate population of two hundred million was staggering. Unfortunately its impracticability was not its only drawback. The assumption of superiority in the civilisation of the West on which it was based played into the hands of those who cared least for India, and used its people as pawns in their personal Empire. In this respect it could only serve to impair the relationship between the communities. For different reasons, the Governor-General-ship of Lord Cornwallis (1786-93) at the beginning of the period also stands out as among the least fortunate for the future of good and fruitful relations; and it is with the negative balance that I want to deal first.

Cornwallis was inspired, as many before and after him, by a deep distrust of the Indian character. Convinced of the necessity for honest and efficient administration in India, he implemented in 1791 a policy which excluded all Indians from positions of responsibility, and effectively from all jobs which earned higher salaries.* This meant not only that able Indians were excluded from work which used their talents, but also from any working relationship with their English overlords. Consequently, at the level where contacts could have been productive of increased understanding and effective coopera-

* Philip Marshall (*Bengal Past and Present*, Vol. LXXXIV, July–December, 1965, pp. 95–120) has sought to diminish the blame attached to Cornwallis. He argues that 'Cornwallis appears to have given effect to prejudices already deeply ingrained among the Company's servants and have completed policies begun by others.' The point does seem a rather academic one since the policy was 'completed' in Cornwallis's administration, and it also reflected his own attitude of contempt for Indian culture and morality.

tion the door was closed and bolted so fast that only militant and prolonged political agitation which began in the second half of the nineteenth century was to succeed in getting it opened again. But Cornwallis was not inspired by the racial attitudes which caused much damage in times to come. He believed that only the English could be trusted to implement the sound administration he was determined to achieve.

It followed from this policy of anglicisation that the members of the covenanted civil service had thrown upon them a burden of work which made even their necessary daily routine so exacting that it left little time or energy for building up the kind of contacts which Jones and Hastings had regarded as important. Respect but not personal affection became increasingly the coldly official relationship between the communities. Conversely, the psychological effect on the educated and able Indian at finding no worthwhile outlet for his talents was in time to have a demoralising and devitalising effect upon the community at large. The higher forms of civilisation do not thrive in circumstances of this kind; and it was not until the influence of western education in the later part of the nineteenth century began to create a new kind of anglicised intelligentsia that this set-back was challenged on any large or potent scale - though the origins of this reversal, as we shall see, began much earlier.

Secondly, Cornwallis's Permanent Settlement of the land (1793), and the establishment of a perpetual land-revenue in Bengal, Behar, and Orissa intended to create a society of landowners on the English model who would act responsibly towards their tenants, in fact gave the Indian 'zamindars'* more power, and the tenants less means of redress. It also effectively ruled out - by placing the 'zamindars' between the English administration and the peasant - the kind of close contact between the district officers and the Indian people which in other parts of the country was valuable and important.

But divisive as Cornwallis's administration proved, it also corrected abuses which had long since been the cause of much trouble. Company servants were paid a proper salary for the

---

* zamindar: literally 'landholder': but the significance of this differed in different parts of the country. In Bengal, as shown here, it implied a permanent settlement.

first time, and their right to trade on their own behalf greatly curtailed This removed a practice which for almost two centuries had led to unhealthy rivalry and strife among the Company servants. In matters of justice too Cornwallis insisted upon racial impartiality, especially in cases where natives had been exploited by Europeans. India should be ruled, he believed, by upright and gentlemanly standards; but arriving, as he did, without any knowledge of the language or customs of the country, Cornwallis was incapable of appreciating Indian civilisation for its own merits as Hastings had done; and it is clear from his correspondence that he saw his life in India as a duty rather than a pleasure: 'I can send you no news from hence that can either amuse or interest you, my life at Calcutta is perfect clockwork . . . I don't think the greatest *sap* at Eton can lead a duller life than this . . .'[1] Moreover, there was implicit in Cornwallis's policy of anglicisation a sense of superiority which was reflected in the way he chose to live: 'Though civil and attentive to the natives, *he has reposed no confidence in any one of them, nor has he had a single individual, either Hindu or Mahomedan, about his person, above the rank of a menial servant, contrary to the general usage of men occupying such stations as he filled.'*[2]

Cornwallis was succeeded as Governor-General by Sir John Shore, later Lord Teignmouth. Although Shore had opposed Cornwallis on the Permanent Settlement, he shared many of his prejudices. These, unlike those of Cornwallis, were the product of a life-time spent in India. Shore had quickly mastered Hindustani, but three years after his arrival in 1769 had come to the conclusion that little improvement or entertainment could be had from conversation with the natives, as 'their ideas were very confined and debased'.[3] This was an attitude which time tended to confirm, increasing his desire to leave the country where fate had cast him. 'So far from contracting a fondness for the country where I have spent so many years of my life, my wishes for leaving it become more sanguine.'[4] He also shared Cornwallis's distrust of the Hindu character which he saw as a 'compound of insincerity, servility and dishonesty'.[5] In the later years of his life, an increasing preoccupation with Christianity led to his working for the moral and religious advancement of the natives through the *British and Foreign*

Bible Society, of which he became president in 1804. His ambition to reform what he disliked, or disapproved of, lacked the shrewdness of Cornwallis who had recognised the strength of the obstacles to the propagation of the Christian religion; but it also reflected the fear of atheism which the French Revolution had induced in English society. Christianity had come to be regarded as the buttress of the established social order. It was the injection of this attitude into the counsels which informed Company policy that started to work against the influence of Jones and Hastings in their attempts to argue the value and age of Indian civilisation.

In 1792 Charles Grant, a former member of the Board of Trade in Calcutta published his *Observations on the State of Society among the Asiatic Subjects of Great Britain, particularly with respect to morals and on the means of improving them.* As an evangelical, Grant was convinced of the need 'for making known to our Asiatic subjects, the pure and benign principle of our divine religion'.[6] He went on to argue that the people of Hindustan were 'exceedingly depraved, and exhibited human nature in a very degraded humiliating state.'[7] They were

a race of men lamentably degenerate and base; retaining but a feeble sense of moral obligation: yet obstinate in their disregard of what they know to be right, governed by malevolent and licentious passions, strongly exemplifying the effects produced on society by great and general corruption of manners, and sunk in misery by their vices...[8]

He attributed this state partly to the effect of their religious customs, and enslavement to superstitions. The Hindus erred because they were ignorant. It was therefore the responsibility of the English to introduce light. Christianity was not, he argued, political by nature; but, by seeking good and general happiness, subjects men to the laws of universal rectitude. The success of a policy of Christianisation in India would constitute our safety. 'In communicating light, knowledge, and improvement we shall attach the Hindu people to ourselves, to ensure the safety of our possessions . . .'[9]

But as well as putting forward his own ideas for reform, Grant also attacked those like Jones who attempted to 'exalt the natives of the East, and of other pagan regions, into models of goodness and innocence'.[10] They had aimed to 'subvert, together with revealed religion, all ideas of the moral government of the Deity, and of men's responsibility to him.'[11] Warren Hastings, in his retirement, recognised, on the other hand, what was socially reprehensible and misconceived in the attitude of Grant, and others like Wilberforce who supported him:

Our Indian subjects having been presented as sunk in grossest brutality . . . it is therefore said that as we possess the power, so it is our duty to reform them, nay, to 'coerce' them into goodness by introducing our faith among them.[12]

*

By its charter of 1698 the Company had pledged itself to active support of evangelical projects. [In this year the Society for the Propagation of Christian Knowledge had been founded.] But unlike the Portuguese, the Dutch and the Danish, the Company preferred not to commit itself to missionary activity directly, and instead gave financial support to other missions where this was thought desirable. In the earlier part of the eighteenth century, official detachment reflected the general dislike of enthusiasm at home; but the growth of non-conformity and evangelicism led inevitably to increased pressure for missionary activity abroad. The Company continued to refuse permission for missionaries to work in its territories, until in 1813 the power of Grant, Wilberforce and other members of the Clapham sect forced this reform upon them.

As early as 1793, however, William Carey had sailed in a Danish East Indiaman, and set himself up in the Danish Mission at Serampore. Carey had formed his views early in life on the necessity for converting the heathen; but he added to his religious zeal a skill in languages of first-rate importance. To begin with, his missionary work met with little success; and seemed to confirm the despair which the Abbé Dubois* was to express a little later of the 'total inutility of the attempt to

---

* 'In thirty years he claimed to have made three hundred converts, of whom two-thirds were pariahs.' (See Mayhew, *Christianity and the Government of India*, 1929, p. 93.)

convert the Hindus'.[13] But Carey's life-work was saved by Lord Wellesley's foundation in 1800 of his College of Fort William which the Governor-General intended to make his 'Oxford of the East'. The story of the College is of particular interest – but before returning to it a little more needs to be said about Carey and the missionary movement. Wellesley recognised that both Carey's skill in languages, and the printing-press run by him at Serampore could be of immense value to his new institution. In 1801 Carey accepted the job of Professor of Bengali at Fort William; in return, the mission received official support from the Government, particularly in the matter of printing. The Serampore Press was contracted to do the College's work; and as such became the means through which grammars, dictionaries, and texts were made available for the first time to students of Oriental languages and literature. By 1806 the Serampore Press was dealing with books in seventeen languages. At the same time, Carey was unobtrusively continuing his missionary work. By 1810 there were four mission stations in Bengal, and the Scriptures had been printed, in whole or in part, in six languages. But Carey, unlike many evangelicals, retained an open and undogmatic mind. As early as 1804 he admitted he had become Indianised; and he records of his relationship with the Hindus: 'Their manners, customs, habits and sentiments, are as obvious to me, as if I was myself a native.'[14]

The double life which Carey led as educator and missionary was to become familiar in the coming century. Permission was officially granted in the Company's Charter of 1813 for missionary work; and the establishment of an Anglican see in Calcutta brought with it an increase in evangelical activity that was reflected in the public support for Missions in India and elsewhere. The total annual income of the Church Missionary Society, and the Society for the Propagation of the Gospel rose from just over £2000 in the first decade of the century to £150,000 in 1850.[15] But as in Carey's case the vital effect of this increased activity lay in education. From the outset mission schools contributed importantly to the spread of knowledge, particularly at primary level; after the Education Despatch of 1854, the encouragement of teaching in the vernaculars made this of particular significance. And although the official attitude of the Company remained one of religious neutrality, the same Despatch made it possible for mission schools to profit from Government Grants, provided they submitted themselves to inspection and maintained sound educational standards.[16] In return, and particularly under the Empire, the missionary skilled in languages and informed about local customs often proved useful to the district officer, employing his knowledge in the service of, for example, journalism, agriculture and public health.

But while the contribution of the missions to education was considerable, their success in the primary purpose of Christianising India remained slender. By the 1880s there were still under half a million protestant Christians, and only a hundred and thirty-eight thousand communicants, out of a total population of two hundred and fifty millions. An acute observer in 1920 remarked that India was still as far removed from being a Christian country then as it had been in 1784.[17] William Hunter in his novel, *The Old Missionary* (1895) allows his central character to express a fear that many must have felt: 'During his long life he had baptised many, but he did not know that he had made a single Christian.'[18] The resistance to conversion was neither passive nor indifferent; and it manifested itself not only to European missionaries; but in cases like that of the school of Hindu widows, started by Ramabai Sarasvati in the 1880s, which foundered on the question of whether Christian instruction should be included in the course. The nature of the problem was one which had been noted by the first Anglican Bishop in Calcutta, Reginald Heber, a man of gentle and shrewd perceptiveness. There was, he admitted, no appearance of a desire among the Hindus for a new religion, except in our schools.[19] Moreover, he recognised in the behaviour of the majority of his fellow countrymen the worst possible example of the Christian ethic in practice. He notes their exclusive and intolerant spirit, forming a caste by themselves, disliking and disliked by their neighbours:

Of this foolish, surly national pride, I see but too many instances daily, and I am convinced it does us much harm in this country. We are not guilty of injustice or wilful oppression, but we shut out the natives from our society, and a bullying insolent manner is continually assumed in speaking to them.[20]

Like Burke he recognised that if the English were expelled, they would leave few relics of the higher aspects of their civilisation; and conversely that the Indian people whom he met could not 'with any propriety of language be called uncivilised.'[21]

Heber aligned himself here more with Burke and Jones, than with Charles Grant. But between the publication of Grant's *Observations* in 1792, and Heber's journey through his extended diocese in 1824, the tide of many great events had flowed in India, which gave a new tone and emphasis to English attitudes. In particular, the defeat and death of Tipu Sultan in 1799, the annexation of the Carnatic in 1801, and the final defeat of the Marathas by the Marquess of Hastings in 1818 had effectively realised Wellesley's aim of establishing British supremacy in India. Against consistently overwhelming odds, the British forces had proved their superior discipline and toughness. During the Second Maratha War (1803-5) a chieftain remarked to Wellesley's brother, the future Duke of Wellington: 'These English are a strange people and their General a wonderful man: they came here in the morning, looked at the Pettah walls, walked over it, killed all the garrison and returned to breakfast.'[22] But neither the success of Wellesley's campaigns, nor his attitude to the Court of Directors had increased his popularity in London. Expensive wars had never been to the liking of the Company who properly regarded their province as trade, and knew all too well that the cost of victory had to be measured in terms of future as well as immediate expenses. Small thoughts of this kind did not bother Lord Wellesley convinced, as he was, that 'Men of mere facts, figures and money-bags' could not enter into the 'enlightened and comprehensive views of uplifting the character of the native of India.'[23]

As this suggests, Wellesley's imperial aims did not end with the fighting. His was a style of government which aimed to impress the might and grandeur of the conquering nation on all its subject peoples. The new Government House which he built in Calcutta indicated in itself the changed role of the

English in India. India was in future 'to be governed from a palace, not from a counting house; with the ideas of a Prince, not with those of a retail dealer in muslins and indigo'.[24] The Governor-General's balls brought together as many as eight hundred Europeans, Persians, and Indians to wonder at the magnificence of the new ruling race; the illuminations at one ball alone cost £3,248. Even in camp, Wellesley insisted on comparable standards being maintained. Costly 'chandeliers of cut-glass were suspended [over the dinner-table], and it was covered with beautiful porcelain and glass-ware.'[25]

But Wellesley also made no effort to conceal his 'frankly contemptuous' attitude towards the Indians. During his stay he made a tour of India to

learn how his administration operated, but because of his ignorance of Indian languages, the haughty demeanour of his entourage, the brevity of his visits, and his inability to meet Indians, Wellesley could learn nothing except the 'admirable effect of the Company's admirable government'.[26]

His attitude to the Vakils or Ministers of the native courts also showed no recognition of their importance. General Palmer in writing to Warren Hastings reflected the change in tone which had occurred:

They are not permitted to pay their respects to him oftener than two or three times a year which I think is as impolitic as it is ungracious. The above-mentioned gentlemen all retain the strongest attachment to you. And indeed that sentiment is general among the natives of my information. I observe with great concern the system of depressing them adopted by the present government and imitated in the manners of almost every European. They are excluded from all posts of great respectability or emolument, and are treated in society with mortifying hauteur and reserve. In fact, they have hardly any social intercourse with us.[27]

Palmer goes on to express his indignation at the ignorance of European magistrates, and the low ceiling of wages for any native employee of the Company. Part of the criticism is of course directed at Cornwallis's anglicisation policy; but with the style and attitudes set by the Governor-General, one is not surprised to find, shortly after his departure, that a Captain Williamson remarks of life in Calcutta: 'Europeans have little connexion with natives of either religion,' and in the same year Mrs Graham regretted that 'every Briton . . . appears to pride himself on being outrageously a John Bull.'[28] In a man of less stature, the contempt of a Wellesley would also have been less damaging. But, after Clive's, Wellesley's name stood out with a brilliance in military and administrative success (in an age where military success still stood high on the list of human achievement) which inevitably shed lustre (whether desirable or not) on his opinions and attitudes. Wellesley set a tone of pride and glory about the conquering race which was never again to be entirely lost, and in the behaviour of small men did incalculable harm.

Wellesley, however, was an exceptional and various man; and in other respects his attempted contribution to the civilisation of Anglo-India was notable: in particular, his view of the importance of a proper training for future administrators embodied in his 'Oxford of the East'. On 10th July, 1800, Wellesley announced the formation of a College at Fort William which would provide civil servants of the Empire with an education in Oriental languages and history, as well as continuing their instruction in traditional European subjects.

In the following four years Wellesley realised his ambition, collecting for the college distinguished Indian scholars from Bengal, and a group of able Orientalists who had carried on the pioneer work done by Halhed and Jones, John Gilchrist, Henry Colebrooke and William Carey. Members of the Asiatic Society were also invited to lecture on the 'History and Antiquities of Hindustan and the Deccan'. At first, the College used the missionary press of William Carey at Serampore, but soon also became a centre for printing and publishing, as well as teaching. Gilchrist started a Hindustani press in 1802; in 1805 and 1807 respectively Persian and Sanskrit presses were also established. By 1810 Colebrooke had published the 'Translation of Two Treatises on the Hindu Law of Inheritance' which aimed to help European students with the chaotic and contradictory Hindu legal system and reconstruct it along modern lines[29] while Carey, as well as producing a Bengali grammar, made the first study of rural dialects in Bengal, and produced a three-volume dictionary, containing 80,000 words.

The students of the College benefited from a view of India that was bound to impress on them its manifold complexities; but it was also important in its provision of employment for the educated Bengalis whom it attracted to Calcutta.* Excluded by Cornwallis from other important activities, the scholars of Fort William formed the nucleus of a new intelligentsia in Bengal; as Western education spread in the course of the century their significance was to become political as well as educational. The College also brought about cooperation between English and Indian scholars on a scale that had never occurred before.

To Wellesley, the College was a matter of deep personal conviction. He even went so far as to say in one of his letters that 'the College must stand or the Empire must fall'.[30] But the Court of directors, influenced by Grant, did not share Wellesley's enthusiasm for the scheme, especially since he had gone ahead without their permission, investing considerable sums of money in its establishment. Grant saw no advantage to an institution which would help the young recruits to the assimilation of a culture and religion that was degrading. He argued that a better and surer way of grounding them in the necessary Oriental languages was for this training to begin before they left England, under the supervision of scholars from Cambridge. The Court's approval was given to this idea in 1805; and in due course, Haileybury came into being†. From this time on, the significance of Wellesley's 'Oxford in the East' declined - at least as an institute for teaching. It continued in existence for the purpose of training civil servants who were expected to serve in Bengal - and as a centre for the Renaissance of Hindu learning and culture. By the time it was finally closed in 1854 it had 'no buildings, no rooms, no professors, no lectures, but only a few Moonshis whom the Government pays but who have no employment.'[31] Nevertheless, Wellesley's College embodied at its inception a great idea; and its death under the influence of narrow sectarian fears

---

* At least twelve distinguished Indian scholars were employed in the early years of the College's existence.

† The East-India College opened at Hertford Castle in 1806, moved to Haileybury in 1809, and continued in existence for fifty years.

represented an important set-back for the growth of contacts and communication between English and Indian civilisation. With its wide-ranging courses in Oriental languages and history, as well as its continuing European education, the University of the East could have served as the centre for the exchange of ideas and information at many levels. Like other possibilities in Anglo-India the opportunity was lost through the assertion of a religious and cultural superiority which proved its weakness by its fear of challenge and criticism.

In the Charter Act of 1813 it was agreed that the Company should provide one lakh of rupees each year 'for the revival and improvement of literature and encouragement of the learned natives of India, and for the introduction and improvement of a knowledge of the Sciences.'[32] This programme concealed more difficulties than it suggested, because it included dispute as to whether the emphasis should fall on Sanskrit, or the vernaculars, in addition to the problem of the choice between Oriental and English education.

In 1814 William Carey proposed the expansion of Fort William College as a training-centre for Indians, to qualify them, in particular, for the teaching of scientific subjects. The Marquess of Hastings, Governor-General from 1813-18, decided to visit the Sanskrit College at Benares, for the purpose of making his own mind up about the value of the education there. He came away appalled by the standards of teachers and taught. A predisposition towards the vernaculars as against Sanskrit was also confirmed by his visit; he further determined to make Calcutta the centre for the Company's new educational schemes. With the help and support of men who had trained in Wellesley's College, and were informed both about the history of Hindustan, as well as skilled in its languages, Hastings presided over the founding of Hindu College in 1816, the Calcutta Book Society in 1817, and the Calcutta School Society in 1818.

Among the declared aims of Hindu College, which became Presidency College in 1855, was the teaching of western secular subjects. This did not involve, as David Kopf has pointed out, any desire on the part of the authorities to anglicise Hindu youth; but reflected that pull towards the West which many educated Bengalis felt at this time, just as many Englishmen had become interested in the learning of the East. The practical usefulness of Western education naturally attracted many Hindus to the College – especially as the spirit in which it was conceived was one of mutual profit. 'The primary object of the institution is, the tuition of the sons of respectable Hindus, in the English and Indian languages and in the literature and science of Europe and Asia.'[33]

The reforms undertaken both in schools and colleges, together with the increasing availability of books, were progressive and heartening. They ensured that a younger generation of Hindus in Bengal would receive an education which both reminded them of the importance of their own traditions and past achievements, while making available to them the scientific knowledge of Europe. But this liberal and unbigoted attitude was also not destined to last. In the very year when the Calcutta School Society was founded, James Mill published his *History of British India* (1818).* Within the next two decades, and partly under Mill's influence, the idea of a golden age in the Hindu past, together with respect for the civilisation that went with it, was to recede before a new burst of European assertiveness. The danger of Mill was not only to be found in his arguments, but in the ammunition he gave to those who through prejudice, lack of curiosity, or simple idleness, liked to think of themselves as unquestioned members of a superior race. Even in Hindu College a change of tone was apparent. The appointment of the Eurasian Henry Derozio as Professor of English literature in 1828, began a fashion for anglicisation that was exemplified in dress as well as attitude. Derozio looked to another golden age which he believed would come for India through Western education. The disruption that was caused by the attempt to implement this can be seen in a father's complaint that his son rejected him now because his English was so poor, and regarded 'Brahmins and pundits', as 'thieves, hypocrites and fools'.[34] Derozio was by no means alone

---

* James Mill came to London in 1802 in search of literary employment; he became an editor of the *Literary Journal* in the same year, and four years afterwards began his *History of India*. He made his name through articles written for the *Edinburgh Review* between 1808 and 1813. After the publication of his history in 1818, he was appointed to a place in India House, and by 1830 had risen to be examiner of Indian correspondence.

in his emphasis on westernisation. Alexander Duff in his Scottish Church College was attempting to turn Calcutta Bengalis into Scottish Presbyterians.

James Mill in his *History of British India* was far from arguing the Christian case; but he was no less implacably opposed to William Jones than Charles Grant had been. 'It was unfortunate,' wrote Mill, 'that a mind so pure, so warm, in the pursuit of truth and so devoted to oriental learning, as that of Sir William Jones, should have adopted the hypothesis of a high state of civilisation in the principal countries of Asia . . . everything we know of the ancient state of civilisation among the Hindus conspires to prove it was rude . . .'[35] The Hindus were inferior to the Chinese in manufactures; prolix and insipid in literature; obscure in their religion; inhuman in their laws. These inadequacies of their past were paralleled in the grossness of their present:

The Hindus are full of dissimulation and falsehood, the universal concomitants of oppression. The vices of falsehood . . . they carry to a height almost unexampled among the other races of men, and in their quarrels they show a coarseness of expression which leaves the eloquence of Billingsgate far behind . . .[36]

Although somewhat more favourable to the Muslim in matters of religion and manners, Mill regards his moral character with much the same scorn: 'The same insincerity, mendacity and perfidy: the same indifference to the feelings of others; the same prostitution and venality, are conspicuous in both . . .'[37] Mill had never been to India; but the influence of his *History* did much to substantiate those prejudices against India and Indian civilisation which were more usually the product of ignorance and incuriosity. It also served to bury the idea of reciprocal profit which had been stressed by the best minds in India since the time of Hastings. Finally, Mill's choice of comparisons for the purpose of denigration effectively placed obstacles in the path of understanding, by misrepresentation of what he was describing.

Mill's assessment of Hindu character makes an interesting comparison with the actual character of the most celebrated Hindu of the age: Ram Mohun Roy. Among a group of distinguished Bengalis who were attracted to Calcutta in the early part of the century, Roy's name stands out because his talents were more varied, and his attitude towards anglicisation more articulate.

Ram Mohun Roy indicates both in his own personal life and in his public acts the need which had arisen in India for a new sense of identity and national consciousness. The decline of Moghul authority, the effects of the Bengal famine in 1769, and the increasingly obvious presence of a race of new conquerors in the land had resulted in a cultural vacuum which had made the last forty years of the eighteenth century a time of sterility, at least in Bengal. Furthermore, it was apparent that however much the English were disliked, they brought with them arts and skills of which India had need, as well as ways of thought which constituted a challenge, if not a threat, to orthodox Hinduism.

By the age of sixteen Roy had written a pamphlet on the idolatrous practices of the Hindus, among whom his immediate family was numbered. Subsequent isolation from them led to his travelling widely in India, where he developed a feeling of great aversion to the establishment of British rule. But this attitude was later modified. His exceptional ability in languages enabled him to converse with the educated English in Calcutta, probably between the years 1797 and 1802 when he is thought to have been employed by John Digby, a student of Fort William College. If this was so, the profit was mutual, because Digby was interested in the renaissance of Hinduism; and Roy had need of the Western viewpoint to enlarge the perspective of his own developing ideas. He was later to write of the English:

Finding them generally more intelligent, more steady and moderate in their conduct, I gave up my prejudice against them, and became inclined in their favour, feeling persuaded that their rule, though a foreign yoke, would lead more speedily and surely to the amelioration of the native inhabitants: and I enjoyed the confidence of several of them even in their public capacity.[38]

But while Roy looked to the West for progressive ideas, he remained deeply rooted in and attached to much in the Hindu tradition. He could not become anglicised to the degree that the

Eurasian Derozio or many Hindus of a later generation did. But because his outspoken criticism of what he did not like in Hinduism estranged him from the orthodox, he found himself in the anomalous position of being attracted to elements in ways of life and thought in both communities, but belonging to neither.

It was not until he was forty-two – and in the year 1815 – that Roy settled down in Calcutta, and emerged from the isolation in which he had previously lived. By that time he had been deeply influenced by the humanistic ideas of Christianity, for the study of which he took the trouble to learn both Hebrew and Greek. But his main preoccupation was still with the Hindu tradition. Shortly after his arrival he published a translation of the *Vedas** which was intended to show that the original Hindu tradition was monotheistic, and the idolatrous worship of innumerable gods and goddesses a later debasement. By translating the *Vedas* into Bengali, and making it available to people at large, he aimed to reveal that the Brahmins had been concealing the truth of their religion from ordinary people, and also that they themselves were ignorant of its true nature. He argued that there was nothing in the *Vedas*, for example, which justified *suttee*. Criticism of this sort did not win him the favour of the Brahmins; but he was equally unpopular with the Christian missionaries when in 1820 he published his *Precepts of Jesus*, which attacked the idea of the Trinity. As with Hinduism, Roy believed that the true monotheistic tradition had been perverted by later fables. Roy's religious views led in 1828 to the foundation of the Brahmo Sabha (later the Brahmo Samaj) – a non-dogmatic society which believed in the ultimate unity of all religions. In the later part of the century the conflicts within the society – especially between Keshub Chandra Sen and Devendranath Tagore – grew increasingly bitter, as the issue of nationalism became involved with dissent from traditional Hindu practice. Roy in a less complex *époque* was looking for a means to retain what he believed to be valuable in Hinduism and Christianity, without

* The Hindu 'Bible' consisting of the *Samhitas* (collections of metrical prayers and hymns of praise), the *Brahmanas* (prose treatises on the sacrifices) and the *Aranyakas* (intended for dwellers in the forest). The most important part of the last is the *Upanishads*.

cutting himself off from his roots in the Vedantic tradition where he knew he belonged.

But neither Roy's thinking nor his work were only religious in form or intention. He also strove for a new spirit of cooperation between the communities through the writing of articles for newspapers, and his friendships among the English. In particular, he recognised the importance of English education, and gave his support to Hindu College. In a letter to Lord Amherst of 11th December, 1823, he argued for 'a more liberal and enlightened system of instruction, embracing mathematics, natural philosophy, chemistry and anatomy, with other useful sciences . . .'[39] He also worked to encourage the missions in educational enterprise; and attempted to get teachers to spread useful knowledge among the native community without pay. In his journal the *Sambad Kaumudi* which he set up in 1821 he argued for the abolition of *suttee*, as well as a revival of the study of Sanskrit literature and Vedanta philosophy. On other humanitarian matters, he was also an outspoken critic of prevailing conditions. He appealed to the Government to make the services of European physicians available to part at least of the female native population; and to the Calcutta magistrates 'to resort to rigorous measures for relieving the Hindu inhabitants of Calcutta from the serious grievance of Christian gentlemen driving their buggies amongst them and cutting them and lashing with whips, without distinction of sex or age.'[40] In spite of his advocacy of English education, and his loyalty to the Government on most issues, Roy did not win the affection of the majority of Europeans in Calcutta. They resented the fact that a 'presumptuous black' should surpass them in knowledge or persuasiveness concerning the important issues of the day. Equally when *suttee* was abolished by Bentinck in September 1829 Roy's life was threatened by orthodox Hindu assassins, who recognised the importance of his influence in bringing this about.

The following year Roy set out for England as the first of the Moghul's ambassadors to the Court of St James. He was also the first Brahmin to lose caste by crossing the 'black water'. But it was characteristic of the middle way he was always trying to find that he took his Hindu servants to prepare his food on the voyage, and cows to supply him with milk! The remaining three years of Roy's life were spent in England, campaigning for the causes in which he believed. Towards the end, it was said that debts and over-indulgence by the high society which wanted to fête him caused a decline in the energy and authority of his work. He died in Bristol in 1833; his tombstone there records his conscientious and steadfast belief 'in the unity of the Godhead . . . and in the worship of the Divine Spirit alone.' It was this 'intense theistic passion' in Roy that constituted the basis of his desire to assert the common origin of all religions, while combating what seemed to him the superstitions and absurdities of his own. Through this means too he worked for a larger degree of cooperation and understanding between the communities in India.

But significant and crucial as the revival of learning in Calcutta was for the future of the Nationalist movement, its academic and intellectual nature gave it little connection either with the mode of living that prevailed in less sophisticated realms, or with the work being done by a new race of administrators which the extension of Company territories had necessitated. They were often required to be soldiers, statesmen, judges, tax-collectors, and engineers – among other things. They were backed by the conviction that for the time being any other available form of government (or so-called government) by the Indians themselves would inflict more damage on a community which had already suffered a great deal. In February 1801 Thomas Munro described the situation in the territories ceded by the Moghul to the Company like this:

The ten years of Moghul Government . . . have been almost as destructive as so many years of war, and this last year a mutinous unpaid army was turned loose during the sowing season to collect their pay from the villages. They drove off and sold the cattle, extorted money by torture from every man who fell into their hands, and plundered the houses and shops of those who fled . . .[42]

The blinding of Shah Alam in 1788 had effectively brought to an end the Delhi kingdom, itself the last outpost of Moghul power. In the years until his death in 1806 the Emperor attracted sympathy but not respect; and after his death the pretence of British allegiance to the rulers who had once granted them permission to trade became increasingly a formality of peripheral importance. The power and glory which had surrounded the Court fell away, until the impoverished ruler found himself compelled to beg for the means to support the enormous household of relatives and retainers, who looked to him for sustenance. To distinguished visitors, the Emperor became a curiosity in a raree show that had to be seen and gaped at, while the British administration pursued its own ends indifferent to a nominal overlord.

Increasingly, the presence of the British was to be felt throughout the northern part of the continent, though with some of the ruling Princes the British still maintained the friendly deference of visitors in foreign lands. The breakfasts given at Lucknow by the Nawab Vizier of Oudh to visiting Englishmen, of sufficient importance, acquired a celebrity for their lavishness and mixture of styles which 'partook of every country'. To Viscount Valentia who travelled in India during the first few years of the century, the scene was 'so singular, and so contrary to all my ideas of Asiatic manners that I could hardly persuade myself the whole was not a masquerade.' 'The room at dinner was very well lighted up, and a band of music played English tunes during the whole time.'[43] This desire to live in the English style was no less pronounced in the Nawab of the Carnatic who arrived in 'an English coach with four horses, and attended by his bodyguard.'[44] Valentia was close to the mark when he used the word 'masquerade'; these were the trappings of formal alliances that often concealed no real liking for the British presence in India,[45] and underlined the English view of the Asiatic ruler as indifferent to the well-being of his subjects. To anyone who travelled far in India, the contrast between the splendour of the Courts, and the disease, poverty, and famine which surrounded them was all too apparent. In these circumstances, British attitudes towards India, and the relationships which followed from them, increasingly crystallised in two ways: there were those who lived in the *ambiance* of English communities in large cities, or smaller stations and had as little to do with India as possible; and those who identified themselves more closely than ever before with Indian life in order to bring peace and prosperity to a ravaged land. Among the last group, the most successful were invariably those who mastered the native languages, and accepted a life of hardship and isolation.

But the civilisation of Anglo-India in the early nineteenth century formed no neat pattern. The anomaly of a trading-company which was rapidly becoming a form of government presented problems which affected behaviour and attitudes as well as political decisions. For those who lived in English communities, self-assurance and assertiveness could be justified by the idea of the ruling race; for the isolated civil servant there remained the question of the permanence and purpose of English administration. Who was to benefit most from it, and in what ways? As Company men the best administrators did not have to think in terms of a permanent Empire to be retained if necessary by force, but of immediate and pressing tasks which humanity demanded to be performed in a land oppressed by lawlessness and famine. Like the best minds involved in the rediscovery of the Hindu past, they were convinced of the importance of what India had to give to England as well as a changed sense of England's obligation to India. Had the development of Anglo-Indian civilisation shown more of the spirit of its representative figures in this period, and less of that self-regarding provincialism which later predominated, its achievement might now appear larger to us. As it is, the voices of a few are heard above the prejudice and dislike, speaking with an independence that is likeable, and a conviction that is persuasive. But the hour of men like Munro, Malcolm, Elphinstone and Metcalfe, to whom I now turn, was not long. Each in his way left a major imprint on his time, but seen in the perspective of what was to come, the voices of these men do not sound as the shaping spirits of the future; rather they indicate a largeness that was lost, or diminished. What follows after them originates in a smaller vision, and less far-reaching concern.

After a breakfast with the Nawab Vizier of Oudh or a look at the mansions of Chowringhee, this letter written by a young officer in the Company's army, to his sister, in the year 1789, is a refreshing change. His name was Thomas Munro; and he was destined to become not only Governor of Madras, but one of the shrewdest commentators that the Company

above (a), Munro; (b) Elphinstone; *below* (c) R. M. Roy; (d) Macaulay

A Durbar Procession: By 1810 every Briton in Calcutta appeared 'to pride himself on being outrageously a John Bull'

Lord and Lady Moira being entertained to a banquet by the Nawab of Oudh, c. 1814 (see Valentia, p 116, and Fanny Parkes, p 154, on these entertainments)

produced on the problems of Anglo-Indian civilisation. He learnt about India, as all who know it well say it must still be known, in the life of its villages, and among those who depended for their survival on its harshly yielding earth:

You may not believe me when I tell you that I never experienced hunger or thirst or fatigue or poverty, till I came to India – that since then, I have frequently met with the first three, and that the last has been my constant companion. If you wish for proofs, here they are. I was three years in India before I was master of any other pillow than a book or a cartridge-pouch; my bed was a piece of canvas, stretched on four-cross-sticks, whose only ornament was the great-coat that I brought from England, which, by a lucky invention, I turned into a blanket in the cold weather, by thrusting my legs into the sleeves, and drawing the skirts over my head . . . My house at Vellore consists of a hall and bedroom. The former contains but one piece of furniture – a table; but on entering the latter, you would see me at my writing-table, seated on my only chair, with the old couch behind me, adorned with a carpet and a pillow . . .[46]

The significance of the contrast between the conventional image of English extravagance in places like Calcutta, and Munro's austerity of life consisted in the possibility which it provided of his making contact with, and understanding the people he later ruled. Whatever truisms have been uttered about the spiritual life of India, plenty of evidence exists that those Englishmen whose own existence was based on austerity and discipline came closest to that mutual understanding and affection on which the idea of civilisation depends.

The strength of Munro's attitudes towards India lay in their derivation from long practical experience. Competent in Persian, Hindustani, Telegu, Canarese, free of proselytising zeal, and even uncertain if British rule was likely to be beneficial to the people of the country (a doubt that an imperialist could not allow himself to indulge in for long) he was guided by an awareness of the irrelevance to India of theories which took their origin in European attitudes and situations – as, for instance, Cornwallis's 'Permanent Settlement' did. Land and revenue problems, like those of law and order, had to be settled by a just appreciation of local conditions. In the later part of his life, Munro formulated a method for achieving this in a way that left no room for the contempt of a Clive or a Wellesley:

It ought to be our aim to give to the younger servants the best opinion of the natives, in order that they may be better qualified to govern them hereafter. We can never be qualified to govern men against whom we are prejudiced. If we entertain a prejudice at all, it ought rather to be in their favour than against them. We ought to know their character, but especially the favourable side of it.[47]

The importance of these ideas alone is sufficient to give Munro a special place in this book, implying as they do the necessity for being able to accept, through understanding, a different cultural situation before applying remedies to it, and for rejecting all notions of prescriptive right to govern based on innate superiority – particularly a superiority based on entirely different cultural assumptions. It was Munro again who in 1813 reminded the House of Commons that 'if civilisation is to become an article of trade between the two countries' England would gain by what she imported. More positively, he attacked the negative aspect of the typical English critique of Indian character:

Foreign conquerors have treated the natives with violence, and often with great cruelty, but none has treated them with so much scorn as we; none have stigmatized the whole people as unworthy of trust . . .[48]

He also recognised that understanding within so different a context could only come from an acceptance of equality:

We shall never have much accurate knowledge of the resources of the country, or of the causes by which they are raised or depressed; we shall always assess it very unequally, and often too high, until we learn to treat the higher classes of natives as gentlemen.[49]

Even more important, he saw that this could not happen until they themselves felt a proper self-respect which depended on a reversal of Cornwallis's policy of anglicisation – and the psychological and social depression which followed from it:

Our present system of government by excluding all natives from power and trust, and emolument, is much more efficacious in depressing, than all our laws and school-books can do in elevating their character . . . While the prospects of the natives are so bounded, every project for bettering their characters must fail.[50]

The profundity of Munro's intelligence comes out with considerable sharpness in three related views: that people – particularly the more able – are degraded by subjugation, that the stability of the future for British India would depend on closer integration and cooperation, and that the limits of British influence are restricted within narrow bounds:

If any person leaving Madras goes to the nearest Hindu village, not a mile into the country, he is as much removed from European manners and customs as if he were in the centre of Hindustan, and as if no European foot had ever touched the shores of India.[51]

Munro's recognition of the extreme delicacy of the English position also made him in some respects conservative. He did not believe in freedom of the press because he thought this could undermine our authority, especially in the native army, and lead to revolt. As he pointed out, the English were maintaining a foreign dominion by means of a native army. Likewise, he saw the sensitivity of all questions that touched on religion. He did not regard the Mutiny at Vellore on 10th July, 1806, when the sepoys killed thirteen officers and a considerable number of men as a treacherous attack by perfidious natives, but as a reminder of the violence which was likely to be provoked when people's deep-rooted and instinctive beliefs were interfered with. Although Munro believed in the use of British power to maintain order, his severe sensitivity to the complexity and problems of the Anglo-Indian relationship, won for him the affection of the districts he administered, to which he brought both peace and a new prosperity. In fiscal matters too he showed his benevolent and large-minded interest in India, believing and stating, as he did, that the taxes on the peasants were too high, and working for a more equitable system of assessment which was ultimately adopted. Munro may be cited as an example of that paternalism to which exception has been taken; but one has only to see him at his daily work to realise that India of the early nineteenth century had no viable alternative, except the continuation of anarchy and misrule:

From day-break till eleven or twelve at night, I am never alone except at meals and these *altogether* do not take up an hour. I am pressed on one hand by the settlements of the revenue, and on the other by the investigation of murders, robberies, and all the evils which have arisen from a long course of profligate and tyrannical government. Living in a tent there is no escaping for a few hours from the crowd; there is no locking oneself up on pretence of more important business, as a man might do in a house . . .[52]

Efficient, direct, impartial, Munro did his job to the best of his considerable ability, while recognising the weaknesses and limitations of the context in which he was called upon to perform it. He saw the need for Indian judges, and village courts of the kind that were introduced a century later. In the meanwhile what was demanded of him was a life that often consisted of infinite drudgery; but to which he brought an affectionate concern that earned its own reward. To men like Munro the idea and practice of civilisation owe a great deal.

What Munro contributed to the province of Madras, John Malcolm and Mountstuart Elphinstone equalled in Central India and the territory of the Mahrattas. But the manner and style of Malcolm's life-work differed from Munro's as much as the problems he faced. 'Boy Malcolm', as he was known, possessed the dash and high spirits traditionally associated with the young army officer. As a keen sportsman he was quite prepared to break off diplomatic negotiations for the sake of a promising tiger shoot; and fortunately for him a major part of his work was concerned with the pleasures of the chase in one form or another. The peasants of Central India had suffered for a long time from the raids and pillage of the wandering Pindaris. Malcolm, who pursued them with the same determination that he showed on his animal hunts, succeeded in restoring order, and with order, cultivation to lands that had long since been laid waste by fear. But the detailed and crowded events of Malcolm's life can find no place here. In his case, as in Munro's, it is an attitude to the particular problems of Anglo-Indian life which indicates qualities in him that were shared by some in the past, but now put forward as a code of conduct which needed to be commonly accepted if British authority was to be preserved. Basically, it was a simple and old-fashioned code which accepted that though his opponents might act with duplicity and cunning, he would apply to his own behaviour the strictest morality; and he set this up as the standard by which the conduct of all Europeans should be guided:

An invariable rule ought to be observed by all Europeans who have connections with the natives of India – never to practise any art or indirect method of gaining their ends, and from the greatest occasion to the most trifling to keep sacred their word. This is not only their best, but their wisest policy.[53]

Malcolm had the position and power to pursue good ends vigorously; but he was also inspired by a view of what he thought the civilisation of Anglo-India should be, and how it could be achieved. In the first place, he worked unremittingly to make a better way of life possible for the peasants by the introduction of stable government to which his own personal prestige contributed a good deal. He concerned himself also to see that the natives in his army were given proper pay and conditions. This was the time of which Sitā Rāma was later to write about life in the army that 'the sahibs could speak our language much better than they can now, and mixed more with us . . .'[54] Malcolm permitted no arrogance or sense of superiority to interfere with his commitment to those under him; and this generosity extended to his general idea of the obligation which the British presence in India involved. In his view we had an obligation to impart knowledge, even if that promoted love of independence and desire for self-government.[55] There existed in Malcolm a strong trace of that code of chivalry which believed in combating evil and protecting the weak: a code that works best in simpler human situations, but which also has a real, and too easily forgotten relevance in more complex ones. His friend Mountstuart Elphinstone expressed his strengths like this:

Malcolm certainly has wide and enlarged views of policy, and, among them the kind and indulgent manner in which he regards the natives (though perhaps originating in his heart as much as in his head) is by no means the least important.[56]

Although a man of very different temperament, Mountstuart Elphinstone shared qualities comparable to those of Malcolm. When the battle against the Mahrattas was finally won near Poona in 1818, Elphinstone turned to regard his participation in the arts of peace with the utmost modesty. A friend who sent him a work of Jeremy Bentham's on legislation received this reply: '. . . My employment is very humble. It is to learn which system is in force and preserve it unimpaired. I shall think I have done a great service to this country if I can prevent people making laws for it until they see whether it wants them . . .'[57] And of the future of English rule in India, he later said: 'The most desirable death for us to die of should be, the improvement of the natives reaching such a pitch as would render it impossible for a foreign nation to retain the government; but this seems at an immeasurable distance.'[58]

Elphinstone had been among the first students at Wellesley's College of Fort William; and his love of learning, particularly in relation to India, continued throughout his life. He was more cautious by temperament than Malcolm - preferring the Muslims to the Hindus, and never able to overcome his distrust of the Brahmins. The precariousness and instability of the British position in India also led him to believe in the censorship of the press; but, on the other hand, his acceptance of the impermanence of British rule made him advocate the employment of natives in high and responsible situations, and attach considerable importance to the improvement of education. Some thirty years after he left the country he summed up his persistent view of the Anglo-Indian relationship like this:

The moral is that we must not dream of perpetual possession, but must apply ourselves to bring the natives into a state that will admit of their governing themselves in a manner that may be beneficial to our interest as well as their own and that of the rest of the world.[59]

Like Munro, Elphinstone had always seen the importance of reciprocity:

It is not enough to give new laws, or even good courts: you must take people along with you, and give them a share in your feelings which can be done by sharing theirs.[60]

Although Elphinstone was critical of much in the contemporary Indian scene, this did not prevent him from forming warm friendships with many Indians. A man without prejudice, and dedicated like his contemporaries to the improvement of the quality of Indian life, both through education and sound administration, Elphinstone reflects once again the importance of the idea, embodied in Wellesley's 'Oxford of the East'.

The last of these 'statesmen', Charles Metcalfe, has already been introduced as a man who greatly regretted the absence of his friends and good books in the early years of his Indian career. But his talents brought him speedy success, and the powerful position of Resident at Delhi by the age of twenty-seven. As an administrator of large ability and vision he worked unceasingly to save the areas under his control from the ruin and despair which threatened them in the decay of the Moghul Empire. An advocate of a two-way exchange between the communities, he regarded with distaste the obstacles created by the conventions of Indian religious practice, and remained implacably opposed to all forms of exploitation by the English. The improvement of the quality of the society in which he lived could only be brought about, he believed, by working for the benefit of the whole of the community, not just a part of it. A man sufficiently large not to be affected by prejudice, Metcalfe had an Indian wife who bore him three children - a fact that his Victorian biographer chose to suppress.

Metcalfe himself saw the Anglo-Indian relationship without sentiment or illusion. He believed that the power of the English depended solely on military superiority, and had no foundation in the affections of the Indian people. This, however, did not deter him from giving freedom to the Indian press during his single year as Governor-General. And he did so without any concealment of its possible implications:

The real dangers of a free press in India are, I think, in its enabling the natives to throw off our yoke . . . The advantages are in the spread of knowledge, which it seems wrong to obstruct for any temporary or selfish purpose.[61]

Again he was realist enough to know that familiarity with the British was causing wonder at the achievements of a Clive or a

Wellesley to wear rather thin; it needed to be replaced by a new kind of endeavour: 'the charm which once encompassed us has been dissolved, and our subjects have had time to inquire why they have been subdued.'[62] This led him to the conclusion which many would have been unwilling to contemplate in the later part of the century on account of its personal and national consequences: 'If India could only be preserved as part of the British Empire, by keeping its inhabitants in a state of ignorance, our domination would be a curse to the country, and ought to cease.'[63] Metcalfe regarded the European presence as justified in India if the result was 'to pour the enlightened knowledge and civilisation, the arts and sciences of Europe over the land, and thereby improve the condition of the people.'[64] If, once again, Metcalfe seems to be arguing from a strongly paternalist viewpoint, it is also one which shows a respect for the difficulty of the task. He had learnt early in his Indian career that 'wisdom wears one garb on the banks of the Jumna, another on the banks of the Hooghly; and another, it may be added, on the banks of the Thames.'[65]

Metcalfe, like his contemporaries in positions of public importance, was concerned with questions of power, and its use, or abuse, in the Indian context. But the central figures of this period looked beyond the horizons of the Company to the wider implications of the British presence in India, and the challenge which it presented to men of imagination and vision. Conservative in the sense that they did not wish to impose reform, they were also realistic in their appraisal of the inadequacies of the contemporary situation.

In spite of the size and arduousness of the tasks which men like Malcolm and Elphinstone faced every day, they also found time and energy to carry on with the pioneering work of Jones and Colebrooke. Malcolm's work on *Central India* and Elphinstone's *History of India*, which he completed fourteen years after his retirement as Governor of Bombay in 1827, were important contributions to the improvement and spread of knowledge about the Indian past. Elphinstone closed his history with the effective end of the Moghul Empire after the Battle of Panipat in 1761; but his eye also looked to the future: '. . . a new race of conquerors has already commenced its career which may again unite the Empire under better auspices than before . . .'[66] Unlike Mill, Elphinstone was not trying to promote his own prejudices, but create through informed and balanced interpretation of the historical past an understanding of the complex cultural differences which would need to be taken into account in the construction of that unity.

But the number of Englishmen whose interest and dedication went as deep as the boldest figures of this generation was limited; and the distance which separated them from the majority of their contemporaries depressingly large. In the year 1812 a spirited young woman, Miss Maria Graham, published an account of her recent travels in India; in it she displayed an undisguised hostility to the behaviour and attitudes of the English she met.

With regard to the Europeans in Bombay, the manners of the inhabitants of a foreign colony are in general so well represented by those of a country town at home that it is hopeless to attempt making a description of them very interesting. The ladies are under-bred and over-dressed, ignorant, vulgar; the civil servants young men taken up with their own imaginary importance.[67]

In brief, 'the small number of rational companions makes a deplorable prospect to anyone who anticipates a long residence there.'[68] But Bombay was at that time still of minor importance; and in Calcutta she does find 'a greater variety of character, and a greater portion of intellectual refinement.'[69] But to her sorrow she also discovers 'that the distance kept up between the Europeans and the natives, both here and at Madras is such that I have not been able to get acquainted with any native families as I did at Bombay . . .'[70] (Miss Graham is probably referring here to the wealthy Parsee families in Bombay who became anglicised to a marked degree, enjoyed many English sports, and did not live under the same religious restraints as the Hindus). The difficulties of social contact between the communities on the eastern coast are explained by Miss Graham in terms of a crudeness which in different ways affects all of them:

If we look round us, the passive submission, the apathy, and the

degrading superstition of the Hindus; the more active fanaticism
of the Mussulmans; the avarice, the prodigality, the ignorance and
vulgarity of most of the white people, seem to place them all on a
level infinitely below that of the least refined nations of Europe.[71]

It is easy enough to perceive the religious prejudice, confirmed
elsewhere in the journal, which accounts for some part of her
attitude to both Hindus and Muslims; but her criticisms of
the English involve a wider scale of defects which in themselves
would preclude any mature civilisation from developing. And
yet if we are to place any faith in the testimony of the Frenchman, M. Jacquemont, who visited India some twenty years
later, Miss Graham understates, if anything, the case against
the English. M. Jacquemont stresses their extravagance, luxury,
drunkenness - but even more seriously, their neglect of
languages, and their open lack of sympathy with the natives.[72]
He is bewildered in particular by a kind of baseless pride which
makes it impossible for an Englishman to appear 'before the
natives except on a footing of superiority and grandeur.'[73]
His own curiosity, skill in languages, and interest in India
enable him to form friendly and easy relations with the
people he meets, while the English in a position of remarkable
power remain ignorant of those they govern. Jacquemont
actually enjoys being cut off from European contacts, and finds
that he learns more in two months on the further side of the
Sutlej, than in two years of British India; at the same time
when he returns to European society he looks forward to a
kind of companionship which he has missed, and the English
are incapable of supplying:

They have no conversation . . . their chief occupation is cursing the
country, drinking brandy and water and smoking hookahs.[74]

At Poona things are even worse than at Simla:

Ah! what stupid creatures the people at Poona are, my dear fellow!
They go out riding and driving, breakfast, dine, dress, shave and
undress, or meet on committees for settling the affairs of a public
library where I have never seen anybody but myself. They sleep,
sleep a great deal and snore hard, digest as best they can, sin no
doubt, as much as they can and read their newspapers from Bombay;
and that is their whole life! . . . I have tried to make some of them

talk about the land in which they live. They know no more about it than I do, who have only just arrived, and they do not speak any of its dialects. They have not travelled about it, and have no desire to do so, or to know anything about it. Oh! the brutish, brutish creatures![75]

The complaint about the ignorance and lack of curiosity in the English was repeated by many others from Colonel Tod whose *Annals and Antiquities of Rajasthan* (1829-32) made a large contribution to knowledge and understanding of that area, to Wilfred Scawen Blunt and Ramsay MacDonald. Among some of the English it even became a fashionable virtue to air one's ignorance. Mrs Lushington who visited India in the 1820s asked the wife of a senior official what she had seen of the country and people, and got the reply: 'Oh nothing, thank goodness. I know nothing at all about them, nor do I wish to. Really I think the less one knows of them the better.'[76] Whether the climate or an innate dullness was more to blame, the plain fact of the matter was, as Jacquemont observed: 'All but the most able of them soon lose all energy and fall into lax indolence . . .'[77] But this in itself determined the tone of society; and meant that the larger spirits found little support in the community at large, while the growth of a belief in English superiority was fostered by a new breed of reformers, as well as the ignorant and incurious. Mill played his part in destroying the authority of Jones and his fellow-scholars; Bentham provided the reformers with a philosophy; and evangelical Christianity armed the new generation of soldier-administrators with a belief in the unique claims of Christendom. Unfortunately these positive forces found easy allies in the worst type of British settler who had never budged from a position of indifference to everything Indian; and with their support the attitude common to Clive, Cornwallis, Grant and Mill of contempt and mistrust for the Asiatic gained ascendancy over the sound and admirable doctrine of Malcolm:

Great and beneficial alterations in society, to be complete, must be produced within the society itself; they cannot be the mere fabrication of its superiors, or a few who deem themselves enlightened.[78]

The change in tone and emphasis is to be associated in particular with the administration of Bentinck and the name of Macaulay. When Bentinck went to India in 1828, it was, he admitted, to govern in the name of Bentham. The contrast between his attitudes and those of a man like Munro who had spent a lifetime's work in the country are striking enough. Bentinck saw, as Mill had taught him to see (without ever going to India) a land

cursed from one end to the other by the vice, the ignorance, the oppression, the despotism, the barbarous and cruel customs that have been the growth of ages under every description of Asiatic misrule.[79]

He was determined to maintain peace and impose social reform. Some of his reforms like the abolition of *suttee* in 1829, the suppression of *thuggee** and some opening up of better jobs for Indians were humane and beneficial. But Bentinck was inspired by that fervour originating in the notion of a higher and better civilisation of which the English were the purveyors. He even considered demolishing the Taj Mahal, and selling its marble, but was restrained when the test auction of materials from Agra Palace proved unsatisfactory.

Macaulay, like many other Englishmen who went to India for financial reasons, lacked sympathy with the country, and knowledge of its people. He remarked after his return: 'There is no temptation of wealth or power which could induce me to go through it again.'[80] And yet tragically it was Macaulay whose influence was to continue throughout the century to make itself sharply felt in the moulding of the British relationship with India.

Macaulay's departure for India in 1834 as Legal Member of the Governor-General's Council was made necessary by the difficulty of remaining in Parliament without Cabinet rank or

* Thuggee: gangs of travellers who at this period fell in with other native travellers on the road and, at a suitable opportunity, strangled and robbed them. William Sleeman (see next chapter) was appointed by Lord Bentinck to suppress them. Before this occurred, they were thought to have been responsible for twenty to thirty thousand deaths each year. The tale of this terrible and wide-spread profession which was inspired by devotion to the goddess Kali lies outside the scope of this book, as the murders were confined to the Indian community (the disappearance of even a single Englishman would have been quickly noticed); but it is vividly retold in Meadows Taylor's fictional reconstruction, *Confessions of a Thug* (1837).

independent fortune. In a few years of exile he hoped to make his financial position secure; and in this he succeeded. But he was also intent on the high aims of his mission which 'were to bestow on the swarming millions of India the blessings of rudimentary legislation.'[81] At the age of thirty-four Macaulay was convinced that the history of progress was to be found in the history of Europe. The achievements of Europe were clear signs of its being a superior civilisation; and he was determined that the people of India should be helped in the direction of enlightenment and improvement by the legislation for which he would become responsible. The reform of the Indian Penal Code which Macaulay was to complete almost single-handed in two years before his departure remains a remarkable memorial to his intellectual grasp, and comprehensiveness of mind. He produced order out of confusion; and a uniformity that was still flexible enough to meet some at least of the varying needs of the sub-continent, while at the same time exercising his formidable imagination to encompass situations that could not arise in England. The effects of Macaulay's Penal Reform inevitably reached out to touch the lives of magistrates and people all over the country; in this respect it also modified their relationship. It would be a task of immense difficulty and value, well beyond the scope of this book, to attempt an assessment of the degree to which Macaulay's Code fostered more or less understanding; but undoubtedly its comprehensive systemisation, and its foundation in such concepts as the needs of public order and the rights of the individual were beneficial to Indian society. But since all law is a matter of interpretation, misunderstanding and confusion between judge and judged, without a common language, inevitably continued to arise in individual courts.

The reform of the Indian Penal Code cannot concern us further here; our attention must turn to the other immense branch of Macaulay's influence on the course of the British-Indian relationship - that concerned with education and language. Here, as in his Penal Reform Macaulay's intention was to do good, but the freedom with which he could act was curtailed by the long-standing dispute in Calcutta between Anglicists and Orientalists. The full story of this dispute has been ably told by John Clive in his recent biography of Macaulay; in particular he has made clear how the dispute was concerned not only with the choice between education in English or the vernaculars, but with the extent to which it was possible for English to be used. When Macaulay arrived in India and was appointed President of the General Committee of Public Instruction he found his future brother-in-law, Charles Trevelyan, 'engaged in a furious contest against half a dozen of the oldest and most powerful men in India on the subject of native education.'[82] It was Trevelyan too who won over Macaulay to the view that the money spent by the Government on native education should be employed in teaching English rather than Sanskrit or Arabic. Macaulay in turn used his immense powers of persuasion on the Governor-General, Bentinck, to gain his support for the anglicist point of view. Macaulay's attitude was at root strictly utilitarian: to start by teaching people what it was needful and useful for them to know. In matters of fact, he believed, a European education was undoubtedly superior to anything which could be provided by an Arabic or Sanskrit one. Through the English language a man might hope to gain 'full and correct information respecting every experimental science which tends to preserve the health, to increase the comfort or to expand the intellect of man.'[83]

But as always with Macaulay it is necessary not only to scrutinise his logic, but to recognise the dangerous and destructive element in his rhetoric. In the immediate context, his tendency to exaggerate and dramatise was not likely to soothe or palliate his opponents; that scarcely mattered. But Macaulay's mastery of language gave too much that he said a memorable authority; and forged through his arrogant insensitivity to the Indian situation a massive weapon in the service of bigotry and prejudice. Macaulay knew his ground, and was entitled to his rhetoric, when in 1832 he warned the House of Commons of the social and political catastrophe which could result from the rejection of the Great Reform Bill; but when the following year he spoke with no less conviction on the Government of India, he revealed, as later in his 'Minute' on Education the danger of the literary mind in practical politics. Like Milton, who established Macaulay's reputation as an essayist, the power of Macaulay's rhetoric could be invidious. Already dyed with the attitudes of Mill he argued before the House that representative government in India was utterly out of the question, and India would continue to benefit from British rule in the future as she had in the past:

I see that we have established order where we have found confusion. I reflect with pride that to the doubtful splendour which surrounds the memory of Hastings and Clive, we can oppose the spotless glory of Elphinstone and Munro.[84]

He also observed – from a distance – that the morality, philosophy and taste of Europe were beginning to have 'a salutary effect on the hearts and understandings of our subjects.'[85] (How little this arrogant superiority would have been appreciated by Munro!) Macaulay had the knack of thinking in epigrams whose neatness half-concluded the sentiments which underlay them. 'To trade with civilised men is infinitely more profitable than to govern savages.'[86] True – but who were the civilised men, and where were the savages? Such reservations never stopped the flight of Macaulay's rhetoric which bore him on the wings of unrepentant self-flattery:

We are free, we are civilised to little purpose, if we grudge to any portion of the human race an equal measure of freedom and civilisation . . . To have found a great people sunk in the lowest depths of slavery and superstition, to have so ruled them as to have made them desirous and capable of all the privileges of citizens, would be indeed a title to glory all our own.[87]

Macaulay spoke as one endowed with that Divine dispensation that grants to particular individuals and nations a monopoly in civilisation, and a freehold in Truth. Not so much as a whisper of mutual profit or reciprocal learning was apparent. This too was the case when on 2nd February, 1835, Macaulay produced his 'Minute' for Bentinck on the basis of which the Governor-General pronounced in favour of the promotion of European literature and science among the natives of India – and English became, by the stroke of an administrative wand, the official language of the sub-continent.

Macaulay's argument ran along these lines: the languages at

present spoken in India provide neither literary nor scientific information; and they are so poor in themselves that it would not be easy for important works to be translated into them. Since we cannot educate people by means of their mother tongue, we will have to teach them some foreign language. Even in matters of literature, the superiority of European achievements to those in Arabic or Sanskrit is apparent; in works concerned with fact or general principles the superiority of the Europeans is immeasurable. Both from an intrinsic point of view, and for practical reasons, English is the most obvious choice for the education of our native subjects.

Not content with invoking the doctrine of superiority, Macaulay was impelled, as usual, to deride the alternative, as he saw it: 'History abounding with kings thirty feet high, and reigns thirty thousand years long, and geography, made up of seas of treacle and seas of butter.'[88] It followed from this that money spent on Arabic or Sanskrit colleges was 'bounty-money paid to raise up champions of error.'[89] And the teaching of the Sanskrit language was an equal folly: 'It is confessed that a language is barren of useful knowledge. We are to teach it because it is fruitful of monstrous superstitions . . .'[90] This course must be rejected in favour of teaching what is best worth knowing: the English language. And as this could not be done for everyone, the end must be a 'class of people who can act as intermediaries between us and the millions we govern: a class of persons, Indian in blood and colour, but English in taste, in opinions, in morals, and in intellect.'[91]

The adoption of Macaulay's proposals produced, surprisingly, just the class he envisaged. Politically this helped them to argue their own case for democratic and representative government which Britain symbolised in her Mother of Parliaments. But the absoluteness and intransigence of Macaulay's attitude to Indian culture, and his conviction of English superiority gave licence to a tone and attitude that inevitably drove the communities apart; under the present system of mixed education, he proclaimed:

We are a Board for wasting public money, for printing books which are of less value than the paper on which they are printed was while

it was blank; for giving artificial encouragement to absurd meta-
physics, absurd physics, absurd theology . . .[92]

In the full flood of his mind Macaulay wanted to wash away
a civilisation belonging to hundreds of millions of people, and
thousands of years – all in a 'Minute'. It was not of course that
India did not have need of Western education in terms of
science and technology, or that at one level, Macaulay's views
were not correct. But in his arrogant dismissal of all that was
un-English, he, like Cornwallis, was closing the door upon
increased understanding or closer cooperation, except among
those Indians able and willing to assimilate the manners of
their masters. The disadvantages and dangers in this were
apparent enough; and Macaulay found himself fiercely attacked
by the leading Orientalist of the time. H. H. Wilson rightly
objected to a policy of making 'a whole people dependent on a
remote and unknown country for their ideas and very words.'[93]
It was also the impossibility of it which impressed W. H.
Macnaughten: 'the notion that the English language would
ever become the language of India is purely chimerical.'[94]
As with many things about the Anglo-Indian relationship,
the legacy of Macaulay's 'minute' is not easy to evaluate.
Clearly his view (shared by Bentinck) that if his plans of
education were followed up, 'idolatry' would come to an end
among the educated sections of the population in Bengal within
thirty years was wholly wrong;[95] but equally too, if Nehru
was right in thinking technology the most important and
valuable contribution of the British to India, Macaulay must
take a good share of the credit for its decisiveness in favour of
an education so largely devoted to fact.
But as with Mill's *History*, the indirect influence of Macaulay's
'Minute' must also be taken into account. It represents a
turning away from the legacy of the Indian past for the sake of
an anglicised future. And because it was implemented as a
practice its influence was to be felt by everyone who came to
India in however important or private a capacity. The language
of the ruling race was the language of India; and it was so
because their culture had shown itself to be superior. Jacquemont had already noticed the inability of the English to ap-

preciate the unfamiliar; Macaulay made the familiar (to him) the only path for progress. He also settled the debate between Anglicists and Orientalists in favour of the former, paying little attention to the obvious need for primary education in the vernaculars. In the same year as the 'Minute', Bentinck took one more step towards the abolition of the College of Fort William by closing the dormitory at the Writers' Building.

After Macaulay's 'Minute', little was heard of the notion of reciprocal advantage. Plenty of men still shared the dedication of Munro; but few did not regard their task as an attempt to enlighten an inferior people, and to rule them for their own good. The Proclamation of Crown Rule in 1858 served to entrench this attitude by the loyalty to national policies and codes of behaviour which it demanded. If in 1810 every Englishman in Calcutta had acted as though he were a John Bull by instinct; a half-century later it had become part of his duty. In spite of the undeniable practical advantages which resulted from Macaulay's 'Minute', he had done a great deal to set the ship moving in that direction which less than thirty years later would cause a Calcutta journalist to say:

As regards Indian literature . . . history, antiquities, the present race of Anglo-Indians (the British in India) . . . are lamentably ignorant . . . Jones, Colebrooke, Wilson . . . respected our fathers and looked upon us hopefully at least with melancholy interest, as you would look on the heir of a ruined noble. But to the great unwashed today, we are simply niggers – without a past; perhaps without a future. They do not choose to know us.[96]

The future was in fact made by those who anglicised themselves fastest and most fully. They learned their Shakespeare and Milton, as they learned their Burke and their John Stuart Mill. But on the English side, though good Orientalists still remained, the desire to understand which leads to comprehension, if not acceptance, passed away. In time, even the idea of it would come to be derided. Three-quarters of a century after Macaulay, an Englishman in a novel would be heard to say, when his companion remarked that he did not understand the Indians: 'Understand! Of course you don't. I don't though I've been here ten years. And what's more I don't want to.'[97]

In a country where traditions and beliefs of great age still retained as much vitality among the population at large as they did in India of the mid-ninteeenth century, there was bound to be conflict of the kind which Roy had experienced when the anglicised Indian wished to assert the persistent value of his national culture in particular respects. History does not repeat itself nor its chances come again. But if the idea and practice of civilisation is to survive, it will be in the continuation of that idea of reciprocal advantage which was shared by Hastings, Jones, Munro and Ram Mohun Roy - not the dismissiveness of Thomas Babington Macaulay who talked most about it.

Chapter 6

Birth of the 'Nigger'

Our Judge . . . there you see him in his court – niggers
– ten thousand pardons! no, not niggers, I mean natives
– sons of the soil – Orientals, Asiatics, are his source
of happiness . . .
G. F. ATKINSON, *Curry and Rice*, 1859

It is indeed because the European officer is a superior
being by nature to the Asiatic, that we hold India
at all . . .
GENERAL SIR JOHN JACOB, *Views and Opinions*, 1858

Of an evening, where the fountains are playing, and
the odour of exotic flowers is on the air, the fall of the
water has a delightful effect both on the eye and ear:
it is really an Indian paradise.
F. PARKES, *Wanderings of a pilgrim in search of the
picturesque*, 1850

IN 1836 the map of India remained practically as it had been
in 1818.* But the annexation of Sind (1843), the Punjab (1849)
and Oudh (1856) in the next twenty years were to make sub-
stantial additions to the territory under direct British rule. At
the same time, wars against the Afghans and the Burmese in
the 1840s were to focus attention on the fortunes of British
arms and the frontiers of the Empire, rather than the domestic
problems of ruling what had already been acquired.

The decisive effect of Bentinck's resolution in favour of
English education reduced the ardour of the debate between
Orientalists and Anglicists which had been in the air for the
last fifty years; and a decline in the reforming zeal of the
Governor-General which manifested itself in the succeeding
administration of Lord Auckland, together with his involve-

* With the exception of the neighbouring territories of Assam, Arrakan, and the
Tenasserim coast.

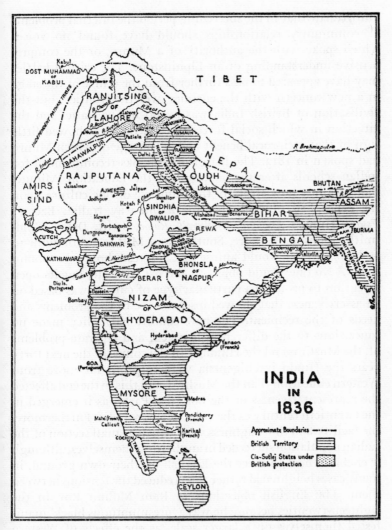

INDIA
IN
1836

Approximate Boundaries ·–·–·–
British Territory ▤
Cis-Sutlej States under
British protection ▦

ment in the disastrous First Afghan War, gave a new importance to the role of the Empire in Asian affairs. If it was scarcely desirable that, as Lord Ronaldshay put it, Bentinck and Macaulay thought of India as 'inanimate clay to be moulded at the potter's whim, not a complex living organism with a distinctive individuality of its own',[1] it was correspondingly unfortunate that in the succeeding period the internal problems of community relationships should have found no voices which spoke with the authority of a Munro, or the comprehensive understanding of an Elphinstone. The critical battles may have appeared to pass further from the centre of the stage in a new concern with the enemies over the frontier; but the civilisation of British India was by no means static, and the direction in which social forces were advancing showed little sign of that reciprocal benefit and advantage of which Munro had spoken in 1813. The list of prize books recommended for Indian schools after the adoption of the Education 'Minute' indicates just how strongly the influence of one culture upon the other had officially become a one-way traffic: Bacon's *Essays*, Hume's *England*, Gibbon's *Rome*, Swift, Defoe, Goldsmith, Johnson, Voltaire, Southey and Mill were 'thought to be books which would amuse and interest those who obtain them'.[2] No one would object to the list in itself; but its open intention to promote a particular type of culture was based on an assertiveness that showed insensitivity to the problems and needs of the recipient. The new educational policy made no concessions to the differences between, and separate problems of, the Muslims and the Hindus.* In the course of the next forty years the Hindu intelligentsia were to profit far more from Western education than the Muslims, and this in the end affected the representativeness of the Congress Party, as it emerged in the twentieth century as the voice of a new India. Furthermore, the facility and thoroughness with which a small section of the Indian population succeeded in anglicising themselves, although it enabled them to meet the English on their own ground, in many cases heightened rather than reduced the tensions between them. The English objections to Ram Mohun Roy in the eighteen-twenties because he was a 'presumptuous black' manifested themselves on a larger scale, as the effects of Western education began to be felt. In addition, the increasingly evangelical fervour of many of the English, together with the hardening of their class attitudes, influenced both their re-

---

* This was partly due to the more militant attitude of Islam to a Christian nation and to less interest on the part of the Muslims than the Bengali Hindus in participating in Government. In both respects the Hindus possessed a motive which the Muslims lacked.

lationship with one another, and with the Indian community. The emergence of a rigid pecking-order in English society reflected the upper-middle class desire for an aristocracy which did not exist, and so had to be invented.* But it also pointed to a change which was occurring in English society as a result of the new industrial age. The bleak and meaningless snobberies which Thackeray depicted in the Newcome family, or Dickens in the Veneerings, were paralleled and exaggerated in India, where a small and isolated community was in need of bolstering its self-assurance.

In the first part of this chapter I intend to illustrate how in the years between the end of Bentinck's administration and the Mutiny, the tone of Anglo-India started to change, not so much by the presence of entirely new attitudes, but rather by a new kind of conformity which ranged the genuine supporters of an anglicist policy on the side of those who through ignorance, prejudice, or sheer indifference found India and all its ways objectionable. Among the English community - and long before the Mutiny had soured relationships further - there were plenty of people who could not abide India, and would not have done so, if circumstances had let them go free. Without pleasure in the country, they also lacked informed interest about it. In contrast to these, a small minority remained knowledgeable and dedicated. While they were impotent to transform the wider scene, they contributed notably to peace and material progress in the parts of India where they served. The second part of the chapter will be concerned with them.

Of all the places in India associated with British rule Simla retains a special significance. The start of its rise to fame as a health resort began in the 1820s. Victor Jacquemont, the French traveller who visited it in 1830, was impressed by an especially shocking example of the English determination never to appear before the natives except on a footing of

* In time this came to apply not only to rank within the Indian Civil Service, which together with the Army, came at the top; but to the other Civil Servants employed in India whose pay and pensions were less than those of the I.C.S.: i.e. members of the Geological, Botanical, Zoological, Archaeological Surveys, the Public Works Dept., the Railways, etc. It took a long time for a member of the Public Works Department to be socially accepted.

superiority and grandeur, in the person of Major Kennedy. He had been one of the first to settle on the future Olympus of the Empire; and he exercised his divine right with extravagance; on an income of a hundred thousand francs a year, he commands 'a regiment of mountain chasseurs, the best corps in the army. He performs the duties of receiver-general, and judges, with the same independence as the Grand Turk, his own subjects, and moreover those of the neighbouring Rajahs, Hindoos, Tartars, Tibetans; these he imprisons, fines, and even hangs when he thinks proper.'[3] To some Simla symbolised a panacea for all Indian ills; to others a proof of the much quoted view that the English left all their morals behind at the Cape. With its bungalows on their terraces, its gardens with flowers, and the Elizabethan style of what became the Governor-General's house, it might almost have been England. Its remoteness, both physically and socially from Indian life, endowed it with a particular charm for the English exile. There, when he was not administering the Empire, he could indulge himself in the sports and pastimes of home: riding, tennis, cricket, picnics, and in the later part of the century, polo.* If you couldn't set out for England, then Simla was about the next best place you could be. 'We pass our lives in gardening,' wrote Emily Eden in the eighteen-thirties with a note of impatience which was scarcely mollified by the reflection that the English endured better and kept better (like meat) at Simla than elsewhere in India.[4] But the price of the exclusive retreat often manifested itself in its restrictedness and provincialism. Miss Eden was too sharp-witted not to observe of the devoted wives who would not go out while their husbands were away at the First Afghan War: 'If the war lasts three years they will be very dull women.'[5] W. H. Russell, *The Times* correspondent who visited Simla in 1858 said of it: 'Here we have ball after ball, each followed by a little back-biting.'[6] But he was also a good enough journalist to get the Indian point of view from a 'native gentleman': '. . . The impassive servants regard the English in their revelry . . . like this: "They are afraid to laugh. But they do

* Polo, which became the main leisure occupation of the English, especially in the Army, started to be played in the 1860s. 'We devoted ourselves to the serious purpose of life. This was expressed in one word – Polo!' (W. S. Churchill: *My Early Life*, 1930, p. 112).

regard you as some great powerful creatures sent to plague them, of whose motives and actions they can comprehend nothing whatever".[7] A large part of the 'mystery' of English social life depended on the rigidity and strictness of its social conventions. A job in the covenanted civil* service was as good as a peerage; and those without titles lived beyond the pale, whatever their wealth.

It was not altogether coincidental that the rise of Simla in popularity occurred when English prejudices were intensifying under the influence of conventional notions of respectability. Simla might even be seen as a symbol of the desire to forget about India; and certainly in the future it came to stand for a collective superior togetherness. In that community, whether actual or metaphorical, the native had no place. He was relegated to a lower division, and judged by a different code of values.

An increasing dislike and disregard for India, especially among those who did not belong to the covenanted civil service, is indicated in the common substitution of the word 'nigger' for 'native', which grew in popularity in the 1840s. The connotations of the word from its use in the New World were suggestive of slavery and degradation. Native, although it signified non-European and so uncivilised, carried none of the dismissive contempt (no doubt grounded in a good deal of fear) of its substitute. In Charles Acland's *Popular Account of the Manners and Customs of India* (1847) he tells of an English expedition to the Neilghirry Hills, on which the local Rajah had offered to accompany the English visitors:

Our party began to move on, when I asked, 'Will you not wait for the Rajah?' 'I should think not,' was the reply, 'we don't want the beastly niggers with us.' And yet these civilised men were glad enough to make use of the beastly niggers' coolies and elephants . . .

The following day the two Rajahs called at the tent. 'They entered as gentlemen, and made the usual Indian salutation. With the exception of myself, I do not think one of our party even rose from his chair . . .'[8]

* Members of the Indian Civil Service were selected after 1858 by public examination. They were popularly known as '£300 dead-or-alive' men because of the pensions which were paid to widows. This made them extremely eligible!

The increasing prosperity of some middle-class Indian families, especially in Calcutta, was also starting to cause unease among the English. In the mid-eighteen-thirties the great shoe question caused a good deal of commotion. The problem was whether natives should be allowed to appear in the Governor-General's presence, without removing their shoes. English opinion was split between the more enlightened anglicists who thought the natives should be encouraged to adopt European habits as quickly as possible; and the conservatives who wanted to keep them in place. Lord Auckland decided in favour of allowing them to come with their shoes on to a levee or a ball, but not to an official reception. Auckland also caused a sensation in Calcutta at this time by going to dine with a native, the wealthy and philanthropic Dwarkanath Tagore, grandfather of the poet. (As was pointed out it was even more remarkable for a native to dine with a Governor-General because 'very few would even sit by while we were eating'.)[9] Even so, fourteen of the Governor-General's servants had to be sent on 'because it would have been quite beneath us to allow the servants of a native to give us any tea . . .'[10] A decade later the Marquess of Dalhousie was appalled to find that 'the old school' objected to native officers being invited to the Governor-General's ball. He determined to change this since they held the CO's commission and the orders from the Court of the Company were very precise as to their being treated like gentlemen. He noticed, however, that there was a growing distance between European officers and native soldiers. '. . . When one sees an insignificant act of courtesy to fine old fellows who have been fighting for you for 30, 40, 50 years, and which can have no effect but that of gratifying their feelings, and disposing them well towards the government one represents, thus perverted into a source of danger to discipline by the distorting force of antediluvian prejudice . . . it really stirs one's bile . . .'[11] But it was not only amongst the 'old guard' that such prejudice existed. It was part of a much more widespread change which the native soldier was aware of as well. One of these, Sitā Rāma, observed that in the second decade of the century, the Sahibs spoke the language and knew their men; twenty years later they only 'speak to their men when obliged, and evidently show that it is irksome to them, and try to get rid of them as soon as possible . . .'[12]

Whether the increasingly bad treatment of the natives in terms of abuse, both physical and verbal, encouraged a sense of superiority, or was the product of it, it alienated not only the sufferers, but those members of the English community sufficiently intelligent or sensitive to dislike it. Such feelings tended to foster a desire to leave India, not stay and change it, as well as dislike for the English who were running the system. Emily Eden is oppressed by the obvious miscarriages of justice which occur when European juries refuse to condemn those charged with a crime against a native; and by the sight of young officers driving fast through the streets under the burning sun, with their servants running after them, just for the show. She also cites with fury the case of an indigo-planter who hunts natives with his bull-dog, among other examples of torture (or even murder) which the low Europeans get away with.[13] From all these horrors the only hope of reprieve is escape.

In both fact and fiction of the period, abundant evidence exists of the brutality with which the English used their servants. In *Peregrine Pulteney*, a novel published in 1844 by William Kaye, this provoked some serious reflection as to the nature of English illusions about India: 'We must be a very sanguine set of people indeed if, when we sow blows and black-guardism, we expect to reap a harvest of gratitude. And yet this is precisely what we do – we beat and abuse our servants, and wonder that they are not grateful in return.'[14] Any feelings of guilt about this could most easily be suppressed and were, by assuming that 'niggers' did not share human feelings, and in many respects were scarcely better than animals. '. . . For niggers – Orientals, I mean – have that peculiar faculty which characterises the ape and the kangaroo; they can only stand erect on occasion. Let a nigger alone, and down he drops upon his hams spontaneously.'[15] This attitude of deprecation came to be applied to all natives, whatever their wealth or position. From the very first evening when W. H. Russell drove on the Calcutta course in 1858 he was shocked by the insult 'offered to those who by no means admit themselves to be the plebeians of the race.'[16] Not only was there no rapprochement between the Indian and the Englishman, but an actual barrier, which neither desired to cross, existed. He hoped that things would be better up country than in Calcutta. He soon discovered they were not.

The distinctions between the races which had always been apparent in, for instance, the black and white town at Madras had now spread generally to the cantonments. 'You find by degrees,' Russell writes, 'that an Indian station consists of two parts: the cantonments, of the Europeans, the native city and the bazaar . . . Belgravia is not so much removed from Houndsditch in feeling, modes of life, and thought, as our western station from our eastern bazaar. There is no bond of union between the two, in language, or faith, or nationality.'[17] This situation had not grown up overnight, but had gradually evolved from the original geographical divisions in the seventeenth century. What was new, however, was the intrusion of racial distinction upon the use of everyday facilities, and improvements made, it might be supposed, for the benefit of the governed. Russell cites in particular the case of the Government bungalows which have been built for travellers:

These buildings, though in theory open to all, are in practice and reality reserved almost exclusively for Europeans . . . These and all such government works are for the white man, and not for the black. The latter buries himself in the depth of some wretched bazaar, or in the squalid desolation of a tottering caravanserai. There would be as much indignation experienced at any attempt on the part of the natives to use the stageing bungalows as there is now expressed by some Europeans in Calcutta at their audacity in intruding upon 'ladies and gentlemen' in first class carriages.[18]

When Russell complains about these distinctions, he is told he doesn't understand 'those niggers yet'; and to this he justly replies that Englishmen don't seem quite the same in India: they 'become very argumentative and theoretical . . .'[19]

The influence of an increasingly large number of English women in India who wished their children to be brought up in a clean and godly manner encouraged this kind of exclusiveness. But the reign of the Memsahib was only just beginning; thirty years later it would have been inconceivable for a Governor-General to have sustained a family relationship with an Indian lady as Charles Metcalfe had done; in the 1830s the natural and easy permissiveness of the eighteenth century, though rapidly disappearing, still lingered on among some families, as Fanny Parkes will shortly relate; and it is for this reason that I have chosen to leave consideration of the blame attached to the behaviour and prejudice of the Englishwoman in India until the time of her undoubted sway in the later nineteenth century.

In 1837 F. J. Shore published an account of his work as Judge of the Civil Court and Criminal Sessions of the District of Furrukabad. In this he made clear that the course of British administration was, by default and intention, moving in the direction of an acceptance that the differences between the two cultures were so large that it was better to recognise this and live with it, than try to understand the nature of the differences, and see where viable compromises could be found.

Shore realised that, in spite of the efforts made by the early Orientalists to inform the British administrator of the nature of Muslim and Hindu law, a judge needed understanding of the community and its people. But the English were in his view taking the opposite path: arrogant and supercilious behaviour was on the increase:

The majority (of the civil and military officers) purposely keep aloof from the people, wrapped in their own dignity, which they think would be lowered were they to hold any communication with the natives, except such as are officially employed; they consequently are shamefully ignorant of the manners and customs of the people, and even of their own duty...[20]

In relation to incompetence, Shore saw that the problems of language were paramount. A magistrate to be efficient needed to be fluent in both Persian and Hindi; he was probably not even really proficient in one. More often than not the proceedings would be conducted in a language which neither the judge nor the defendant understood – and without a common language between them. Shore further observed that, as the

rule of the English became more firmly established, the bitterness aroused by their not understanding Hindi increased. In a
situation of complex social and religious relations of the kind
which existed in India, a judge needed the more urgently to
understand what was being said and done. As Kipling was later
to remark with succinctness, this type of understanding was not
only acquired in courts of law; it meant mixing with the
Indians in everyday life, and being able to talk to them in their
own dialect. As things were, the native member in Council
probably knew as much about Punjabis as he did about Charing
Cross.[21] Shore, for his part, was no less scathing about the
hopelessness of 'trying to teach a hundred million illiterates,
almost all of whom were slaving from morning till night to
scrape up a bare subsistence, a foreign language.'[22] Shore did
what remarkably few English commentators possessed the
imagination to do: and that was to ask how effective and
practical it would be arbitrarily to introduce Mohammedan
or Hindu law in England. The ordinary Indian stood at a double
disadvantage when he was involved in proceedings against an
Englishman: the Indian did not understand the law; and the
accused Englishman usually had greater economic power to
indulge in the well-accepted custom of bribes. In the end Shore
saw the legal issue in black and white terms which were un-
answerable, but never properly implemented. The people had
the right to demand that the business of the courts was conducted in the vernacular; the English if they were to continue
as rulers had a duty to learn those languages, and by these
means strive to form some community of feeling with the
people whose land they inhabited. Until this happened, the
Indians were not very likely to feel cordial to the English.

But Shore also saw that in spite of, or perhaps because of,
their increasing authority, the English were alienating themselves further: 'In the present times when an Englishman does
treat the natives with merely common civility, he is looked
upon as a wonder.'[23] A Munro or a Malcolm would have reacted
to Shore's observation with a proper aristocratic contempt, not
least for the lack of independence of thought. Standardisation
of behaviour and conformity of attitude were accepted by the
young Englishman almost as soon as he arrived in the country.

Ignorant about native character and unable to speak more than a few words of any Indian language, they would yet insist that they hated the natives, who had no good qualities, and almost every bad one; in short, that they were a degraded lot. In the eighteenth century such attitudes were shared by many; but there was an important difference between each side holding a low opinion of the other's integrity and the unquestioned assumption of a conquering nation towards its subject peoples, especially in matters such as the law.

Even during his own career Shore was aware of the deterioration in community relations. The English used to pay some attention to the natives and treat them with consideration and civility. The Muslims who in the past would eat with the English no longer did. Even the class of servant prepared to work for the English had declined. Shore ultimately placed the blame for this deterioration in good relations on the anglicisation policy of Cornwallis. The idea that the natives were not fit to be trusted had both degraded them, and helped to crystallise an attitude of public disapproval which even manifested itself in the idea that 'a man who treats the natives with too much civility and attention will be in bad odour with his Government.'[24] Shore also attached a good deal of importance to colour, which had had little attention paid to it in the seventeenth and eighteenth centuries. The English have got to endeavour, he says, to conquer their dislike of the colour of the inhabitants of India, so far as to treat them with a little civility. 'Many English are apt to imagine, that because their skins are black, it is impossible that they should possess the common feelings of human nature.'[25] Such an attitude discloses not only the increasing emphasis placed on race in Anglo-India, but a hardening and unimaginative response to their situation among the English community at large. This served both to draw them together as one large family in any matter of conflict with the Indians, and to make the Englishman who fell out of step in any way an object of public disapproval. It was an attitude which many had already learnt well at their public-schools.

But Shore did not rest content with unconstructive criticism. He argued the desirability of 'getting Indians to join us socially at our meals';[26] and a larger understanding of the differences between the two cultures, through an improvement in the ability of the English to speak Indian languages, and an end to the adoption of conventional attitudes and generalisations about the natives. This in itself would involve the admission with proper pay of Indians to jobs and responsibilities they were quite capable of undertaking. But above all he urged the necessity for the English to gain familiar and intimate knowledge of the Indians by breaking out of their own small communities, when in fact they were tending to enclose themselves more.

The British in India did not like criticism; and Shore left the country without the promotion he deserved. If his views failed to do justice to the larger spirits of his time, he nevertheless recorded accurately the existence of tendencies which were gradually altering the tone of Anglo-Indian society. The distance which separated the communities in matters of livelihood was now having its effect on the way each thought about the other; and not least in the acceptance of the gulf between them as uncrossable.

The forces that served to limit the viewpoint of the English or, to put it the other way, caused a deterioration in community relationships, are not easy to define. But without any doubt the evangelical bias of Christianity in the early Victorian period did a great deal to foster intense disapproval of heathen practices and idolatries. Equally certainly when the Mutiny did come, the fear of conversion to Christianity was among the most often quoted reasons given for its outbreak. But this had also been true at Vellore in 1806. Shore himself had complained of the narrow-mindedness of some of the missionaries who could see no good qualities in Hinduism, and could only catalogue its crimes and vices. Another observer at this time also remarked on the ignorant vituperation of Hinduism by Christian missionaries, and the indolence of English chaplains who could hardly speak intelligibly to their servants.[27] But of far wider significance was the Christian 'soldier' who might well justify the imperial ambitions of the English by reference to the task of bringing Christianity to India. While the Company continued to implement a policy of official neutrality in matters of religion, it did not prevent the Empire builders of

(a) Simla with a view of Lord Auckland's house, not long after Emily Eden's stay there; (b) The snows from Simla with a lady in a jampan admiring them

Fête at Annandale: see Emily Eden's description of a similar occasion on p 19; she remarks of the natives seated on the hill: 'I sometimes wonder they do not cut all our heads off and say nothing more about it.'

'Sowing, ploughing and breaking clods': the India
which most English people did not, and could not, know

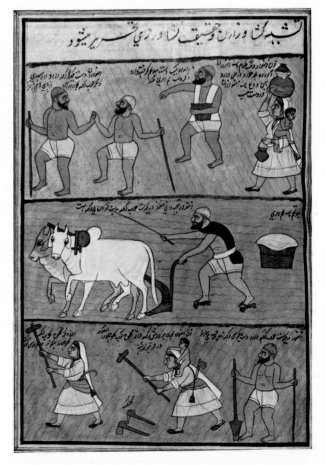

Mutiny: the wages of ignorance

the mid-century from laying their hands to the Christian plough in a private capacity. In particular, men like Herbert Edwardes and Henry Lawrence who were destined to play central parts in the Mutiny displayed that austere type of 'muscular Christianity'[28] which was to prove effective in encouraging respect and loyalty, but was restricted by the narrowness of its vision.

Sir Herbert Edwardes, for example, believed, on the one hand, in the utter depravity of the natives, and, on the other, in the duty to evangelise India, which was the responsibility of the private Christian. India had in fact been given to England, he believed, rather than to the Portuguese or the French, because 'England has made the greatest effort to preserve the Christian religion in its purest apostolic form.'[29] Force of circumstance, and Will of Providence decreed that we should govern India - a belief that was confirmed by the outcome of the Mutiny. Speaking at the inauguration of the Clive Memorial in Shrewsbury on 18th January, 1860, he said: 'The Giver of Empires is indeed God. But God works through human means, . . . and in honouring the instrument we do but honour the Providence that wields it.'[30]

Incredulity that Edwardes really believed this should not be allowed to conceal the strength and authority which faith of such sort gave to him and other earnest Victorians in India at this time. Edwardes found his vocation in India; but by no means all derived his satisfaction from the struggle against paganism. Honoria Lawrence, the wife of Henry, confided in a letter that she found nothing attractive in the native character and was tired of living among the seven deadly sins. 'There is something very oppressive,' she went on, 'in being surrounded by heathen and Mahommedan darkness, in seeing idol-worship all around, and when we see the deep and debasing hold these principles have on the people, it is difficult to believe they can ever be freed from it . . . I hear it said on every hand that missionaries are not effective, but no one seems to have found the way of making them more so.'[31] In a later part of the letter she revealed the personal significance for her of Christianity, and the strength which she derived from it in the arduous life she led - in camp from October till May or June. 'The deep and debasing hold' of heathen principles, once observed, provided the platform for justifying British rule on moral as well as religious grounds.

The irony of the situation was that, outside the small group of rulers and evangelicals, English society showed few signs of that higher morality on which the argument rested. For the most part it was a crudely and openly materialist society which W. D. Arnold did not spare in his novel, *Oakfield* (1854): 'There is an utter want of nobleness in the Government of India . . . the evil is a money-getting earthly mind that dares to view a large portion of God's world, and many millions of God's creatures, as a more or less profitable investment, as a good return for money laid out upon them.'[32] In his view the lowest ranks of English society were 'gross', and the highest 'false and mammonish'. Their concern for the well-being of India was limited by their own material objectives. Those who wanted to do good conceived it in terms of dragging the Indian population (or some of it anyway) to the Olympian heights on which they already resided. It was not an attitude that appealed to Russell's good judgment, or his liking for honesty. In 1858 he was especially incensed by a sermon preached on the theme that the English Empire would not fall as other Empires had fallen because it was Christian. He retorted: 'I believe that we permit things to be done in India which we would not permit to be done in Europe. Our Christian zeal in Exeter Hall* will not atone for usurpation and annexation in Hindustan, or for violence and fraud in the Upper Provinces of India.'[33] A viewpoint like this shed a bizarre light on the faith of Governor-General from 1864-9, Sir John Lawrence, 'We have not been elected or placed in power by the people, but we are here through our moral superiority, by the force of circumstances and by the will of Providence.'[34]

The tone of a civilisation is to some extent set by its leaders; and the generation of men who went out to India in the two decades before the Mutiny and distinguished themselves in it (like Edwardes, Nicholson, and the Lawrence brothers) were strongly motivated by Evangelical Christianity. Unfortunately, their rejection of India for its morality and religion had all too

* Exeter Hall was used as a meeting-place by Evangelicals in this period.

much in common with those who rejected it for more worldly reasons. In these two decades too, the effect of the new industrial age was beginning to make itself sharply felt in India. Especially during the Governor-Generalship of Lord Dalhousie (1848–56), the building of railways, the initiation of a post-office and telegraph service, and the development of civil engineering began slowly but significantly to change the nature of Indian life. The first railway station in Bombay was built beside a new Hindu temple: 'the works of the rulers and the ruled – the last triumphs of science side by side with the superstitions of thousands of years ago.'[35]

But age had not withered the infinite variety of the last; and the new technical skills of the English provided another instance of superiority which was inflamed when the 'childishness' of the Indians impeded progress. Lacking a sufficient respect for accuracy, and obdurate in any conflict with their religious beliefs, they often created a real obstacle to efficient work. Colonel Sleeman cited the characteristic case of a Mohammedan law officer who told him: 'I would not hold the evidence of all the telescopes in the world as against one word uttered by the humblest of the prophets named in the Old and New Testaments, or the Holy Koran.'[36] The similarity to the case of Galileo points to the size of the time-lag which existed in the scientific evolution of the two nations at this time; and it is paralleled accurately enough in other instances too. It was on 10th January, 1836, that Pandit Madhusadan Gupta became the first Hindu to dissect a human body for the purpose of teaching anatomy.[37] Three years later Lord Auckland presented the first diplomas for Indians to practise as surgeons. With a start of more than two centuries it was not surprising that impediments existed to the marriage of minds. But the lack of training in the exact sciences which characterised Indian civilisation helped to harden the prejudice against it. Equally oppressive and irritating to the Englishman in his new drive for tangible achievements were the religious objections – and those of caste – to improved sanitation. The majority of illnesses were still ascribed to evil spirits or the evil eye[38] – and in some places blights to crops were said to result from an increase in adultery that had come in with British rule! As had been true in Europe, the advance of the sceptical spirit upon which scientific inquiry depended did not occur in a hurry; early attempts to start Colleges of Technology met with little success. W. Medlicott in his final report to the Government of India as Director of the Geological Survey in 1886 said that in his view the scientific education given to Indians in the previous fifty years had been largely wasted; it had not produced one single case of original scientific work. 'Of imitation there is no lack, but of creative power there is no sign.'* In the last decade of the century John Lockwood Kipling, Rudyard's father, still regarded the absence of training in scientific discipline as a major problem in Anglo-Indian relations, in spite of the advances which education had succeeded in bringing about. 'First-hand observation, and accurate statement of fact,' he wrote, 'seem almost impossible to the Oriental, and education has not hitherto availed to help him.'[39] In particular among the literate Hindus, 'love of wordy abstractions and indifference to practical considerations' remained a trait to which the English took exception.

The assumption of cultural superiority, in science and in religion, on the part of the English; and the absence of scientific training, together with the problems created by their beliefs, on the part of the Indians, tended to range East against West more rigidly than before. In the second quarter of the nineteenth century, the exclusiveness of the English, intensified by their situation in India, manifested itself in the foundation of clubs. At the outset these were usually formed for the purpose of some commonly enjoyed sport, such as golf, yachting or cricket. And although these clubs did not express a racial attitude at their inception, they had the effect of separating the English in their sports and pastimes from the rest of the community. By the end of the century they had become to the Indians hated signs of the English Eden to which they were only

* Dr J. B. Auden, to whom I am indebted for drawing my attention to the Medlicott report ('Records', *Geological Survey of India*, Vol. XX, 1887, pp. 11–13) has kindly provided me with the following note upon it: 'Yet some seventy years later D. N. Wadia of Medlicott's own Department was elected to the Royal Society for outstanding work in the Kashmir Himalaya. The Bengali physicist Bose collaborated with Einstein in formulating the Einstein-Bose equation. C. V. Raman became Nobel Laureate in physics. This list could be greatly extended.'

admitted through the back-door as servants. Clubs also tended to minimise interest in Indian affairs.*

Few books were now written of the stature achieved by the first great inquirers into the Indian past and present; and none to rival those of an Orme, a Jones, or a Tod.† But there were still the occasional eccentrics in the tradition of Coryat whose sharp and individual gaze brought a new life to the Anglo-Indian landscape. Among those solitary travellers who looked on what they saw with curiosity and spirit was Fanny Parkes who described herself as a 'pilgrim in search of the picturesque'.[40] She started to discover it when she made a journey by herself down the Jumna on her pinnace, the *Seagull*. Before turning to figures better known in their public life, Fanny makes a rewarding companion. On her travels she got to know aspects of Indian life which few who stuck to official circles, or tight communities, ever saw. Fanny had arrived in Calcutta with her husband, a member of the Civil Service, in 1822. At the beginning she liked her Indian life no more than most people did; she looked forward mainly to going home. Even when she and her husband were received at the court of the King of Oudh, she didn't take pleasure in being entertained with animal fights, and the balls and breakfasts did not appeal a great deal more. Fanny had begun to suffer from the inertia of the Anglo-Indian life. 'Oh! how I long for the liberty and freshness of a country life in England – what would I not give for a fine bracing air, and a walk by the sea-side, to enable me to shake off this Indian languor, and be myself again!'[41] Existence seemed to be a perpetual fight against the climate and the servants, until she was weary of life; she couldn't even find a soul with whom to exchange an idea.

But Fanny revived when she decided on her two-month pilgrimage up the Jumna to visit the Taj. Unperturbed by minor misadventures like getting stuck on a sandbank in the

* They also indicated social distinctions among the English. Calcutta Civil Servants lived in the *United Service Club*; commercial men or 'box-wallahs' in the *Bengal Club*. Even after the Second World War a proposal to amalgamate the *United Service Club* and the *Bengal Club* was turned down as outrageous. [Dr Auden also assisted me by providing the information for this note.]

† Although not published until 1829-32, Tod's work in Rajasthan was done in the years 1813-19.

middle of the river, she arrived to find in the garden of the Taj
what she felt to be an Indian paradise, spoiled only by the
behaviour of some of her fellow-countrymen. 'Can you imagine
anything so detestable? European ladies and gentlemen have
the band to play on the marble terrace, and dance quadrilles in
front of the tomb!'[42] Their treatment of Agra Palace was no
better; the turret of Noorjahan had been turned into a cook-
room, and the ceiling, the marble, and inlaid work had been
reduced to a mass of blackness and defilement, while the tomb
of Akbar at Sikundra was falling into decay.

During her stay in the area she made the acquaintance of
Colonel Gardner, who had married the niece of Akbar Shah,
and now lived in a predominantly oriental way. He told
Fanny: 'I have been happy in my marriage; but I would not
advise a European gentleman to marry a native lady.'[43] Fanny
was interested to learn that his son had not been educated in
England, and conducted all his business in Persian. She was also
able to penetrate the mysteries of the *zenana*. From this time
on, Fanny's travels became of absorbing interest to her. Her
powers of description, and her curiosity about the details of
Indian life enabled her to convey a strong sense of its anachronisms and oddities, as, for instance, when she visited
the Nawab of Fathigar: 'The rooms of his house are most
curious; more like a shop in the China bazaar, in Calcutta,
than anything else; full of lumber, mixed with articles of
value. Tables were spread all down the centre of the room,
covered with the most heterogeneous articles: round the room
were glass cases, full of clocks, watches, sundials, compasses,
guns, pistols and swords . . .'[44]

Fanny's closest friend was the Baiza Bā'ī at Allahabad, who
even offered to provide her husband with another wife when
Fanny had to return temporarily to England. Fanny declined
the offer, unless the Baiza Bā'ī herself would be . . . By this time
she had come to the conclusion that one might be happy for
ever in India if one could roam about with a good tent and a
good Arab. As *The Wanderings of a pilgrim in search of the
picturesque* suggests, Fanny combined a desire to be informed
with an eye for the striking scene. In particular she was impressed, as not many were, by Benares: 'I walked to see a tomb

on the top of the high cliff a little below Rāj Ghat;* it is
enclosed by stone walls in a garden, and is a handsome monument; many tombs are on the outside by the ravine. It is a very
picturesque spot.'[45] Like many others in India she was also
struck by the speed of decay. Even the beautiful ghat constructed by the Baiza Bā'ī fell into the river during a five-year
interval between two visits. 'Probably,' Fanny reflects with
resignation, 'the masons were dishonest, and that fine structure
which cost her 15 lakhs to rear a little above the river is now a
complete ruin.'[46]

The pleasure which Fanny derived from her travels and
friendships in India between 1835 and 1845 distinguishes her
at once from the majority of English women who spent any
time in the country; and in fact from the English community
at large. But though they refreshed her, they did not make her
forgetful of the hardships that her less fortunate compatriots
had to endure: 'What can be more wretched than the life of a
private soldier in the East: his profession employs but little of
his time. During the heat of the day he is forced to remain
within the intensely hot barrack-rooms: heat produces thirst,
and idleness discontent.'[47] The dullness of life in a small cantonment where even Fanny could not find a single person to
exchange an idea with was magnified by the conventions and
restrictions of English and Indian life. On the other hand,
Fanny is justifiably angry at the indifference and ignorance of
the majority of the English in the more favourable circumstances at Agra. (When a few years later, a group of English
officers went to visit the ruins at Kunauj, they summed up the
experience in words which would have aroused Fanny's spirit:
'It was a "do" - a sham, nothing but old bricks and rubbish.'[48]
Not only had the interest and respect shown by men of Jones's
and Colebrooke's time been replaced by ignorant dismissal; but
it had become part of a pervasive rejection of Indian life which
only a few like Fanny were intrepid enough to overcome, just
as she would have nothing to do with the dreary conformity of
English life. She also proves the point that it was not wholly
the climate that could be blamed for the English inertia: the
'type' who came out East had also contributed. Aliph Cheem,

* ghat: a landing-place on a river.

the pen-name of a verse writer of the 1870s, called W. Yeldham, expressed this part of the truth when he said:

> But India wanted a class of men
>   Of the intellectual type,
> With a mind to study, an eye to ken
>   Weightier things than snipe . . .[49]

The hunting instinct and a liking for a hard open-air life were common enough among the young English setting out for an Indian career in the 1840s. As a future Lieutenant-Governor of Bengal, George Campbell, admitted:

Like all Britishers, too, I was infected with that survival of the hunting age of mankind – the feeling that it was necessary to a man and a gentleman to take every opportunity of killing something, and it has taken me some fifty years completely to emancipate myself from that superstition . . .[50]

As the last remark illustrates, he was a man sufficiently flexible in his ideas for them to evolve and develop with his experience of India, and its people. It wasn't so much a lack of the intellectual type that mattered, as a convention-bound and unimaginative response to the country of their work which typified the Englishman of this period. Michael Holroyd in his biography of *Lytton Strachey* has caught it well in writing about Lieutenant-General Sir Richard Strachey, Lytton's father: 'He was not merely a soldier: he was also a scientist, civil administrator, explorer, engineer and mathematician. Yet, though his restless energy overflowed into so many, various channels, his imagination remained exclusively matter-of-fact, and his whole conception of life was of a perfectly unexceptional kind.'[51]

But in spite of the increasing conformity of the English in the second quarter of the nineteenth century, there still remained in India a number of individuals who served it with a freedom from prejudice and an impartiality which rivalled the great generation of Company administrators. An attitude of sympathy and interest which was to be given a severe shock by the Mutiny still prevailed among them. Philip Mason in *Prospero's Magic* quotes the nice example of the young Bartle Frere in Bombay in the 1830s sitting cross-legged on the floor by the side of an Indian clerk from whom he was learning how the treasury accounts were kept.[52] It was in Bombay in this period too that the close relationship between the English and the Parsis was symbolised by the parties of Sir Jamsetjee Jejeebhoy. For the first time Parsee women began to live with much the same freedom as the English.

But it is in particular to the lives of two men that I want to turn now, as a corrective to the view already established of the increasing distance between the communities. They were men who passed their lives in attempting to make the existence of the people in whose districts they worked a little more endurable and free from basic human wants. As in the case of Munro, the price of such a life was often isolation and relentless, arduous work; it was also a life which called for the largest reserves of personal courage and resourcefulness, with few psychological or material compensations for them. Solitary men do not make up a civilisation nor leave a permanent imprint on its nature; but they do at times play an indispensable role in preventing things from getting any worse, and bringing a temporary alleviation to otherwise intractable problems. Among the notable men of this sort was Meadows Taylor, who arrived in Bombay on 1st September, 1824. After a short and unhappy commercial career there, he got a commission in the Nizam of Hyderabad's army. It was in that state that the greater part of his working life was to be spent. From 1841-53 he administered the principality of the young Rajah of Shorapoor for the Nizam's government; there he enjoyed a freedom of action which few possessed in Company days, and none under the Empire. Taylor quickly proved himself an able linguist; he soon gained command of Mahratta, Telegu and Hindi, and by the end of his life had mastered several of the other languages of Southern India. Free from prejudice, he believed firmly and simply in the necessity for respect of all the people with whom he came in contact. 'The highest', he said, 'are on a par with the oldest and proudest aristocracy in the world. The lowest are entitled to be treated as members of an old and civilised society.'[53] These were sentiments to which Burke would have warmed.

In Hyderabad itself, unlike the English towns, no apparent

social barriers existed between the races; and Taylor enjoyed its mixed community. Later when he went to work as Resident in Shorapoor, he found himself without any European associates. The account of his life there makes it clear that for all his interest and sympathy, only the extreme pressure of his work enables him to carry on. 'If it had not been for my daily work, which lasted from seven in the morning till eight at night, and sometimes longer, I could not, I think, have endured the entire isolation of my life, all official praises notwithstanding . . .'[54] On one visit to Hyderabad he notices with particular sharpness what he has missed, and it confirms the experience of many others in similar circumstances. 'What a treat it was to hear some music, and exchange ideas with men of one's own kind after the life of solitude I had led so long.'[55] The need for people who speak 'one's own idiom' (and that is perhaps not so far removed from the harmony of music) cannot be replaced by a shared language; the differences of educational and cultural background will even perhaps intensify a sense of loneliness, when elementary conversation is possible, and no more. But Taylor was not a man to turn his hand from the plough.

In spite of the hardship which Taylor's life imposed on him, his presence succeeded in suppressing violence, and increasing prosperity, as well as inspiring the loyalty and affection of those around him. At any time - and with little risk - he could have been killed. But in such matters as roads, sanitation, cultivation of waste land, effective policing, resource in times of famine, and administration of justice, Taylor proved his worth. It was based on an impartial dedication to the people and their interests, which was all too seldom the characteristic of an Indian ruler. In this respect Shore had perhaps exaggerated the disadvantages of English administration as against the possible alternatives. The tribute paid to Taylor by the Mahrattas of his district before he left was by no means a mere form of words. 'It will be difficult for us to obtain another superior like you, and we considered it good fortune when we obtained service with you.'[56]

Taylor himself, however, recognised that much in his life's work could be no more than a holding-action; and that as soon as he moved on, the hard-won prosperity and peace would quickly disappear under the influence of internal political squabbles and strife. There is something particularly poignant in this when it is seen in the light of his affection for the country, and its people, whom he persistently served to the best of his ability. His social contacts were of the widest kind from the *ryots* with whom he worked all the time to the descendant of the Rajahs of Vijayanagar who told him he was 'the only Englishman with whom I ever felt on easy terms of friendship.'[57] Only ill-health in the end compelled Taylor to leave India for, as he said, 'I loved the country and I loved the people.'[58] He exemplified this in his last word of advice to the Indian traveller, which could have been heard to advantage by many occupying higher office than Taylor did: 'use true courtesy to natives of all degrees.'[59] Its Confucian simplicity and directness was typical of the man. But when Taylor steams away from Bombay at the end of a good and valuable life, the recollection of his knowledge of the transience in his influence and contact remains in the mind. The value of his daily work in saving people from violence and injustice, in improving irrigation and helping to reduce disease is indisputable; but Taylor's markedly English personality, and the Indian community he serves, remain part of different worlds.

The second Englishman of this period whose career I wish to consider is William Sleeman. Sleeman made his name in the period of Bentinck by his work for the suppression of *thuggee*.* He published his first work, the *Rambles and Recollections of an Indian Official* in 1844; and it showed his attachment in particular to the rural life of India. Like Taylor he is quite without moral or social prejudice; he is deeply attached to the *ryots* and has found among them 'some of the best men I have ever known'.[60] Keenly aware of the effect of economic circumstances, as well as religious beliefs, on human values, he strove to diminish the number of crimes which resulted from each. He was only able to achieve this by his close knowledge of, and familiarity with, the people in their villages; and an informed understanding of the kind of existence they had to endure. But he saw also that much of the European criticism of lawlessness and superstition had applied equally to Europe in the not so

* See footnote on p. 130.

distant past. The Hindus 'go on through life reading and talking of these monstrous fictions, which shock the taste and understanding of other nations, without once questioning the truth of one single incident or hearing it questioned. There was a time, and that not very distant, when it was the same in England, and in every other European nation . . .'[61]

As with most people who thought at all about the nature of Anglo-Indian civilisation, Sleeman recognised the key role of language, and the difficulties which existed on both sides, either for sufficient numbers of the English to speak the vernaculars well, or for the Indians to acquire sufficient proficiency in English to make equal and useful converse possible. He intensely dislikes the prejudices of his fellow countrymen and women, especially the custom of blaming everything that goes wrong on the natives, which is common among the young. Sleeman had no illusions about how slender the influence of the English upon India had been. Just beyond the boundaries of our civil and military stations, so few signs existed 'of that superiority in science and arts which we boast of, and really do possess, and ought to make conducive to the wealth and happiness of the people in every part of our dominions.'[62] But he too sees an almost equally great need for the reversal of the policy adopted by Cornwallis: 'To give the Hindoos and Muhammadans a liberal share in all the duties of administration, in all offices civil and military, and to show the people in general the incalculable advantages of a strong and settled government.'[63]

In 1849 Lord Dalhousie sent Sleeman on a journey through the kingdom of Oudh to report on the state of the realm, and provide him with first-hand information, to help him decide if he should annex it. Sleeman, Resident at the Court before his travels began, knew that the King himself took little or no interest in the affairs of state, his life being fully occupied with food, eunuchs, and women. Around him in the court at Lucknow wealthy land-owners enjoyed the luxuries of city-life, without either interest or concern for poverty or crime in the land which belonged to them.

Sleeman had broken his thigh bone the previous April; and this meant that the first part of his journey was made in a *tonjohn*,* and the second on an elephant. The elephant does not under normal circumstances hasten; so Sleeman had plenty of time for observation, and for talking to land-holders and cultivators who came each day to ride or walk with him. He also saw all he wanted of the waste and dereliction of the countryside because of the prevailing lawlessness. Nobody bothers to improve a house because there is no security of life or tenure; nobody wants to get a murderer or thief arrested because if he is of any importance he will simply buy himself out of gaol at Lucknow, and return for his vengeance. The massacre of families, the pillage of estates, represent a way of life in which the strongest survive by the sword until they in turn get supplanted. The best that a man can hope for is to live in the service of a ruler so ruthless that his power is not jeopardised. Such is the system which the King and his court at Lucknow approve, as it leaves them free to pursue their own pleasures.

. . . these great landholders, who have recently acquired their possessions by the plunder and murder of their weaker neighbours, and who continue their system of pillage, in order to acquire the means to maintain their gangs, and add to their possessions, are those who are most favoured at Court, and most conciliated by the local rulers; because they are more able and more willing than others to pay for the favours of the one, and set at defiance the authority of the other.[64]

The implications of this are tragic not only in individual human terms, but in the potential beauty of Oudh, as a 'universal parterre'. In many places, Sleeman sees the signs of a land that could become as fair as anywhere in India, if it was not laid waste 'by the continual dread of man and beast.'[65] Obviously little can be done to improve the situation until some kind of order is restored, and the elementary struggle for existence and power replaced by the controlling influence of stable authority. This exists, in the form of an army and an administrative system, just beyond the boundaries of Oudh in the Company's territories (where incidentally criminals find sanctuary till their deeds are forgotten). But when Sleeman asks the direct question whether the people would prefer rule by the

* tonjohn: a 'sedan' or portable chair.

Company, and an end to violence, the answer is an unequivocal 'No.' Better the bloody system we do understand, than the rules and regulations of yours, of which we have heard terrible accounts, and which we know we should never understand.

In the Indian view, British justice means the wrong man getting punished, because of the different ways in which the truth is ascertained. As one Brahmin puts it to him: 'The truth, sir, is seldom told in these courts (i.e. the English ones). There they think of nothing but the number of the witnesses, as if all were alike; here, sir, we look to the quality. When a man suffers wrong, the wrong-doer is summoned before the elders, or most respectable men of his village or clan; and if he denies the charge, and refuses redress he is told to bathe, put his hand on the peepul tree, and declare his innocence . . . A man dares not, sir, put his hand upon that sacred tree and deny the truth - the gods sit in it and know all things; and the offender dreads their vengeance . . .'[66] With differences of this sort, the possibility of any shared and viable civilisation is slender. As Sleeman realises, much that he dislikes in the customs of the country would have been perfectly familiar to a European living a few hundred years ago; but the body-clock of nations cannot be changed by the substitution of one form of government for another.

It is not therefore surprising that while he feels intensely the need to do something, he is also aware of the slender potentiality in the situation as it existed: 'I feel like one moving among a people afflicted with incurable diseases, who crowd around him in hope, and are sent away in despair.'[67] But it nevertheless emerges from his journal that in many individual cases Sleeman was able to use his authority to relieve suffering, and secure redress from grievous wrongs. Against the background of an Anglo-India in which religious prejudice and social snobbery were pre-occupying the minds of his contemporaries, Sleeman stands out a dignified and reflective figure, who remained firmly opposed to exploitation and annexation. On his return journey home, necessitated by a break-down in health, Sleeman wrote a letter which was published posthumously in *The Times*. It expressed that deep-rooted conviction in standards of morality which ought to be rigorously maintained, and for which the great tradition of Anglo-Indians had always fought:

I desire a strict adherence to solemn engagements, whether made with white faces or black. We have no right to annex or confiscate Oudh; but we have a right, under the treaty of 1837, to take the management of it, but not to appropriate its revenue to ourselves.[68]

In spite of Sleeman's advice, Oudh was annexed in 1856; and there were some who believed this to be one important cause of the Mutiny. However that may be, Sleeman emerges as a man who through his moderation, shrewdness and freedom from prejudice worked for improvement in relations between the communities. His information was gathered through personal experience, which permitted no illusions about the complexity of the problems in front of the British as rulers in India.

The strength of mind and coolness of reflection which he persistently showed need also to be seen in the perspective of men, senior to him in rank, but who based their authority on windy assertions, incapable of proof and doubtful in truth. In 1854, General Sir John Jacob wrote: 'We hold India, then, by being in reality, as in reputation, a superior race to the Asiatic ... If ... we really are a morally superior race, governed by higher motives, and possessing higher attributes than the Asiatics, the more the natives of India are able to understand us, and the more we improve their capacity for so understanding, the firmer will be our power.'[69] It was of the utmost importance that England should be represented by straightforward, open, liberal English Gentlemen, not by clever and cunning diplomatists. The Indians wanted nothing more than 'to be governed by men who inspired respect by their moral nature, derived from intercourse with the people.' The native had little power for evil or good; and would therefore respond when an appeal was made to his highest and most generous feelings. While English officers were alive and did their duty it was impossible the sepoys would mutiny.[70]

This Old Testament morality which placed both the Law and its Vengeance in the hands of the Lord may have 'become' a General commanding an army, but in human situations more subtle than war it had little to offer. Even so convinced an evangelical as Herbert Edwardes had recognised the danger which existed ten years before the Mutiny in the withdrawal from Indian life which a sense of superiority brought about. In a novel he planned to write about a mutiny against the English, he assigned four causes to its outbreak: the adminis-tration of the law in English, English education, secret native organisations (of the kind which Sleeman had put down) and the withdrawal of English officers more than ever from their men, as a result of the large European society in the great cantonments. This meant that 'few are now left who can discourse with them in their own languages.'[71] Both among those who abjured India, and those who believed they possessed for disposal a unique and universal truth in the Christian religion, the vital spirit of reciprocity was disappearing. Among the more educated the pragmatic doctrine of Bentham encour-aged an impatience with the ancient superstitions and traditions of Indian life. This was to be exacerbated as the growing in-fluence of Western science altered radically and quickly the way in which the majority of Europeans viewed the world, making even wider the gap between them and the still relatively static civilisation of India. In addition, the influence of the public schools on those who went out to India manifested itself in a team spirit that all too often meant racialism. On the credit side, that same education also inspired the self-reliance and indepen-dence of mind which characterised many of the best District Officers. But such men worked largely alone. Around them existed the mass of English people in India, practical in their concerns, prone to snobbery and unbrightened by any real spark of curiosity about the land where they found themselves living. Ironically, as the network of railways, canals and postal services which they helped to create spread over the country, the possi-bility of communication grew steadily less.

Chapter 7

Mutiny

Barring humanity-pretenders
To Hell of none are we the willing senders;
But if to sepoys entrance must be given
Locate them, Lord, in the back slums of Heaven.
Englishman, 1858

To men of keen sensibilities the few minutes preceding
the execution must appear like cycles of torture; but to
brutes like the savages of Cawnpore and Delhi – they
can have few terrors ...
Household Words, edited by Charles Dickens, 1858.

If we Christianise one man, we have made one friend.
If we Christianise a race, we have got an army. If we
Christianise a province, we have founded a government.
If we Christianise a people we have made an Empire.
HERBERT EDWARDES, 'The safety of a Christian policy
in India', 1860

In spite of the signs of growing estrangement within the
civilian communities, and an increasingly rebellious attitude
in the Bengal army, the Mutiny, when it broke out, came as a
shock. When the telegraphs began to tick on 10th May, 1857,
with news of the massacre at Meerut, and the march of the
sepoys on Delhi, it was as though a nightmare, long since
half-anticipated but never really believed in, had passed into
waking life. In crossing the boundaries from sleep to reality,
the ugly dream bore with it the dark terrors and panic from
which the censors of the mind and the conventions of everyday
life normally provide protection. The haphazard massacres
which followed indicated the abyss beneath the surface which
was best papered over by regarding the war as holy and the
issue as moral. When Meadows Taylor first heard of the
Mutiny, it struck him as a 'great struggle between light and

darkness, civilisation and savages.'[1] If this was so, it didn't seem as though the difference mattered that much, since each side rivalled the other in brutality.

The causes of the Mutiny, and what its occurrence signified, have been the object of thorough and detailed scrutiny by English and Indian historians. Here it would be neither possible nor desirable to attempt an account of its causes, or its historical significance in relation to the stirring of latent nationalism. As far as the theme of this book is concerned, the Mutiny represents a breakdown; the emotions shown and the atrocities committed on both sides indicate how large a degree of fear, distrust and hate a superficial friendliness had concealed. There was in those months of 1857 and 1858 no *difference* of feeling or attitude; East and West met in a lust for blood and revenge that cut through all social and humane restraints. The eruption of these forces inevitably left their scar on the society which the following year was taken under the protection of the Crown. While not very much appeared to have changed, the development of East-West relations was decisively affected by the Mutiny and the Proclamation of Empire. Each in its different way gave a new feeling and tone to the Anglo-Indian relationship. As everyone knew - and India most of all - Empires were not for ever. But the effect of the Mutiny on English and Indian attitudes to each other must await the next chapter. They themselves need to be seen in the baneful glow of those words and deeds which showed how shallow was the confidence and how bitter the resentment in the shared community of Northern India. As Harriet Martineau gloomily put it in 1858: 'One may span defiles and torrents more easily than bridge over the chasms which yawn between races of men.'[2] If nothing else, the Mutiny proved once and for all the need for caution and humility in race-relations: and those who thought they understood the 'native mind' were the victims of pride and delusion. It also became apparent that the 'raw material' of the sepoy did not only perform as his puppet-master intended; but had a will and intention of his own, even if he had not yet learnt the lesson of deploying forces to their best advantage, or the essential role of cooperation in victory.

Thomas Metcalf's assessment of the Mutiny as 'Something

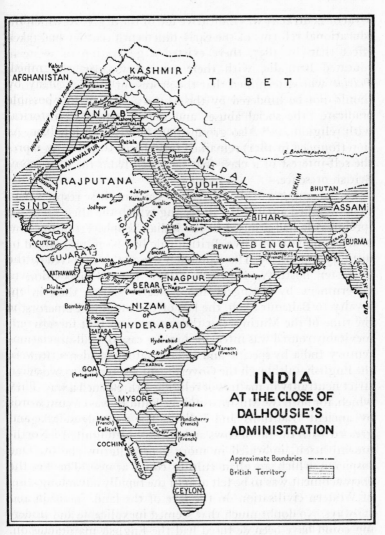

Kabul
AFGHANISTAN
KASHMIR
Srinagar
TIBET
INDEPENDENT PATHAN TRIBES
Peshawar
R. Jhelum
R. Chenab
PANJAB
Rawalpindi
Multan
R. Ravi
R. Sutlej
LAHORE
KAPURTHALA
Patiala
R. Indus
BAHAWALPUR
Delhi
RAMPUR
NEPAL
R. Brahmaputra
SIKKIM
BHUTAN
KHAIRPUR
RAJPUTANA
AJMER
Jaipur
Karaulie
OUDH
NORTH WESTERN PROVINCES
Lucknow
R. Gogra
ASSAM
SIND
Jodhpur
R. Chambal
Gwalior
R. Jumna
Benares
BIHAR
BURMA
HOLKAR
SINDHIA
JHANSI
Jaitpur
Allahabad
ARAKAN
CUTCH
REWA
BENGAL
GUJARAT
BHOPAL
Chandernagore (French)
Calcutta
BARODA
R. Nerbudda
UDAIPUR
KATHIAWAR
Surat
R. Tapti
BERAR
(Assigned in 1853)
NAGPUR
Nagpur
Sambalpur
Diu Is.
(Portuguese)
Bombay
NIZAM
OR
Poona
HYDERABAD
SATARA
Hyderabad
R. Krishna
Yanaon
(French)
GOA
(Portuguese)
KARNUL
MYSORE
Madras
INDIA
AT THE CLOSE OF
DALHOUSIE'S
ADMINISTRATION
Mahé
(French)
Calicut
Pondicherry
(French)
R. Caveri
Karikal
(French)
COCHIN
TRAVANCORE
Approximate Boundaries ----
British Territory
CEYLON

more than a sepoy mutiny, but something less than a national revolt . . .' is judicious and sane.[3] If the rebellion against the English had in any way been coordinated or shared a common goal, under a decisive leader, the Europeans would undoubtedly have been exterminated in a very short time. But for the thousands who mutinied, there were millions who remained loyal or neutral. It was indicative too of the degree to which the educational reforms of the early nineteenth century had taken effect that, by 1857, there existed a generation of western-educated Bengalis, with their own newspaper, the *Hindoo Patriot*, who determined that the process of English education should not be hindered by the Mutiny, since it alone 'could eradicate "the social abuses and moral outrages" connected with religion . . .'[4] Also groups like the British India Association (founded in 1851) remained loyal because they represented the self-interest of a class that benefited from the continuing British presence.

The advantages of the British presence in these respects have to be weighed against the ill-feeling which the alien nature of foreign rule had aroused in the Indian people. From the time of the conquests of Clive, British rule had been maintained by military supremacy. The repression which this involved helped to foster hostility. Nowhere was a natural opposition to government by strangers more clearly shown than in the loyalty to Bahadur Shah, the last of the Moghul Emperors, at the time of the Mutiny. But the antagonism that foreign rule inevitably roused was intensified in the case of mid-nineteenth-century India by specific and inflammatory incidents. Rule by the English – although the Government attempted to preserve a strict neutrality in matters of religion – threatened a way of life which, for both the Muslims and the Hindus, was circumscribed by ancient traditions and beliefs. The cartridges, allegedly greased with the fat of cows and swine which ignited the sepoy mutiny itself, indicated in more general terms the fear and suspicion which an alien culture could arouse. The English encroachment was to be felt also in the rapidly advancing signs of Western civilisation on the face of the land, in canals and railways. No doubt much that seemed inexplicable and menacing could have been de-fused had the English maintained the close personal relationships of the previous century; and there were many of the older officers who claimed that at an earlier period the Mutiny would have been suppressed long before it broke out because knowledge of its imminence would have been widespread, and precautionary measures taken. This does not seem to be borne out by the evidence of the Mutiny at Vellore in 1806; but something of the reverse is no doubt true: that the increasing pace of Western development, together with the increasing distance between Indians and Europeans, had a cumulative effect in creating hostility and suspicions. Once initiated, the Mutiny quickly took on the guise of a religious war. By making Christianity the enemy, both sections of the Indian community found a common cause; and this was the emphasis which the proclamation from Delhi in 1857 exploited:

To all Hindoos and Mussulmans, Citizens and Servants of Hindostan, the Officers of the Army now at Delhi and Merut send greeting:
    'It is well known that in these days all the English have entertained these evil designs – first to destroy the religion of the whole Hindostani army, and then to make the people by compulsion Christians. Therefore we, solely on account of our religion, have combined with the people, and have not spared alive one infidel, and have re-established the Delhi dynasty on these terms.'[5]

Christianity served to conceal a good number of things inimical to the Indian way of life; and it is therefore the more remarkable that the call to rebellion was not met in a more unified and concerted way, which the English could certainly not have withstood. The hostility, like the Mutiny itself, was sporadic, mainly unorganised, but when it occurred, vehement. In matters of land-tenure, technological development, and legislation for the remarriage of widows (though little advantage was taken of it in the early years) Lord Dalhousie had hastened the pace of changes brought to India from without; and all of them touched at some point the central coordinate of religious practice. Syed Ahmad Khan, who later distinguished himself in the cause of Muslim education, saw the origins of the Mutiny in the desire for a change of rule, and the conviction that the British were tempting converted Muslims to adopt European ways. But he also blamed the insolence and contempt with which his fellow-countrymen were treated. The legislation introduced by the British often displayed ignorance of the habits and customs of the people; and when even 'natives of the highest rank' came into the presence of officials with an 'inward fear and trembling',[6] few opportunities existed for making things better. Worse still, the sepoys who had remained loyal to the British during the Mutiny still found themselves treated as 'damned black pigs'.

As is well-known, the unexpected violence on both sides led to atrocities. The massacre of women and children at Delhi and Cawnpore in particular roused the bloodlust of the English. The events at the latter, though well-known, bear repeating as an instance of the degree to which the English were incited to indiscriminate violence – without providing any exoneration of the form that it took which was wholly repulsive. When the sepoys of the Nana Sahib refused to carry out his orders to shoot the English women he had imprisoned, he had them butchered with knives. Later their bodies were thrown down a well. General Neill, the British Commander who saw the room of the massacre, pronounced judgment on all mutineers: 'I wish to show the natives of India that the punishment inflicted by us for such deeds will be the heaviest, the most revolting to their feelings, that they must ever remember.'[7] He gave orders that each miscreant, after sentence of death had been pronounced upon him, should be taken down to the house in question under a guard and forced into cleaning up a small portion of the blood-stains. The task was to be made as revolting to his feelings as possible . . . After properly cleaning up his portion the culprit was to be immediately hanged. Even among the more civilised English the desire for revenge on those who slaughtered women and children was scarcely less powerful: 'I do not suppose,' wrote Alfred Lyall on 12th May, 1857, 'that I am naturally ferocious, but (after the massacre at Delhi) I would shoot down any native on the slightest pretext without the least compunction.'[8] In England, too, Dickens's *Household Words*, while, in principle, attacking execution by blowing the criminal out of the mouth of a cannon, exonerated it in the Mutiny, since the mutineers planned the destruction of every European – man, woman and child – on the island of Bombay.[9]

But there was a difference between proposing and disposing. W. H. Russell who observed the behaviour of the English at first hand was by no means so uncritical. He comments as many were to do after him on the pitilessness shown by Neill on his march from Allahabad; his executions were so numerous and so indiscriminate that 'one of the officers attached to his column had to remonstrate with him on the ground that if he depopulated the country, he could get no supplies for the men.'[10] Another English civilian actually boasts to Russell that he has hanged fifty-four men in an hour for plundering a village; and he sees Englishmen look on with pleasure while a sepoy is roasted alive.[11] At the sack of the Kaiserbagh in Lucknow, he witnesses the lawlessness and uncontrolled lust for plunder that has been allowed to take possession of the British army; he is shocked by the senseless destruction and pillage. 'It is no exaggeration to say that the marble pavement is covered two or three inches deep with fragments of broken mirrors and chandeliers which have hung from the ceiling; and the men are busy smashing them still . . .'[12] He sees the men as being 'wild with fury and lust for gold . . . literally drunk with plunder...'[13] It was the same sort of story in Delhi: every native was killed; the troops were completely disorganised and demoralised by the immense amount of plunder which fell into their hands and the quantity of liquor which they managed to discover in the shops of the European merchants at Delhi.' Such demoralisation was partly initiated by the reports which had reached the army of the treatment of civilians at the hands of the mutineers a few months before. To many it confirmed rather than changed what they felt about the natives. As one observer said to Russell: 'If niggers have souls, they're not the same as ours.'[14]

Almost as disturbing as the acts of revenge were the expressions of vindictiveness among the English at home, and in India. John Nicholson who was to be killed during the recapture of Delhi wrote to Edwardes: 'Let us propose a Bill for the flaying alive, impalement or burning of the murderers of the women and children at Delhi. The idea of simply hanging the perpetrators of such atrocities is maddening . . .'[15] At the Cambridge Union one speaker urged:

When the rebellion has been crushed out from the Himalayas to Comorin; when every bayonet is red with blood; when every gibbet creaks beneath its ghastly burden; when the ground in front of every cannon is strewn with rags and flesh and shattered bone – then talk of mercy.[16]

The butchery at Cawnpore was avenged with bodies hung up to be eaten by pigs, men blown from guns, massacre at the roadside, desolation of villages - this was the vengeance which God permitted and ordained to those who had seen the heathen rise against them. As General Neill remarked to Henry Tucker, the Commissioner at Benares:

I fear in your case your natural tenderness . . . The magistrate bears not the sword in vain. The Word of God gives no authority to the modern tenderness for human life which would save even the murderer . . .[17]

The Evangelical Christian has become the licensed avenger of the Lord. Remote from the strife, though uncertain each evening whether he would wake to see the next dawn, Meadows Taylor remarked:

The civilisation of mind, which most of us thought had made progress, proves to be only skin-deep, and not to have affected the masses of the people at all, and will have to be commenced again . . .[18]

But Russell knew how shallow that civilisation of mind had beeen among the majority of the English. Even before he got to India an English major had remarked to him: 'By Jove . . . those niggers are such a confounded sensual lazy set . . . that you might as well think to train pigs . . .'[19] Once there, he had noted how native employees were treated like slaves, mosques were used for picnic breakfasts without any concern for the sacrilege or offence, and physical violence used on servants at the whim or caprice of the master:

I was very much shocked to see in this courtyard two native servants, covered with plasters and bandages, and bloody, who were lying on their charpoys moaning. On inquiring, my friend was informed by one of his guests, they were So-and-Sos servants, who had just been 'licked' by him.[20]

Russell remarks that it is a 'savage, beastly and degrading custom', but the master had no fear of being punished by law. The colour of one's skin in India has become both a passport and guarantee of rank.[21] And yet even during the Mutiny, the situation was not as simple as distinctions of colour might suggest. Among many of the English there was a remarkable conviction of native loyalty which circumstances justified.

Russell quotes as an example of this the Englishman who tells him: 'They're all niggers alike; but I can trust my fellows . . .'[22] But again the pattern of the reliability of such trust was varied; in some places and regiments no trouble broke out. In Allahabad where the sepoys had volunteered to help with the suppression of the Mutiny at Delhi, massacre broke out on the approach of General Neill's army: those who had seen no sign of rebelliousness in the morning were dead by lunch. In the early part of the Mutiny the question of confidence or non-confidence in the native was a raging one; subsequent experience justified this degree of uncertainty. But as Lawrence and his rulers proved in the Punjab it was the last moment for indecisiveness. The English had seen how shallow their roots were in the country; but that merely brought their superior discipline and tactical skill to a harsher test. It was the hour of the soldier, and civilians, like Mark Thornhill, could do little except hope to avoid capture by the sepoys scouring the country for the purpose of killing the Europeans they found.

At the time when the Mutiny began, Mark Thornhill was a magistrate at Muttra in Upper India; he lived with his wife and two children 'in a degree of state which has long since been abandoned.'[23] He admits that, in spite of his job, and having lived many years in India, he was almost entirely ignorant of the habits of life among the natives. But he soon discovered when the news of the rising at Delhi reached his servants, the 'deep impression and hold upon their loyalty that the splendour of the ancient court had made upon their imagination.'[24] All around him, and his beautiful house with its English garden, he sees the fabric of his authority disintegrate; and the divisive effects of the differences between Muslim and Hindu disable any attempts at defence. The mob at Muttra destroys the Government records and account-books, 'because they regard them as the machinery by which we enforced our severe taxation.'[25] He finds himself forced to admit that the citizens had no love for our Government, or any desire for its continuance. Among the native soldiers, who have always been given only the oldest uniforms, and whose dirtiness is a reproach to the care with which they have been treated, he sees for the first time murderous dislike which makes his own life, and that of all Englishmen hang on the finest of threads. His house is ransacked, and his assistant, Mr Colvin, murdered. The ability of his fellow-countrymen on whom he has previously relied appears as their ignorance of the real state of feeling among the natives. He is compelled to recognise a want of harmony between them and the English which has not impressed itself on him in the course of his career as magistrate. But equally he is disturbed when the English army, sent out to traverse the country at the end of the Mutiny, proves itself 'a scourge and a terror'.[26] Vanished into thin air was that forbearance which only ten years previously H. B. Edwardes had praised in the British army encamped before Lahore: 'The lofty, dignified and magnanimous attitude of the British army . . . did honour to the European character; and the forbearance of the British troops, to British virtue and discipline.'[27] In the void which the Mutiny revealed, the claws of the ruling race were more obvious than its magnanimity.

The transfer of power from the Company to the Crown at Allahabad on 1st November, 1858, was also an official proclamation of the sovereignty of the English at the end of the Mutiny. By this act the British Government took over responsibility for the management of affairs in India, and secured to the people who lived there, and their interests, the backing and support of Imperial power. In the future the allegiance to the Crown was to play an outstanding part in the loyalty of the Indians to the British Empire.* W. S. Blunt, a sharp and outstanding critic of that Empire, nevertheless saw this as its one hopeful aspect in 1885:

There is no question that the Indian populations are possessed with a strong feeling of personal attachment for Her Majesty the Queen, and while they grow yearly more and more estranged from their Anglo-Indian masters, they yearly look with more and more hope to England and to her who sits upon the English throne. This is a sentiment of the utmost value, and one which may yet prove to be the salvation of the Indian Empire, in spite of all the Anglo-Indians can do to wreck it . . .[28]

* At the time of the Mutiny, the deep veneration for the Moghul Emperor – although robbed of his power and wealth – had been apparent. Some of this feeling was no doubt transferred to the Queen-Empress to whom allegiance was due, partly as a final court of appeal against injustice.

But to the Englishman serving in India the proclamation brought no such brightening hopes. Russell with his usual sharpness recognised the change which had occurred amongst them:

One great and distressing result of the violent shock which the Mutiny has given to the whole of the social relations of India, is a deep dislike to the country and to its inhabitants, which is evinced by a constant cry for 'Home!'

A little later he returns to this theme:

It must be borne in mind that now nearly every man is sick and disgusted with India – so much so, that I believe not one out of twenty would remain there, if he was offered this moment, in England or Europe, the fourth or fifth of his present salary in India.[29]

A feeling of bitter execration towards the natives as a result of the Mutiny had made a deep impression on the English mind. With the increased opportunities for furlough, and the opening of the Suez Canal little more than a decade away, the old spirit of dedication which had ruled in the hearts as well as the minds of men like Munro and Meadows Taylor was loosening its hold.

In 1888 Kipling published a story in dramatic form called 'The Gadsbys'. It tells of a young man who makes a promising start to a career in the Indian army: a respected member of a good regiment. Gadsby notes with increasing disturbance that the natives exist only as servants: 'Objects to which reference is made.'[30] But the real crisis comes for him when he gets married and has a child; he decides in spite of the disapproval of his unmarried friend, Mafflin, to chuck the regiment and go home, where he is fortunate enough to have money and a country house. As he says: 'I'm sick of the strain and worry for their sakes out here.'[31] Marriage has crippled his sword-arm. It was fear for the women and children, as well as their ultimate dependence on the sword arm, which the Mutiny had indelibly printed on the minds of the English.

With the Proclamation of Crown Rule, the context of Anglo-Indian relationships had also changed. Although the Queen confirmed the Charter of 1833 in her assertion of that 'perfect equality which was to exist, so far as all appointments were concerned, between Europeans and natives,'[32] it was now no longer only a question of the best man for the job; but the retention of power by an imperial race. The development of Anglo-Indian relations in the second part of the century was affected by this as much as the wounds which the Mutiny itself had caused.

Chapter 8

The Wide Arch of Empire

I doubt whether one vestige could now be found . . .
of those old loyal feelings that twenty years ago
animated so many of the best and most influential of
our subjects.
ALLAN OCTAVIAN HUME, 1872

Thou hast racked him with duns and diseases,
    And he lies, as thy scorching winds blow,
Recollecting old England's sea breezes
    On his back in a lone bungalow.
ALFRED LYALL, *Poems*, 1908

Sir, if our English friends will kindly disabuse their
minds of all bias against us, if they will take a calm
and dispassionate view of everything, if sentiment will
give way to reason, then they will find that in treating
the natives of this country with courtesy, consideration,
and equality, consists the best safeguard of the British
rule.
G. K. GOKHALE, 1889

THE transfer of power from the East India Company to the
Crown which took place officially at Allahabad on 1st
November, 1858, was witnessed by Russell and described by
him as a 'cold and spiritless' affair.[1] It could scarcely have been
much else with the wounds of loss and atrocity still so green in
men's minds. The effect of the Mutiny had been, as Russell said,
to cause 'a deep dislike to the country and its inhabitants.'[2]
Feelings of this sort had recurred, to a greater or lesser degree,
in the course of British relations with India; but now in the
wake of the Mutiny their commonness and their vehemence
became symptomatic of a relationship changed both by bloodshed and England's official assumption of an imperial role.
The loyalty to the Crown, demanded of both English and
Indian subjects, was rarely able to conceal the unease which

one race felt in the presence of the other, except as master and servant. The appearance of an Englishman at a native gathering became sufficient to change its tone of spontaneity. The significance of this was not only contained in the psychological strains which it imposed, but in the estrangement between the communities that it intensified. On the one hand, the Indians began to admit that the Sahib was not what he was; and on the other, a man so devotedly imperialist as Lord Curzon could see that 'the average young Englishman who has been ten years in the country no longer has the affection for the people, or the love for India, that his forerunner possessed in the days gone by.'[3] He regarded the greatest danger now threatening British rule in India as racial pride, and the undisciplined passions of the inferior class of Englishman in the country. Curzon was writing almost fifty years after Russell, and his remarks do not say much for the progress of relationships between the communities in the first half-century of Crown rule. But they do indicate the permanent change in tone that existed in Anglo-India after the Mutiny and the Queen's Proclamation. In the first part of this chapter I shall be concerned with the attitudes underlying this change.

Although trade remained an essential factor in the British relationship with India, the new generation of Indian Civil servants rightly conceived their role in terms of ruling men. Few practical changes occurred in their work, but their relationship to the Indian community was inevitably different in kind and quality to that of the Company merchants. The power of the Empire invested individuals with authority of a different order in which their responsibility became larger, but at the same time more deeply influenced by bureaucratic control. Of equal significance in the development of the Imperial relationship was the reawakening of the Indian national consciousness, to which I shall return in the second part of this chapter. The peace which the British maintained throughout the greater part of the sub-continent after the Mutiny permitted the growth of new political and social relationships within those Indian communities most affected by contact with the West. As administrators like Munro and Elphinstone had foreseen, the price of educating India (or a part of it) would be a powerful challenge to British authority and rule. In fact, the growing demand for self-government which Indian nationalism produced radically altered the relationship between East and West, and caused a form of estrangement between them that could not be removed until the political issue was resolved. As in the ensemble of an opera, the main singers came to pursue their own individual problems and feelings without reference to those of the others. The result in the real event was not harmonious; but it did show with increasing sharpness how little even then the principals understood or had to say to each other. And yet in spite of this there remained on both sides deep and important loyalties that were larger than the divisions of race and politics.

Among the more interesting accounts of the changing British attitudes to India after the Mutiny is that contained in the travels of a Bengali Hindu, Bholonauth Chunder, in the late eighteen-sixties. Chunder, as an anglicised Indian, was sympathetic in many ways to English rule and influence. The spread of English education had reduced the power of priests, and of superstition in general. In technological progress he noted in particular the beneficial effects of the railways and the printing-press, paying to the influence of the latter a somewhat generous compliment: 'Nothing less than Hindustan ought to be given away to the English in grateful reward for their introducing the *art of printing*, which is emancipating thousands of minds from the yoke of a superstition that held us brutes for centuries . . .'[4] But Chunder also feels the anomaly of his personal position. Politically, morally and intellectually he finds it easy enough to anglicise himself; but in more personal things like thought, habit and feelings he knows there to be a vast geographical distance fixed between himself and the Englishman.[5] An educated Hindu of his type finds himself torn between the orthodoxy of his fellow-countrymen which understands but cannot share, and the attitudes of the conquering race to which they make it clear he can never belong, even if he wished to. Keenly aware of the importance of England, in making India a nineteenth-century nation, he perceives with bitterness the change that has overtaken the relationship: 'In 1781 Warren Hastings publicly rode through

the streets of Benares behind the howdah* of the Shahzada,†
carrying a fan of peacock's feathers in his hand. In 1860 every
native in Benares has to salaam to a passing European.'⁶ On
a smaller scale he cites an example of the change between 1857
and 1860 concerning two Europeans on their way to Agra:
'They were travelling by an European *dawk*,‡ and soon out-
stripped us to justify how everything native stands at a dis-
count.'⁷ Whether Chunder was right in his interpretation of
this particular incident or not, he indicates the pressure which
the Mutiny imposed on Europeans to make a point of asserting
their superiority. As a young artillery officer who claimed to
know nothing of politics remarks in the 1870s: 'If a nigger
cheeks us, we must lick him.'⁸

Chunder's travels implicitly make the point that the Mutiny
not only tended to emphasise the worst faults of the English,
but to obstruct what could have been a rewarding cooperation
between the English and the educated Indians in the pursuit of
common ends. It needed a powerful and binding force to heal
the moral and psychological inertia which had settled upon a
land afflicted by frequent famine, and ruled by princes all too
indifferent to the fate of those in their care. In his view, the
English could act as this binding force if their new determination to assert their superiority did not end in their losing all
contact with the needs and hopes of the Indian people.

Chunder's concern with the deterioration in Anglo-Indian
relations after the Mutiny was shared by the more reflective
English. In 1864, G. O. Trevelyan published a book that was to
become well-known: *The Competition Wallah*. His intention was
'to arouse interest at home in the native population of our
Eastern dominions . . . and to make plain the feeling which is
entertained towards that population by the European settlers
in India.'⁹ He is concerned not merely with the lack of sympathy
towards them, but the actual injustice with which they are
treated. He includes mention of the better-known instances of
prejudice – such as the exclusion of Indians from first-class
carriages (by custom, not law), the insolence of the imperial
race towards them, and the disgusting habit of giving servants

* howdah: the great seat on an elephant.   † Shahzada: the son of the Shah.
‡ dawk: the mail-coach.

a licking. But he also comments on subtler problems which arose from the increasingly complex and involved relationship of the British to India: Indians who had been taught correct English at Government schools from the models of Addison and Goldsmith now 'use on all occasions the literary English of the last century.'[10] The ribaldry this caused inevitably aroused resentment and bitterness. But Trevelyan's sharpest attack is reserved for the 'damned nigger style' with its dismissive and violent attitude to those for whose benefit the English are meant to be ruling the country, and 'to whom we shall have one day to account for the manner in which we govern it.'[11] In relation to his rights as man and citizen, Trevelyan argues, the *ryot* is the equal of the Viceroy: behaviour which ignored such rights resulted from the decay of attitudes common enough among earlier generations of Englishmen; but noticeably absent since the Mutiny. Trevelyan depicts the change in the following way:

I have lately read through a file of *The Friend of India* for 1836, with great pleasure, not unmingled with regret . . . The tone of the articles indicated the existence in Anglo-Indian society of a spirit which has passed away and left but faint traces. In those times the well-being of the Hindu was the first and dearest care of our leading civilians. Their successors honestly do their duty by the native population, but that duty is no longer a labour of love.[12]

In the earlier period, Trevelyan continues, officers were not ashamed to call natives friends, and 'would have been very much ashamed to talk of him by the appellation of "nigger", even without the customary prefix.'[13]

As we know from other contemporary sources, Trevelyan exaggerated his case when he said that 'at the commencement of 1857 humanity and philanthropy were the order of the day.'[14] But the Mutiny did bring to the surface latent hostilities which would never again be forgotten, and made themselves apparent with special force in any issue where English authority and supremacy looked as though they were being challenged or whittled away - as, for instance, in the Ilbert Bill controversy of 1883, to which I shall shortly return.

Trevelyan, as well as observing the increased estrangement

produced by the Mutiny, is concerned with its deeper causes. In his view the unexpectedness with which the Mutiny burst upon the English indicates their failure to understand the feelings and character of the people of India, either in relation to their own civilisation or to the English. In the end he finds himself to be in agreement with those who believe that some almost insuperable barrier does exist between the people of East and West which stands in the way of any really close identification. An incompatibility of sentiment and custom causes even the firmest friends of India to think that 'a complete amalgamation is quite hopeless.'[15] But if there is to be an elementary improvement in the relations between the two communities, it depends on a change in the tone of the European settlers. Only among the most highly educated does pride and insolence diminish. He admits he knows of no non-official person in India who would not dismiss as loathsome cant the idea that we hold India for the benefit of the inhabitants. To Trevelyan the consequences of this are intolerable. 'If we do not exterminate them,' he says, 'we cannot continue to humble and wrong them.'[16] The latter part of the sentence might have been written by Burke; but in his time extermination would scarcely have been a practical remedy. With improvement in fire-power and proliferation of political activity in the form of mass meetings and processions, the English came to possess a deadly instrument for imposing their authority. When it was used at Amritsar in 1921 and accounted for more than three hundred killed and a thousand wounded, Churchill was among the few in England to denounce what he saw as a defection from the standards which justified and adorned the British Empire. Some sixty years earlier Trevelyan had perceived in the English treatment of natives an inhumanity which led in that direction. To those like Bartle Frere who had known India since the thirties, the changes wrought by the Mutiny were immense and for the worse. 'You can have little idea,' he wrote in 1868, 'how much India is altered. The sympathy which Englishmen felt for the natives has changed to a general feeling of repugnance, instead of a general feeling of content with their Indian lot.'[17] Opinions might differ on the source and degree of the change; but none denied that it had happened, or of the dangers which went with it. As George Campbell, later to become Lieutenant-Governor of Bengal remarked: 'There is very great truth in an opinion quoted by Lord Shaftesbury, to the effect that one of our greatest difficulties now is the feeling of bitter execration towards the natives which has taken so firm a hold of the Anglo-Indian mind.'[18]

The spectre of the Mutiny was by no means easily or quickly exorcised. When Edward Lear visited India twenty years later, he found it a common topic of conversation among English families, and its places of massacre tourist attractions. Uninteresting as Arrah appeared to the passing eye, it had come to symbolise the power of the English to survive the revolt of the heathen, just as Plassey and Assaye recalled his ability to win military victories against excessive odds. This exultation at British achievement is matched by despair about the Indians. Especially irritated 'by the odious curiosity of the loafing Brahmins,' Lear consoles himself with the reflection that ' " we cannot change the natives" as has been safely remarked.'[19] The word 'safely' gives a good indication of the complacency and dismissal which Mutiny and Empire did much to encourage in a country where they were already not unfamiliar. To an increasing extent the colour of one's skin determined the way in which one was treated. The danger that Russell perceived in the ill-feeling between the two communities, which was the legacy of the Mutiny, lay in its power to aggravate the evils which in some measure caused the revolt. Prejudice, ignorance, and lack of sympathetic interest were numbered among these. In the future, however, other attitudes that Empire helped to create accounted for much that was damaging too.

The administration of the Indian Empire began from an awareness, sharpened by the Mutiny, of the inaccessibility to European understanding of much in the native mind. The Mutiny had also provided further proof of that mind being degraded, just as the British success in quelling it proved them once more to be the superior race. But a difficult question remained. Was the Indian a vassal of his Imperial masters, or was he a citizen proud, as the Englishman's ancestors might have been once, to be called a 'civis Romanus'. Officially, the Crown had a duty to protect all of its subjects, and protect all of them equally. But as everyone knew, the dignities of citizenship did not spread far into the Mofussil, or the indigo-plantations. European juries on the whole would not convict their fellowmen accused of crimes against natives, while a servant suspected of bad behaviour might be sent on the whim of the Memsahib for flogging by the magistrate, and afterwards dismissed. The notion of equality before the law to which previous administrators had attached the greatest importance was now openly regarded as 'sufficiently aggravating' to the European settler, while the principle of 'perfect equality' confirmed in the Queen's Proclamation, far from being implemented was rejected outright by senior servants of the Crown. In 1878, Sir Giles Couper, the Lieutenant-Governor of the North-Western provinces noted:

. . . it seems to me the time has come for us to cease from putting our heads in a bush and shouting that black is white. We all know that in point of fact black is *not* white; and the sooner we plainly recognise and act upon that fact the better it will be for our influence and hold on the millions we govern. That there should be one law alike for the European and the Native is an excellent thing in theory, but if it could really be introduced in practice we should have no business in the country . . .[20]

Sir Giles regarded the idea of equality as an error of fact; others looked at it more sombrely as a political blunder, the more so as the Indian community began to press in various forms, both extreme and moderate, for its implementation. By the first year of the new century the Secretary of State for India, Lord George Hamilton, was to tell the Viceroy, Lord Curzon, that he regarded the inclusion of the reference to equality as 'one of the greatest mistakes that ever was made.'[21] Mistake or not, the status and rights of the Indians, within the new imperial family arose in many contexts. B. G. Tilak, at his second trial for sedition in 1908, insisted on their relevance: 'The point is whether I was within my rights and whether a subject of His Majesty in India can or cannot enjoy the same freedom which is enjoyed by British subjects at Home, and the Anglo-Indians out here.'[22] Tilak got the answer: deportation and six years' imprisonment, for using incitement to violence as part of his political programme in India. The parallel between Tilak's case and that of the Italian liberator and patriot, Mazzini, who had argued the necessity for force in the political struggle for Italian freedom was pointed out by W. S. Blunt. Although the Indians had become British subjects, the English still possessed rights and status of a different order. This concern for the status of the Indian, and the attitude adopted to him both at home and abroad remained with Blunt for many years, and is reflected in the following note for 9th September, 1907:

In America six hundred Hindoos* have been set upon by a mob and beaten, an act of race fanaticism. If this had happened to Englishmen in Turkey we should have had the whole British press breathing fire and fury, now not a paper has any article about it, except a feeble one in *The Times*. Our people are afraid, and though the Hindoos are British subjects, nothing will be done.[23]

It was not an issue which became easier as the tiny English minority of rulers found themselves faced with an increasingly organised and militant Indian opposition. Fear and mistrust were inevitably part of the Mutiny's legacy; but fear, as before, was also begotten by ignorance. As Harriet Martineau observed at the time of the Mutiny, the improvement of relations depended on a free career for Indians in every department of social life. In this way 'men of different race would be brought face to face, and cease (whether the dark or the white) to look upon one another as "monsters".'[24] But among the Anglo-Indians there were far more who believed the only solution to India's problems existed in 'severe repression'. If you were dealing with children, legal niceties over status were not really relevant. The majority of Empire-dwellers regarded the natives as useful for serving, and in moments of frustration also for kicking. The Mutiny provided a psychological excuse for getting rough, and the Empire a political reason. The degree to which the English on the whole looked down on and disliked the other inhabitants of their Empire emerged with especial

* The Hindus were working as factory hands at Bellingham in Washington State. Four hundred were reported, in *The Times* of September 7, 1907, to be in prison; and another 750 to be fleeing to Canada.

force on the occasion of the celebrations in Delhi to mark
Queen Victoria's assumption of the title of Empress in 1877.
The official celebrations were intended to unite both peoples in
an act of common allegiance to the Sovereign. But neither
chivalric ideals nor Victorian good manners greatly influenced
the occasion. Rajahs from all over the sub-continent had been
invited; but the people murmured if they remained sitting
down when the Viceroy stood; they talked discontentedly of the
'Black Raj'.[25] At parties the Indians sat and sulked in corners;
and the young subalterns were overheard making loud remarks
about them, expressing 'a wish to cut off their ears to get their
jewels.'[26] It seemed to an observer that they expected the natives
to be just like Englishmen in fancy-dress; and that the Anglo-
Indians as a whole were incapable of making allowance for
prejudices which were the inheritance of ages.

But a balanced view of British India is never obtained while
the focus of attention rests exclusively in Calcutta, Delhi, or
Simla. For the District Officer, Crown Rule meant a pressure
towards conformity, and the steady expansion of the empire
of paper, but no reduction in the burden of practical work.
With a covenanted civil service of less than a thousand, an area
larger than England, France, Germany, Italy and Spain put
together was administered. Famine, plague, lunatic asylums,
rebellions, gaols, roads, education, land requisition, tax were
some of the responsibilities a district-officer had to tackle. It
was not surprising, as one of them put it that, 'I felt like a man
wandering about with a dim lantern in the dark.'[27] In addition,
the confusions and problems which resulted from trying to
administer British India, whether from Simla or Calcutta, as
though it was one country, inevitably involved delays and
frustrations and muddles which did away for ever with the
dashing and adventurous life of a man like Malcolm; and
transformed him into a civil servant who was forced to
administer with his pen, not his instinct – or his sword. If
government became questionably more professional, it also
became less inspired, and the talents it required of a more
conventional sort. Whether the individual was affected by the
changing situation or the changing situation attracted a
different sort of individual has no easy or simple answer. But it

is difficult not to compare unfavourably an evening of the 'usual district gup'* in the period of Empire with one spent in the company of William Jones or of Mountstuart Elphinstone. They both knew their India and were capable of talking about it with the concern and interest of the well-informed. The libraries of travellers in the seventeenth and eighteenth centuries reveal the range of their interests; a Company servant like Henry Strachey in the 1760s took with him his Orme and his Bernier as well as the standard introductions to Oriental languages, and a wide range of classical authors. In Anglo-India of the nineteenth century a lack of intellectual stimulation and a dearth of books was a frequent complaint of the more intelligent, and ignorance about India became a common criticism of the English from educated Indians, who, also made unfavourable comparisons with the men of Jones's time (see p. 136). Even detailed knowledge of his own area might not be acquired by the District Officer if his moves were sufficiently frequent, and his subordinates, for this or other reasons, also not well informed. Meanwhile, the legislative machine above him was turning out complicated Acts on English models which in a particular district might aggravate the problems they were intended to correct, as was the case in the land-reforms of the Punjab.†

The conformity which a bureaucratic system imposed on its officers affected attitudes as well as policies. With a strict hierarchy of rank, rigidly observed, the civil servant anxious for promotion did well not to quarrel with his superior, or attract the attention of 'Government' by too much independence of judgment or action. In some ways this was a good thing; but at the same time, the importance attached to status prescribed his attitudes to superiors, and did not encourage too much familiarity with natives. As one District Officer put it with a professional evasiveness, 'the doing of the work left little time for solving of the problems.'[28] It also left little time or energy for enlarging or invigorating interests. Even Simla, which was admired and loved by many, proved all too often a

* gup: gossip.
† The Punjab Land Alienation Bill of 1899 was intended to prevent land passing into the hands of money-lenders as payment for debt, but did not succeed.

sufficiently dull place. Colonel Deane's efforts in the 1890s to encourage amateur dramatics were not only impeded by the audience's greater interest in the players than the play (even when it happened to be *Macbeth*). He had problems on the other side of the footlights too:

> Tis also sweet when soldiers brave
> Doff regulation swords,
> And corked and rouged, sublimely rave
> Upon the station boards.
>
> The only draw-back seems to be
> This well-established fact,
> That every amateur thinks he
> And he alone, can act.[29]

Even the ruling race, it seems, had its weaknesses. But India was a land that proved the value of exceptions; and in the following account of the lives of two members of the I.C.S. in the later part of the nineteenth century, I want to illustrate both the increasing conformity of behaviour and attitude – but also how some men still found in varying ways a creative potential which they used for increased understanding and the benefit of both communities.

John Beames was among the last generation of Company servants educated at Haileybury. He says of his time there: 'India was not talked of or thought about except by the few who really worked, nor did we as a rule care or know or seek to know anything about it ... it was "beastly hot" ... and "there were niggers there".'[30] By the time Beames took up his appointment as Assistant Commissioner in the Punjab, the Mutiny was over and Crown rule established. In spite of his training Beames quickly succumbs to the challenge of his work, which he sees with a perspective of the ruler, not administrator. 'Governing men ... is grand work, the noblest of all occupations, though perhaps the most difficult.'[31] He also soon discovers in his post at Champaran that he does not stand alone in the claims he makes for his authority: the English planters in the area dislike the interference which the magistrate practises in what they regard as their own domain. The policy of the planters is to diminish as far as possible the authority of the magistrate, so that they can exercise their right to despotic control over the *ryots*. Baldwin, the manager of the indigo factory, blatantly regarded the natives as his subjects.[32] As well as conflicts of this sort, the range of Beames's duties in relation to the control of disease, and famine, and sanitation keep him busy enough; but outside his work the amusements are slight.

The station of Ballasore where he acted as magistrate and collector between 1871 and 1873, he describes as a 'dull little place', and the few European officers there were so 'stupid and uninteresting, that I was forced to keep myself constantly occupied at one thing or another to prevent myself perishing from *ennui*.'[33] Among Beames's more important interests was the study of language; and he succeeded in producing a Comparative Grammar of the Modern Aryan languages of India which remained a standard work for many years. His social life, so far as he had any, appears to have been exclusively European. In his next post at Cuttack, he spent a good deal of time at the English Club. Among his companions there he mentions George Faulkner - a man so thoroughly English in manners and feelings that 'though he had been forty years in India, he could not speak a dozen words of any Indian language.' Like Hickey a hundred years previously, he enjoys his 'India',[34] since it enables him to live as an Englishman - but with a great deal more style than he could have enjoyed at home.

The Englishman's club, like his house, defended him from the filth in which he commonly regarded the natives as living. If a Lieutenant-Governor came to visit, as much as possible of the 'natural every day dirt and misery'[35] was bundled out of sight; it was not good for Government to get too many glimpses of its own inability to cope. Eight hundred pounds a year was the kind of sum which a District Officer might get for the making and upkeep of roads and communications in an area of over 6,000 square miles.[36] For the Europeans, technological advances like electric light and refrigeration, while improving their own circumstances, made them dislike even more the medieval dirt and disorder in which most of India continued to exist, and also intensified the exile's longing for home where modern amenities were readily available; it also increased his sense of estrangement. When Beames enjoys his work, as he does at Cuttack, it is on account of the friendliness of the other European residents. The Indians when mentioned are usually regarded with disapproval. Many of the Rajahs are 'wild, jungly, uncivilised creatures, mere savages in fact',[37] the Bengalis are the 'funkiest race in the world'; and the servants who 'get very high wages are the worst scum you could dream of in a nightmare.'[38] Beames does however often admire the scenery.

His case is by no means untypical. A hard-working and efficient District Officer who knew his languages; he had no liking for those who went native, and little patience for many native habits and customs. Critical in particular of Government's ignorance of every-day life in the Mofussil, Beames for all his prejudices and conventionality did useful work; but his way of life constantly underlined what had become not only a division between two cultures with little in common, but an approved distance between the ruler and the ruled, itself reinforced by the greater comforts and pleasures now becoming more available to the English community.

Beames never allowed himself to be carried far into the no-man's land between race and race. Sturdy and reliable, but lacking in imagination, he provides an interesting contrast to Andrew Frazer who spent what he described as thirty-seven years of work and sport in the Central Provinces and Bengal between 1874 and 1911. It is characteristic of Frazer, as of all those who worked for the improvement of relations, that he saw as first principles the importance of knowing the language, courtesy, and an active desire for cooperation. He thought that an Indian gentleman ought to be treated in the same way as a European gentleman, not only because that was the natural way to behave, but also because it was politically and socially desirable. 'I have known some few Europeans,' he remarks, 'who seem to think that no one is to be trusted except a European. This is a frame of mind, in Indian and European alike, which is altogether inconsistent with the sound administration of the country.'[39] Throughout his Indian career he speaks warmly and affectionately of his Indian friends 'whom I have learned to love as we love our friends at home.'[40] The contrast between this and the 'damned nigger' style needs no underlining. Like other men of his type Frazer insists upon the unrepresentativeness of Calcutta for any understanding of Indian life. But boorish provincialism does not set in for Frazer when the city-lights grow dim. The pleasure which he derived from the people he met was unfortunately available only to few:

I took the lady into dinner, and talked with her at one side of the table in Marathi; for she knew no English. On the other side of the table, her husband was talking to my wife in English; for my wife did not know Marathi. Sometimes the conversation became general in Hindustani, which was known, more or less, to all of us.[41]

Without prejudice in his social attitudes, Frazer also saw the importance of education in the vernaculars.[42] If these were sacrificed to English, the true interests of the vast majority of the people would be forsaken for the doubtful advantage of the few. He used the same argument when Lieutenant-Governor of Bengal against the nationalists who were becoming militant for reforms. The job of England, he said, was to govern in the interests of the whole country, and this was not necessarily the same thing as governing according to the views of educated Indians.[43] He saw his job as trying to secure the best possible form of government for India and its people at large. It was not to him a place of exile – but a place where he found his life's work – and a place where he had friends whom he loved. At the same time he reserved his harshest criticism for a man who sank to the level of the East. The job of the Englishman is to help to benefit and elevate the Indian people. As a convinced Christian he believed in missionary work and conversion. For Frazer Christianity is inseparable from his definition of civilisation. 'To give them civilisation without Christianity is to withhold that to which our civilisation owes all that is best in it, and by which alone it can be kept pure and healthful.'[44] He also accepted the traditional conservative view of Christianity as a potential stabilising power for the moral and political well-being of India. And so he equally disapproved and disliked those Hindu revivalists – like B. G. Tilak – who by the end of the century were, as he saw it, associating religion with violence and sedition in the minds of half-trained youths. Paradoxically he approved Christianity in the service of British rule, but not Hinduism in the service of Indian nationalism!

Frazer's Christianity is a natural part of the man; he sees it in no way as an obstacle to his work. He believed that it was his job to live in the Indian community without haughtiness or aloofness; he also found it one of the deepest pleasures in his life to live with the people he governed.[45]

Frazer's standards were high, and not unlike those of Munro - perhaps only a little too like them for the changes which had taken place in Bengal by the first decade of the new century. The young nationalist at that time was not interested in being benefited or elevated; he just wanted to get the Englishmen out. As Lala Lajpat Rai put it shortly before his deportation: 'The soil of India belongs to our ancestors and to us, . . . and the English have no right to deprive us of it.'[46] Men like Rai knew all about benevolent paternalism, and they wanted no more of it. The frame of mind which Frazer typified, kindly and convinced, was unfortunately to have little relevance in the increasingly abrasive conflicts of the twentieth century. As linguist and humane administrator, Frazer was a gifted man. Reading an account of his life, it is easy to forget how deep and extreme the prejudices of the majority of the English community remained.

Some attributed much of this to the Englishwoman who rigidly maintained the observation of status and rank, within her own community, and in relation to the natives. She insisted, in Blunt's experience, upon reproducing as nearly as possible her mode of life in England, except that she lived about five times as well and often the less she knew or heard of the natives the better. 'No collector's wife will wear an article of Indian manufacture to save her soul from perdition, and all the furniture, even to her carpets, must be of English make.'[47] (The economic effects of this for India were as serious as its social ones.) Her husband, like the doctor, or the judge, may be quite happy to meet the Indian on equal terms. '. . . But their wives will hear nothing of the sort, and the result is a meaningless interchange of cold civilities . . .'[48] Even worse, they looked upon India as a house of bondage, its inhabitants as 'outside the pale of humanity', and the day of their departure as 'the one star of hope on the horizon.'[49] Prejudices of this sort were inevitably exacerbated by the Mutiny and encouraged by the idea of Empire.

But Blunt, like others who walk this ground, is in danger of idealising a pre-Mutiny Utopia which did not exist. Thirty or forty years ago, he remarks, the general feeling of the natives towards the English civilian was one of respect or even of affection. (It is of interest to compare this view with that of Charles Metcalfe at the time of which Blunt was speaking: 'We have no hold on their [i.e. the native] affections; more than that disaffection is universal.')[50] The English official, Blunt continues, took pains to know the people, and occasionally married among them, or at least contracted semi-matrimonial relations with women of the land.[51] Such behaviour was more normal in the eighteenth than the nineteenth century, though Metcalfe himself, as already mentioned, had three children by an Indian woman. In the course of the nineteenth century inter-racial marriage became less common and more disapproved of. Bishop Heber noted gratefully that 'connection with native women was by no means a fashionable vice, except among elder officers of the army.[52] Instead of this boat-loads of young (and some not so young) English girls disembarked each year in the 'Presidency towns', hoping to find a 'noble, true and loving lord.' Their hopes and their charms are commemorated in these lines, amongst others:

> With boots and shoes, Riverta's best
> And dresses by Ducé.
> And a special licence in my chest
> I'm going to Bombay![53]

It was a hit-or-miss business in more ways than one; and a rude awakening for those who had visions of Palladian Calcutta, since the bungalows of Bombay were by comparison no better, as one traveller remarked, than a 'comfortable English cow-house'.[54] If she was successful in getting her man, she would more than likely find herself sooner or later in the Mofussil, where her existence – whatever its compensations – would be lonely, monotonous and constantly at risk from disease.

Mrs King, a civilian's wife who was in India from 1877-82,

wrote an account of her experiences intended to help those who followed her. Her husband was posted first to Meerut where the Mutiny started; and this no doubt magnified her initial misgivings: 'We live on a volcano in India, with the elements of an eruption always seething below the surface.'[55] Once she goes out on camp with her husband she enjoys herself more – though there too she admits to missing white faces; and her sense of insecurity is heightened by the native habit of exaggeration which 'makes it impossible to know what to believe.'[56] (The significance of fears like this in relation to a general feeling of dislike must vary from person to person; but their effect is, one suspects, in the majority of cases considerable.) Mrs King consoles herself with the reflection that the native is not yet educated up to the point where they could mutually understand each other. By contrast with the eighteenth century such a remark indicates how the emphasis now falls on a race; the other race is no longer regarded as composed of individuals, but as a group who have to be judged by standards which make allowances for their failings. Gone is the grand opera rhetoric of Macaulay against Nuncumar; Mrs King's is the world of the minuet where the natives are complimented on their politeness and good manners. When it comes to anything more personal her tastes are exclusively European. 'Last night we had some people to dinner, and afterwards we all adjourned to the club to see Herbert Roberts, the Champion hand-stroke billiard-player, who is making the tour of India this cold season.'[57] Far from disapproving the separate development of the two cultures she deplores the attempts at fusion which she comes across. The town of Ulwar has been modified by English style and taste, and its interest destroyed. She is equally hostile to the art-school at Jaipur where poor imitations of English designs destroy what is charming and characteristic in Indian work.[58]

Mrs King clearly had an eye for the authentic; but her observations of differences in custom or taste conform to the pattern of rejecting what she finds alien, or, at best, accepting that it cannot be assimilated. She has little of Fanny Parkes's engaging enthusiasm, or Lady Falkland's inquiring curiosity, though, in fairness, it has to be admitted that her opportunities were less, and the rigours of her life not the kind to stimulate interest.

India in the hot season for a woman in a small cantonment must have felt at times like existence in a void. Mrs King complains of its absolute monotony, with nothing to look back upon and nothing to look forward to, except the distant Utopia of the hills. Even there the way of life might be more varied, but not much less trivial. In the cantonments which were often dusty and dreary, the men and women came and went, like shadows, neither staying nor wishing to stay for long. Even in three months away from Meerut, Mrs King finds that society (and that naturally means European society only) has changed considerably. 'The Buffs are gone, the artillery is changed, nearly the whole of the civil staff, the chaplain, and many others. We seem almost strangers in the place.'[59] When on a rare occasion she goes to visit the wife of a Babu (again characteristically unnamed) the encounter does not go well. She discovers that 'natives do not like being asked any questions about their domestic affairs.' 'Does this not alone constitute a gulf', she asks, 'between the two races, impassable almost to friendship? It shows such a radical difference in the tone of thought.'[60] At other levels too elements of Indian life repel her. 'It is hardly credible, but it is a fact, that turkeys in India are killed always by having their tongues pulled out or cut out, thus dying a slow but frightful death.'[61] When the sun begins to burn Mrs King is of the opinion that there's no place like home. But her idea of home is very different to an Indian home, typified for her 'by dirt and the absence of any decency in the arrangement.'[62] Economic, as well as educational, differences do undoubtedly separate her from her Indian neighbour; but they do not account for the causes of unease, especially as Mrs King prides herself on not being one of the school who find nothing pleasurable or interesting in India. She listens with delight when Lord Ripon on a visit recounts the pleasures of shooting from an elephant, and the beauty of the forest scenery.

The freedoms which she takes for granted are wholly denied to the Babu's wife whom Mrs King thinks of as living in prison. Often there was just not enough in common between the English woman and the Indian women of her town to make a close relationship possible, until towards the end of the century they started to engage in common work or causes. It was in 1886 that the first Hindu woman qualified as a doctor, and in the near future Cornelia Sorabji* was to start her work on the problems which arose from the *zenana*. As teachers too, English and Indian women began to share the same kind of hardships: 'The walls and the floor of her schoolroom are of baked mud, the latter overlaid with matting, whereon the great-eyed children squat solemnly in rows . . .'[63]

But it was partly for her husband's sake (fraternising too much with the native was not a good thing if you wanted promotion) and largely through anxieties for her children that the female of the species was more deadly in her prejudice than the male. One Englishwoman in the 1863s makes a common enough complaint, that the native servant wants constant supervision, even in every-day matters like sweeping and dusting, but more especially in relation to the children:

As far as possible children should be prevented from acquiring native dialects, as with the language they are almost certain to imbibe ideas and knowledge most prejudicial to them in every way . . . At all events the greatest stress should be laid on their not understanding any language which their parents do not: when they comprehend the quarrels of the lower classes, which, I am told, are literally untranslatable, as our English has not words to express their grossness, there is no guarantee that they are not falling into the depths indeed.[64]

The traditional view of the native as a moral defective carried its weight here too. By the age of seven (if the child lived that long) it was considered desirable to prevent him catching an everlasting cold, by sending him (or her) back to England for school. This left Mama with the uncomfortable choice between leaving her husband, and letting her children leave her. It did not encourage her liking for India, but was almost certainly not her first experience of its impermanence. Orders for her husband to move far away to another cantonment often came at short notice; furniture had to be sold and new stuff bought when they arrived. Sometimes their house might not even have been built. In austere circumstances like this the Englishwoman naturally wanted to create around her what she con-

* See footnote on page 28.

sidered the decencies and amenities of domestic life. On the one hand, she was made idle by the servants; and on the other expected to endure the deprivation of friends and family. Unless she maintained some vivid interests as Fanny Parkes did, she succumbed easily enough to the petty snobberies and scandals of cantonment life. As the natives had nothing to offer her socially, she found her contact with them sufficient as servants. Even an invitation from the local Rajah was likely to be accepted by her and her husband as a duty or penance.

The insistence of the Englishwoman on her status could be paralleled with only slight modifications in all the European capitals of the period, except that in India it was becoming increasingly the case that the colour of your skin determined whether you used the front-door or the tradesman's entrance. In all too many cases, the questions of difference in attitude or potential understanding were disposed of long before they were raised. 'Niggers after all could only exist as niggers.'

It was not until the Ilbert Bill controversy of 1883 that the full strength of British feeling against greater equality with the Indians was demonstrated with a force that none could ignore. Warning signals had from time to time been given. The view of Sir Mordaunt Wells in 1860 that there could be no equality between Europeans and Indians was shared by many men in positions of power and responsibility. The following year a petition criticising his behaviour as a Judge was signed by 5000 Indians, including Devendranath Tagore.[65] Fitzjames Stephen, the Legal Member of the Viceroy's council between 1869 and 1872, justified rule by a gifted English minority on the grounds that 'the Indian people were ignorant to the last degree' . . . 'and the principles of law and government were the sum and substance of the English legacy to India.'[66] It did not say a great deal for the efficacy of forty years of English education; but the anachronism had a sharper human twist, elegantly expressed by Charles Dilke in 1868: '. . . while by the Queen's Proclamation the natives are our fellow-subjects, they are in practice not yet treated as our fellow-men.'[67] The Ilbert Bill looked on the surface like a piece of legislation intended to clear up an anomaly that resulted from the decision to allow

Indians to enter the Indian Civil Service. By 1883 the numbers who had passed were scarcely in double figures. When they became magistrates, they were not empowered to try white British subjects, as their English colleagues could – although it was clear that no distinction ought to be made between those who had been successful in an open competitive examination.

The Ilbert Bill was intended to give the Indians equal powers as magistrates. But the opinion of the English community in India was so vehemently and vociferously opposed that Lord Ripon was compelled in the end to drop the Bill, and to modify his extensive plans for liberal reforms. The ultra-conservative, Fitzjames Stephen, in a letter to *The Times*, expressed the attitude of many less articulate than himself when he said of British government in India: 'It is essentially an absolute government founded, not on consent, but on conquest.'[68] The public controversy over the Bill in India left no doubt in the minds of the Indian community how hard the struggle was going to be for any improvement in their political position. But perhaps most surprising of all was the openness and crudity of the English attack: 'Would you like,' *the Friend of India* asked, 'to live in a country where at any moment your wife would be liable to be sentenced on a false charge, the Magistrate being a copper-coloured pagan?'[69] Less personal, but no less vehement was the opposition of *The Englishman* which saw the Bill as the start of a policy of Indianising the administration of the country: 'the European community are fighting against their own ruin and the destruction of British rule in India.'[70] The manifestation of solidarity amongst the English led inevitably to a strengthening of Indian opposition, so that when Ripon's successor, Lord Dufferin, arrived in India, it was to find that 'the impotence of Ripon's good intentions'[71] had intensified the conflict between people of different colour. The failure to implement a more liberal policy in India and to secure greater parity in the rights of the English and Indian had the effect of strengthening Indian determination to achieve these ends by themselves – and particularly when Ripon's successor, Lord Dufferin, after appearing at first to favour a liberal policy, showed little inclination to implement reforms in practice.

The year 1885 was a critical one in Indian political history. Lord Ripon's Viceroyalty came to an end in tumultuous popular expressions of appreciation for the work he had done in the service of the Indian people. In the same year - and due, in good measure, to the exertions of Allan Octavian Hume, a retired Scotsman dedicated to the idea of racial equality - the first meeting of the Indian National Congress occurred. More than half the members of the Congress, presided over by an eminent Bengali barrister, W. C. Bonnerjee, were lawyers, and the product of westernised education and professional training. It will be recalled that at the time of the Mutiny members of the British-India Association remained loyal to the English because they were convinced of the overriding value to India of that education. Thirty years later, their successors wished to make plain to their English masters (who showed little enough interest in the Congress meeting) that Congress was in no way opposed to the rule of the English, but sought to make Indian opinion known on issues of public importance, and to secure greater participation in government through democratic means. Far from being revolutionaries they were anxious to impress the English with their political maturity by proceeding in a proper and constitutional manner. There were those at the Congress who did not only regard the British presence in India as beneficial, but as a 'divine dispensation' for the well-being of India.[72] Among the leaders of both Hindu and Muslim communities this reverence for the English relationship was apparent. When the following year, the Muslim leader, Syed Ahmad Khan, decided against Muslim representation at Congress, he was motivated by the dominance there of Hindus. He wanted to make it clear that Congress did not represent the Indian people. The significance of this for the future was large. Not only did it weaken the Congress case in the eyes of Government, but initiated a split that was in the end to lead to the tragic division of India in 1947. The contrast between Syed Ahmad Khan's mistrust in 1886 of the Hindus, and his praise of the English for all their faults, is striking:

Although I do not absolve the English in India of discourtesy and of looking upon the natives of that country as animals and beneath contempt, I think they do so from not understanding us; and I am

afraid that I must confess they are not far wrong in their opinion
of us . . . the natives of India . . . when contrasted with the English
in education, manners and uprightness, are as like them as a dirty
animal is to an able and handsome man.[73]

Syed Ahmad Khan knew that the Muslims had fallen far behind
the Hindus in their acquisition of Western education, which he
regarded as essential to the social and political prosperity of the
Muslim community, and as a pathway to more cooperation
with the English. He regarded the absence of community of
feeling between the two races as due to the absence of community of ideas and interests. Education was the means to
remove these obstacles, and bring about the kind of friendship
between the races which he believed in. His foundation of the
Muslim Anglo-Oriental College in 1875, which among other
things prepared students for further training in England,
embodied this conviction.

In the course of this book it will not be possible to pursue
any further an account of the Muslim break-away in terms of
their future relationships to the Hindus and the British. Nor
am I going to try to provide anything like a comprehensive
account of the early history of the Congress Party.[74] I intend
rather to illustrate how in the years between 1885 and 1914 the
differences between the English and the Indians became in their
manifestation predominantly political and nationalistic; this
at times helped to conceal more basic difficulties, but also at
others to illuminate them. As the twentieth century passed on,
the question was not only who profited or benefited from the
relationship, but on what kind of authority British political
power was based. Bit-by-bit the English hegemony was worn
away, like a coast worn down by the sea, until the island went
under the ocean.

In 1885 the process had scarcely begun. While the leaders of
Hindu and Muslim communities had acknowledged the benefits
to be derived from Western education, the problems of their
eligibility for posts of responsibility remained unchanged. All
Government jobs with a salary of more than £800 a year were
reserved for covenanted civil servants appointed in England.
Although Indians were allowed to compete, the reduction of

the maximum age limit to 19 in 1876 made it practically impossible for them to do so – especially since the examination could only be taken in England. A quarter of a century after the Indians became eligible for the service, only about a dozen out of 1000 were working in it. An increasing number of Indians found themselves equipped with the advantages of a Western education, but no scope for using it; they also had to live with the divisive effects of a break with tradition in their own families and communities. The plight of the Indian educated at Eton and Oxford who finds that he is expected to be nothing and to do nothing 'except to practise economy and marry – a nigger' was a sorry one.[75] The concessions which the English in India made towards fuller participation of Indians in the administration of the country were slow and grudging, because they believed the Englishman's job was to rule. But the obstinacy of the English also helped the Indians to realise the strengths and depths of their own cultural and national ties.

Surendranath Banerjea provides an interesting example of a man who found a personally satisfying position in an eclectic mixture of Hindu orthodoxy and Western ideas. A member of the Brahmo-Samaj, he inherited that tradition of cultural fusion which originated in Ram Mohun Roy. Much in his life and career shows the Anglo-Indian relationship at its best; a man of wide and civilised interests Banerjea's effectiveness was only curtailed when the struggle was not merely one for political power, but for seizing power by whatever means and justifying them in that case. The politics of violence had no place in Banerjea's character; and he lived to regret them in his own countrymen, and in the English.

Banerjea was sent to England in 1868, where he became one of the first Indians to pass the open competitive examination for the I.C.S. In England Surendranath was impressed both by the lack of prejudice against him – in marked contrast to the situation in Anglo-India – and also by 'those great institutions which have helped to build up English life and the fabric of British constitutional freedom.'[76] By contrast he felt keenly the degraded conditions of his own country – and not least in the restraints of the caste system on progress and reform. Banerjea became even more aware of its inhumanity when on his return to Calcutta he found that not only he but his family also were treated as outcastes by orthodox Hindus.

His career in the I.C.S. came to an end when a few months after his return to India he was accused of dishonesty, summarily tried and dismissed the service. But Banerjea was too large a man to ruin his life by resentment. He determined to work for an improvement on the system which made possible such a miscarriage of justice. From then on two principal causes took up the greater part of his life: the improvement of education, and the foundation of a political association that could give to the Indians an opinion and voice in the counsels of Government. It was characteristic of the man that in spite of the grounds he had for bitterness against the British he 'never amidst all his labours, trials and sufferings . . . ever varied in his love for, and loyalty to, Great Britain . . .'[77]

The pressure of Banerjea's politics was always most keenly directed against those measures which in any way discriminated between Indians and Europeans, as, for instance, Lord Lytton's *Vernacular Press Act* (1877) which aimed to control the press in Indian languages on the ground that 'the only political representatives of native opinion were the Babus, who had been educated to write semi-seditious articles in the Native press, and who really represented nothing but the social anomaly of their position.'[78] Sedition was a crime that came in with the Empire; and could all too easily be used against anyone whose opinions earned the disapproval of the Raj. Banerjea recognised too that the British determination to retain control was reflected in subtler ways. He cites the example of Sir Ashley Eden, the Lieutenant-Governor of Bengal, who in his official social life made no distinctions between Europeans and Indians, but professed a profound distrust of all progressive institutions of 'representative government'.[79] He said it was 'a sickly plant in its own soil, and as to its being bred in India, that was out of the question.'[80] This did not correspond to Banerjea's observations in England, or to his political hopes for India.

Large changes were occurring too in the widening sphere of Indian political life. It had become possible – as it would not have been a quarter of a century before – for a Bengali lecturer to help in the education and political instruction of the Punjab. By the early 1880s, he notes that 'the efforts of the last years had stirred a strange and hitherto unfelt awakening among our people, and had created new hopes and aspirations. It was not enough that we should have our full share of the higher offices, but we aspired to have a voice in the councils of the nation.'[81] Under Lord Ripon, the repeal of the *Vernacular Press Act*, and intended reforms of local government looked as if they were going to open the way for the fulfilment of some of these hopes until the controversy over the *Ilbert Bill* swiftly dammed them.

But the English position was becoming increasingly delicate. The failure of Lord Dufferin's administration to bring about any major reforms hardened the determination of the moderate Congress leaders to secure political advancement by constitutional agitation in England and India; this led to a growing feeling of unity among the Indian people, and an increasing demand for representative government.[82] Another important moderate of the time, G. H. Gokhale was acute in pointing out to the moralistic British how unethical their position was:

The position virtually amounts to this, that it is the administration of the finances of one country by the Executive Government of another, under no sense of responsibility to those whose finances are so administered. And for years past we have been treated as a vassal dependency, bound to render services to the suzerain power, and to place our resources, whenever required, at its disposal. As a result millions upon millions have been spent on objects which have not advanced the welfare of the Indian people so much as by an inch . . .[83]

Just as he was direct in denouncing economic exploitation, he was openly critical of the anglicisation policy which dated from the administration of Cornwallis, and in some departments earlier. It had become in his view a moral evil:

The upward impulse, if I may use such an expression, which every school-boy at Eton or Harrow may feel, that he may one day be a Gladstone, a Nelson, or a Wellington, and which may draw forth the best efforts of which he is capable . . . can never be reached by us under the present system . . . Our administrative and military talents must gradually disappear owing to sheer disuse . . .[84]

Partly because they were so keenly aware of the benefits which India had derived from England in the form of education, and political ideas, neither Banerjea nor Gokhale liked the violence which some argued was necessary to win the political battle. They preferred to beat the English at their own game of constitutional reform. But as the years passed and the goals in which Banerjea and Gokhale believed did not grow any closer, the sound of fiercer voices began to be heard. It was in particular during the Viceroyalty of Curzon (1899-1905) that the political debate took on a far more sombre tone. Or to put it another way, the absence of political debate and consultation turned even Banerjea into a radical. Banerjea had never regarded Curzon as a blessing because he 'loved the people of India after a fashion they did not appreciate.'[85] But it was in the *Universities Act* of 1904, and the *Partition of Bengal* in 1905 that Curzon antagonised the Indians to an unprecedented degree, as much by his method as in the matter.

The *Universities Act* which Curzon regarded as an essential step towards the improvement of academic standards, was seen by them as an attack on higher education for the purpose of limiting the number of political malcontents which it produced; and the *Partition of Bengal* which Curzon regarded as an administrative necessity to ease the burden on one Lieutenant-Governor was greeted with the passionate outcry of a people whose local allegiances were being violated. To make matters worse, the leaders of the community were only informed when the decision was taken. As Banerjea said, 'we felt that we had been insulted, humiliated, tricked.'[86] The hostility of Bengalis to partition was expressed in the *swadeshi* movement, which involved a refusal to buy British goods, and a new determination to encourage the production of the necessities of life in India itself. But the significance of the movement extended far beyond economics; it brought the political issue between the English and Indians into every home, and made it a matter for the individual conscience. Tagore used the movement as a background for his novel, *Home and the World* (1919), which portrayed the conflict it caused between husband and wife, and the challenge to the values of the individual which it presented. It also helped to make the aims of the Congress movement more radical than before: unification of the Indian peoples for the pursuit of common political ends; establishment of friendly relations between the Muslims and the Hindus, and the association of the masses with public political pressure for reform.[87]

Even so the aims of Banerjea and Gokhale remained modest: 'self-government within the Empire' achieved by 'constitutional means'.[88] Banerjea, who regarded the connection with England as 'divine dispensation', abhorred the methods which his more radical contemporaries advocated. A moderate in the best and positive sense of the term, he reflected the moving together of the streams which had flowed out of the educational disputes in the earlier part of the century:

Our fathers, the first fruits of English education, were violently pro-British. They could see no flaw in the civilisation or culture of the West . . . In due time came the reaction . . . and from the adoration of all things western, we are now in a whirlpool of a movement that would recall us back to our ancient civilisation.[89]

In the twenty years of the existence of Congress, a growing sense of common involvement and unity had begun to emerge in the complex interrelationships of Indian society; this deepened the Indian belief in, and adherence to, the innate qualities of their own culture. In the nineties the Temperance movement was significantly connected with nationalism, through a shared dislike of the English addiction to alcohol. But Indian nationalism was not created only by moderate men like Banerjea and Gokhale who believed in moral pressure and reasoned argument. Had the politics and attitudes of the British Government - particularly under Lord Salisbury - been less dominated by a sense of imperial mission, and more by the challenge which existed in the creation of a society of harmonious and mutual benefit, men of the political temper of Banerjea, and the first president of the Indian National Congress, W. C. Bonnerjee, would have been able to contribute their statesmanship and knowledge of Indian affairs to it. In the early years, Indian nationalism in Congress was characterised by a lack of resentment, except towards the indifference of English politicians about Indian affairs. At this time the possibility of a closer rapprochement between East and West did perhaps exist, and was thrown away through pride of Empire, and misjudgment by men in public life of the pressure of the times. As it was, the movement which grew in force and numbers as the twentieth century progressed aimed ever more sharply to drive the English right out. Not unexpectedly the pressure towards that end came from men more radical than Banerjea and Gokhale.

Lala Lajpat Rai conceived the idea of writing his autobiography in 1907 while a British prisoner in Mandalay Fort to which he had been deported for his political activities. To his mind, the Indians and the English belonged to opposed and hostile camps: the friends to freedom were few and must be increased; the enemy if not numerous was mighty.[90] This might was expressed most oppressively in the suppression of truth, if that was thought to endanger the security or interests of the rulers. It was a classic view of authoritarian government which neither sought nor welcomed criticism from its subjects. Rai's attitude to the Raj was based both on love of his own country, and a desire for political liberty which he derived from Mazzini. The discontent which he knew to exist in India he attributed to the policy of what he described as 'defiant imperialism', initiated long before Curzon came out to India, but perfected by him.[91]

In the first decade of the century Rai's political extremism stands out as an indication of how the tone of Anglo-Indian society was being changed by an active dislike of the British. The following story from his autobiography provides a striking example of its causes. In 1905 he was travelling from Bombay to Ceylon with Lala Ganga Prasad, a well-known Arya Samajist . . .* They were the only passengers on the second-class deck of the British-Indian steamer; the cabin allotted to them was a very bad one, the heat extreme. The captain, an Englishman, looked upon them with contempt and never let them set foot on the first-class deck, for which, although they were able to pay, they were not even eligible to buy tickets.[92]

The incident on the steamer was typical of the organisation

* The *Arya Samaj* as founded by Salasvati in the second half of the nineteenth century; it was part of the revolt of Hinduism against idol worship.

of social life in trains, hotels, clubs, travellers' bungalows –
and on the street. Everywhere the Indian was treated as an
inferior being. The political views which Rai expressed in a
speech at Lyallpur the following year reveal a natural response
(already quoted) to this situation: 'The substance of the speech
I delivered was that the soil of India belonged to our ancestors
and to us, and that the English had no right to deprive us of
it.'[93] His political activities in pursuance of this idea led to his
arrest and deportation on 9th May, 1907.

To Rai, and his fellow radicals, the one important issue was
how real political power might be wrested from the present
possessors of it; and here Rai accepted the position of Mazzini
that it might involve crime – a view taken also, it will be
remembered, by W. S. Blunt, particularly in the context of
contemporary India. What Blunt shared with Rai was the
rejection of the idea of the subjugation of a number of races
by a single race or a single man; and the recognition that
when such a thing had occurred, and been built into a system of
government, a good deal of force was likely to be necessary to
get rid of it.

But for all the strength of feeling in Rai, there was little
organising political ability. It was this which distinguished
his contemporary B. G. Tilak, and brought him the patronymic,
Lokamanya, or 'revered by the people'.[94] Tilak was inspired not
only by political ideas, but by a militant Hinduism which he
made part of his politics. In his native state of Maharashtra,
Tilak initiated festivals in honour of Sivaji, the Mahrattan
leader who championed Hinduism against Aurengzebe, and
compelled recognition from the Moghul of his right to rule in
his own kingdom. In 1893 he also initiated the Ganapati festival
which in honouring the favourite deity of the Deccan helped
to create a new sense of cohesion and community among
people at large.[95] Tilak himself made no distinction between
religion and politics, so that in honouring the gods or wor-
shipping the heroes of the past, he also preached the nationalist
cause. The revival of Hinduism went hand-in-hand with the
campaign for a renewed Hindu state. Tilak even went so far as
to justify political murders which 'assumed a different aspect
from ordinary murders owing to the supposition that they

were doing a sort of beneficent act.'[96] In 1897 he was tried for
the first time for sedition. With great skill he argued his case
on fine shades of idiomatic meaning; and 'challenged a foreign
people's capacity to rule over a land whose languages they
neither spoke nor read with fluency.'[97] Far from trying to
overthrow the government by seditious articles, he claimed,
he was in fact supporting them, as anyone properly familiar
with Marathi could see. The six European jurors found Tilak
guilty; the three Indians found him innocent; and he was
sentenced to eighteen months' imprisonment. Tilak's appeal
went as far as the Privy Council, but they refused to review the
case. It did not help Tilak in the eyes of the English that a
union between orthodox Hinduism and political terrorism was
already well-established in Maharashtra; or that sympathy for
him had strengthened a little further the sense of national
unity.

Gokhale, like Tilak, came from Maharashtra; but it would
be difficult to think of two men more dissimilar in temperament or politics. Tilak placed his whole faith in complete
Independence, and the restoration of Hindu orthodoxy. Gokhale believed that only madmen could think in terms of
Independence.

The only means for Indians and Englishmen to reach a serious level
of understanding lay in responsible association. This meant not
merely refraining from hostile acts against the order to which we
are loyal, but also a readiness to rush to its support if its existence is
in any way threatened.[98]

It was equality between the races, and equality before the
law, for which Gokhale worked and in which he believed. Tilak,
more concerned with liberty than equality, continued to
encourage the people to revolt against their European masters.
He realised as Gandhi did later that a revolution could be
brought about by non-cooperation:

Though down-trodden and neglected, you must be conscious of your
power in making the administration impossible if you but choose to
make it so. It is you who manage the rail-road and the telegraph, it
is you who make settlements and collect revenues . . . You must
consider whether you cannot turn your hand to better use for your
nation than drudging on in this fashion . . .[99]

By 1907 the differences between Gokhale and Tilak had resulted in a split in the Congress Party which was not to be healed till 1916. Meanwhile among the British the clamour grew louder for stronger measures against promoters of sedition. The view expressed by Lord Lytton thirty years earlier that 'already great mischief has been done by the deplorable tendency of second-rate Indian officials, and superficial English philanthropists to ignore the essential and insurmountable distinctions of race qualities, which are fundamental to our position in India'[100] had hardened under increased pressure. The radical solution favoured by some among the British community was indicated after the attempted assassination of the Viceroy, Lord Hardinge, in 1912. E. M. Forster was staying at Dewas when the news came through, and got a first-hand account;

M says that after the news came, several Englishmen – officials of high position too – were anxious for the Tommies to be turned to fire at the crowd, and seemed really sorry that the Viceroy had not been killed, because then there would have been a better excuse for doing such a thing.[101]

It was fortunate for the British and the Indians that in the struggle for *swa-raj* after the First World War, India should have found a leader who shared the humanity of Gokhale and the fervour of Tilak, but who was himself greater than their sum as preserver of peace: M. K. Gandhi.

Banerjea, Rai, Tilak, Gokhale all point the way to the struggle which was not to be resolved till 1947. They stand at a watershed which was in the end to pour the whole force and strength of Indian life into a massive demand for the British to go. But it is not so much with those who look forward that this chapter has to end, but to the man who more than any other stands for the glory and riddle of the Empire. A figure isolated by his own self-devised splendour, Curzon is also illuminated by the last blaze of that imperial flame which was handed down from Clive to Wellesley, Dalhousie and him. As Gokhale remarked with some pertinacity: 'He has no sympathy with popular aspirations, and when he finds them among a subject people, he thinks he is rendering his country a service by trying to put them down.'[102] Curzon's concern for Empire led him far beyond the nascent desires and wishes of ordinary men in his time; and in doing so the imperial dream obscured the possibility of a new and closer entente between East and West.

A man in many respects of the highest principle, and rare imagination, Curzon bestrides the narrow world of Anglo-India, angrily rejecting its prejudices and injustices which impoverish his conception of what the Empire had to be. While still at Balliol he had written:

There has never been anything so great in the world's history as the British Empire, so great an instrument for the good of humanity. We must devote all our energies and lives to maintaining it.[103]

This service owed to the Imperial vision was in Curzon's case backed by a unique personal knowledge of the terrain on which the sun never set. A fearless and tireless traveller in his years after leaving Oxford, Curzon saw with his own eyes the frontiers which required defence, and the immense lands within them that had to be administered for the well-being of their people, not only different in contrast to the English, but to each other. It was to India as the jewel of the Empire that his eyes and thoughts most often turned during the period of his political apprenticeship which like everything he touched in his early life shone under the influence of his particular gifts. In 1897 he talked to the Prime Minister, Lord Salisbury, of the great work that could be done in India by the Viceroy, though 'a good deal of energy and application would be wanted and what very few men take to India - a great love of the country and pride in the imperial aspect of its possessions.'[104] Curzon, neither then nor later, saw that these two emotions in an Englishman were scarcely compatible, or even possible, for any Indian touched by the new movement of emerging nationalism. Two years after his conversation with Salisbury, Curzon found himself at the age of forty endowed with the responsibilities he had clearly defined.

It was unfortunate that Curzon's love of the country did not extend to its people, especially since each year that passed intensified the frustration and anger of the educated at their inability to participate in government. Curzon's attitude to this problem was prejudiced, unconstructive and wrong: 'We cannot take the Natives up into the administration,' he wrote to his life-long friend, Alfred Lyttleton. 'They are crooked-minded and corrupt. We have got therefore to go on ruling them and we can only do it with success by being both kindly and virtuous. I daresay I am talking rather like a school-master; but after all, the millions I have to manage are less than school-children.'[105] It was a shocking misjudgment of the political situation which then existed in India, and a blindness to merit and ability not like his own. Gokhale himself diagnosed his major weakness which he described as a lack of 'sympathetic imagination'.[106] He then went on to attack Curzon for his hostility to what Mr Gladstone 'used to call the principle of liberty as a factor of human progress.'[107] Particularly in relation to partition, Curzon's failure to consult eminent Bengalis about the proposed move was seen as a deliberate rejection of their ability. Gokhale stressed the significance of this in terms of all it said about the lack of understanding and cooperation that still existed between the eastern and western communities:

If men, whom any other country would delight to honour, are to be thus made to realise the utter humiliation and helplessness of their position in their own country, all I can say is 'Goodbye to all hope of cooperating in any way with the bureaucracy in the interests of the people!' I can conceive of no graver indictment of British rule than that such a state of things should be possible after a hundred years of that rule![108]

In Curzon's view the lack of cooperation resulted from the incapacity of the natives. 'It is often said, why not make some prominent native a member of the Executive Council. The answer is that on the whole continent there is not an Indian fit for the position.'[109] It would not be easy to think of another sentence which expressed so concisely the dangers of the imperial attitude, and the degree to which it had, during the previous forty years, contributed to increasing estrangement, hostility and bitterness. Above all, it was an admission that the problem had been shelved: what British India meant to Curzon was rule by the British. So sure was he of this Imperial mission that he failed to see how much the time was out of joint for it.

But while Curzon remained unimpressed by the claims and abilities of the Indian people, he did prove a fearless custodian of the standards and values which befitted the Imperial race. He regarded them not merely as desirable in themselves but as essential to the holding of the Empire: 'Above all I see . . . that we can only hold this country by our superior standards of honour and virtue and by getting the natives to recognise them as such.'[110] His message to the Englishman in India was conceived in the highest moral tones:

To feel that somewhere among those millions you have left a little Justice or happiness or prosperity, a sense of manliness and moral dignity, a spring of patriotism, a dawn of intellectual enlightenment, or a stirring of duty where it did not exist before – that is enough, that is the Englishman's duty in India.[111]

Where Englishmen fell short of their duty in these terms, Curzon campaigned against them bitterly. Not long after his arrival, a private of the Scots Fusiliers battered a punkah-coolie to death with a dumb-bell and, after unnecessary delay, was brought to trial and acquitted. Curzon was disgusted, not only at the manner in which the trial had been conducted, but the lack of concern because the murdered man was only a punkah-coolie.

That such gross outrages should occur in the first place in a country under British rule; and then that everybody, commanding officers, officials, juries, departments should conspire to screen the guilty is, in my judgement, a black and permanent blot on the British name. I mean, so far as one man can do it, to efface this stain while I am here.[112]

Curzon kept his word, and although it meant estrangement from senior officers in the army, he waged war against the physical abuse of natives, and the practice of one law for the whites, and another for the blacks. He would never be party to the theory that 'a white man may kick or batter a black man to death with impunity because he is only a " d——d nigger".'[113]

In spite of his convictions about British imperialism, he contemplated without any pleasure the fact of Englishmen in India becoming a white caste. The young officer of the Indian

THE MEMORIAL WELL CAWNPORE INDIA

"SACRED TO THE PERPETUAL MEMORY OF A GREAT COMPANY OF CHRISTIAN PEOPLE-CHIEFLY WOMEN AND CHILDREN-WHO, NEAR THIS SPOT, WERE CRUELLY MASSACRED BY THE FOLLOWERS OF THE REBEL NANA DHOONDOPUNT of BITHOOR, AND CAST, THE DYING WITH THE DEAD INTO THE WELL BELOW ON THE XVᵗᴴ DAY OF JULY 1857."

The shadow over the Empire: 'a feeling of bitter execration towards the natives as a result of the Mutiny had made a deep impression on the English mind . . .'

(a) The natives 'have to be judged by standards which make allowance for their failings'

The First Indian National Congress, 1885.
W. C. Bonnerjee, the first president, is seated
in the middle of the third row; he is bearded
and dressed in black

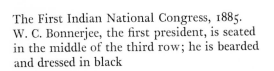

(b) A Punjab Court-Room, *c.* 1860: the proceedings might be
conducted in a language which neither magistrate nor
defendant understood

(a) W. Rothenstein:
Rabindranath Tagore, *c.* 1911

(b) E. Burne-Jones:
Rudyard Kipling, *c.* 1899

Civil Service knew and saw less of the Indians than before; and this was a loss to them both. But it was also a problem higher up on Olympus after almost fifty years of Crown rule. Lord Ampthill who took over as Viceroy for seven months from Curzon in 1904, during his absence in England, noted that he did not come into personal contact with more than a dozen Indians;[114] and, furthermore, that all the English in India were bound together in a conspiracy to conceal whatever an Englishman does. It was not part of Curzon's view of an imperialist that he should be in need of protection.

The sensitivity and refinement which Curzon showed in his attitude to many human issues was also expressed in his appreciation of Muslim and Hindu art. He determined to ensure that the beauty of the past should be preserved; and those monuments of historical interest and aesthetic value in India which had been shamefully treated by the English should now be restored and preserved. He believed in the reverence that was owing to all that had 'evoked human genius or inspired human faith.'[115] In Bijapur he had seen feats of vandalism 'of which only the British people could have been capable.'[116] The debt owed to Curzon for preserving works of art and restoring ancient monuments is immeasurable. What Nehru said of this aspect of his work may well still prove to be true: 'After every other Viceroy has been forgotten Curzon will be remembered because he restored all that was beautiful in India.'[117] In this respect he renewed the tradition of the scholars and historians who at the end of the previous century had made available once more the glories of India's ancient civilisation.

Curzon himself stands on a lonely eminence. Behind him the Empire on which the sun never set; in front, the shadows of broken beliefs, of revolutions and wars, and the popular voice raised against the authority of the past. In that modern world the figure on a pedestal had no place; but there was also one part of the wisdom of the old that he had forgotten or mislaid. No dialogue between East and West could occur, when one side (or one man) set itself up to be the sole guardian of virtue, honour and insight. As false self-assurance provided no shelter when the season of fortune should pass, it stamped the Imperial

Race with a pride that demonstrated more of its ignorance than its superiority. Curzon - 'a being rudely wise and darkly great' - exemplified the flaws of the Empire over which he ruled.

It was the revival of an image of India that belonged to the far distant past that importantly affected the awakening of Indian national consciousness at the beginning of the nineteenth century. In this rebirth the anomalous and pervasive relationship between England and India played a significant part. Whether consideration is given to Ram Mohun Roy at the beginning of the century, or Surendranath Banerjea at its end, the renewal of Indian life was conceived in the context of modifications which derived directly from the association of India and England. It does not, I think, overstate the case to say that the English presence in India, and the foreign rule which it came to embody, acted as a catalyst upon the fragmented society of India, and helped to draw considerable parts of it into an unprecedented unity. At the same time, in more practical ways, the English were setting in motion forms of modernisation, such as the railways,* which in addition to benefiting the community, came in time to alter its traditional ways of life. But beneficial and productive as the relationship was in some respects, the achievement of Anglo-India as a civilisation falls short of much that might have been hoped from it, and this is reflected clearly enough in the quality of its art. The relationship between what men create, and the environment in which they live is a complex one; but the great periods of human culture, whether in the India of Asoka Maurya, of Periclean Athens or Elizabethan England are represented by what they bequeath to posterity – an art that embodies a new synthesis of human will and aspiration, which justifies the first and embellishes the second.

In the final chapters of this book I wish to examine the extent to which the literary art of Anglo-India, in the century or so before the First World War, confirms or modifies the view of that civilisation provided by the sources already considered. As the political theme begins to dominate in the late nineteenth

---

* By the first decade of this century more than thirty-one thousand miles of railway had been built.

century, and the conflict between East and West expresses itself
in increasingly public terms, so it is easy to forget the more
individual and personal problems, which were also changing
beneath the surface of important public events. The literature
of the period provides an interesting illustration of the pulse
of that change; and it is dominated by the twin figures of Kipling and Tagore. Their view of Anglo-India reflects their own
place in the different traditions to which they belong; but they
also shed light on the nature of those traditions in contrast to
one another.

One further point perhaps needs to be made about their role
as artists. In the period before the First World War the artist
still existed in a context where political strife did not inevitably
play a central part in human affairs, and where the values of
civilisation could be regarded without the interfering glare of
opposed ideologies. The old and inspiring idea that good and
right would triumph over might was modified by the advantages which technology all too obviously gave to the richer and
more advanced cultures. From the time of the First World
War, the justification of the British presence in India, on the
grounds of moral superiority, could easily be challenged by
reference to the machine gun, available to lend its support
when traditional forms of leadership and appeal broke down. In
the final chapters of this book the peril in which the old order
stands will need little emphasis. The increasing vehemence
and violence of the political dispute makes this clear enough;
but it can also obscure the more permanent rifts of mis-
understanding which lie beneath ephemeral tensions, however
bitter.

Chapter 9

The Foothills of the Himalaya

... a bivouac in the Himalayas, when one is alone and
far from any kind of assistance is not the spot to
indulge in any prejudice about colour.
F. MARION CRAWFORD: *Mr Isaacs*, 1882

Doth he curse Oriental romancing,
  And wish he had toiled all his day
At the Bar, or the Banks, or financing,
  And got damned in a commonplace way?
ALFRED LYALL: *Poems*, 1908

I saw God, not with fleshly eyes, but with the inner
vision, from the Himalayan hills, the holy land of
Brahma.
DEVENDRANATH TAGORE: *Autobiography* (trans. 1916)

An approach to Kipling and Tagore through the minor
writers of the nineteenth century in India would serve little
purpose if it were only intended to emphasise the artistic
limitations of the lesser by contrast to the greater. But as well
as highlighting their successors' achievement, some of the
minor figures serve to indicate where the boundaries of understanding and communication lay, in a form that might well
have been more opaque if the fabric of art had been deeper and
finer. In fact, the range of characters and situations encompassed by the English novelists of India in the nineteenth
century reveal a great deal about the nature of English pre-
occupations, and the boundaries of imaginative sympathy
within which they are contained. On the Indian side, the earlier
attempts at writing English verse combine a considerable grasp
of English, and knowledge of the English poetic tradition,

without in fact contributing anything significant to it. The intuitive understanding of meaning and association beneath the surface of language, on which poetic effect often depends, is scarcely ever apparent.

The adoption of English as the official language of India in 1835 did nothing to make it a natural and flexible instrument for communication. And in spite of the swift mastery achieved by many Indians, especially in Bengal, its effectiveness for communicating finer and more traditional ways of thinking and feeling was inevitably limited. Furthermore, the question of language soon became involved in the nationalist conflict. As early as the 1870s Bankim Chandra Chatterjee, who was to become one of the most respected and admired Bengali writers of his age, was voicing a reaction against the effect of anglicisation. Although he had written his first novel, *Rajmohan's Wife* (1865) in English, he recognised the need for a literature of the people of Bengal in their own language. The influence of English had already penetrated the consciousness of his fellow-countrymen so far that it would actually be 'degrading' for the young Bengali 'who writes and talks like an Englishman, to be caught writing a Bengali book.'[1] He himself started to reverse this trend by writing his future novels in his mother-tongue. He objected strongly to the renunciation of their natural culture, and the fashion for everything English from food to poetry. He argued that a single great idea, communicated to the people of Bengal in their own language would produce 'grander results than all that our English speeches . . . will ever be able to achieve.'[2]

By no means all Bengalis who could speak English shared Chatterjee's views; and the Muslim community was still moving in the opposite direction. Under the leadership of Syed Ahmad Khan the promotion of English education was going forward as fast as possible; and he himself was taking encouragement from the diminution of prejudice against it. He had been among the first leaders of his community to recognise the political and social significance English now possessed for material and educational advancement. As in the case of the Hindu community half-a-century earlier, change at this level could not be expected to be dramatic, and the pace of absorption was inevitably slow.

The English writer, although not trying to fit his ideas and feelings into the wrong clothes, also had his own problems. As a member of the ruling race and a small expatriate community (described by James Mill as a 'few Europeans holding millions of natives in obedience by an army composed of those very natives'[3]) he recognised in other Englishmen the bondage of needed loyalties. Often isolated from his fellow-countrymen by the special and rigorous conditions of his work, the Englishman combined a lack of bookishness with a dislike of criticism in public. W. D. Arnold was sharply rebuked after the publication of *Oakfield* for his candour about the attitudes he had observed in the Indian army, and intensely disliked. There was something improper about telling the truth when it reflected badly on the guardians of the Empire, whose justification was meant to be moral as well as physical strength. Arnold accepted that his view of the Indian army reflected the exception, not the rule; but defended himself on the grounds that he was attacking a class of men who disgraced the service, and ought to be exposed.[4] Kipling (who was as usual a good many moves ahead of his contemporaries) disarmed potential criticism of his writing as a member of the Raj, by making fun of the situation in his first collection of verses, *Departmental Ditties*, 1886:

> Never young Civilian's prospects were so bright
> Till an Indian paper found that he could write:
> Never young civilian's prospects were so dark
> When the wretched Blitzen wrote to make his mark . . .
>
> . . . Posed as young Ithuriel, resolute and grim,
> Till he found promotion didn't come to him,
> Till he found that reprimands weekly were his lot
> And his many Districts curiously hot . . .[5]

Some of the animosity which Boanerges Blitzen attracted may simply be attributed to the philistinism of which Matthew Arnold complained in England; but the unwritten code of the English in India also exerted its inhibiting pressure. A strong sense of 'never letting the side down' militated both on the grounds of loyalty and courtesy (at a time when such concepts had rather more popular support than they do now) against the depiction of one's fellow exiles in unflattering terms. Equally, the hard and frugal lives of the majority of the more intelligent members of the civil service left little opportunity or time for the cultivation of life's more sophisticated pleasures, even where the taste or temperament for them existed. An untuned piano, and a few books, might be the only companions of the District Officer; and during the months in camp Nature alone was likely to compensate for Art. If, for some at least, the transforming vision of Wordsworth had modified their response to Nature, it was a pity that the greater social fusion and ease of the eighteenth century in India was not also commemorated in a more potent memorial. There was truth in Val Prinsep's observation of 1879 when writing of the great mosque in Delhi, the Jumna Musjid: 'Yet all this sense of beauty is to be found in this people even now; and we have left it unacknowledged, almost to die out.'[6]

*

If there are two characteristics shared by English life and letters in the nineteenth century, they might be described at one ex-extreme as severity, and at the other, as good-humour of a particular kind. The first manifests itself in social and moral behaviour, is self-righteous and assertive. It rejects with hostility those who do not share or who fall outside its codes. Conscious of being more right than anyone else, and therefore superior to them, the Englishman recognises too the duties, obligations and self-sacrifice which is demanded of him. This type of severity and moral earnestness is counter-balanced by a geniality which does its best not to allow him to take things too seriously; the old colonel, for example, 'is not naturally an indolent man, but the prominent fact about him is that he has nothing to do.'[7] In the earlier part of the century, the novels of W. B. Hockley contained a good deal of the severity which in the later part was often replaced in verse and prose by its lighter associate. I want to begin by tracing the evolution of these two characteristics along the path which leads to Kipling, both for their own intrinsic interest, and for the purpose of illustrating in the end how he incorporated and transcended them in a far deeper imaginative penetration of Anglo-India than had been achieved before. After this, I shall turn to look at, and compare, some of the very different themes and traditions which culminate in Rabindranath Tagore. The boundaries of this interest will inevitably preclude anything like a comprehensive survey of the poetry and fiction of the period, but will take in what remains of greatest relevance to the theme of the book.

*

The Poetical Remains of John Leyden were published in London in 1819 – two years before the death of Keats, and three before that of Shelley. As a young man Leyden had qualified as a surgeon and gone out to Madras in the Company's service, arriving in 1803. Like the best men of his time, he applied himself to the study of Indian languages and literature; but they did little except to confirm him in the rightness of his own beliefs. He came to regard the Hindus as 'utterly worthless and devoid of probity,'[8] and their religion as 'wicked, shameless, impudent and obscene.'[9] Swift and sweeping in his condemnation of others – it is no surprise to learn that he himself was beyond reproach: 'scrupulously and inflexibly virtuous in the discharge of his public duties' and 'attentive in private life to the duties of morality and religion.'[10] It does not sound the stuff of which poets are made; and a scrutiny of the *Remains* confirms the view. But he does express in a number of poems a contrast between the innocent delights of childhood, and the corruption of his life that resulted from a passage to India. Even exultation over the English victories at Seringapatam (1799) and Assaye (1803) did little to console him for dislike of the country which had lured him to destruction by appealing to his greed. Many others, before and after, shared the feeling he expressed in an *Ode to an Indian gold coin*:

> For thee, for thee, vile yellow slave
> I left a heart that lov'd me true!
> I crossed the tedious ocean-wave,
> To roam in climes unkind and new.[11]

The moral and physical dislike of the country which this poem expresses works forcibly against any understanding or appreciation of it. If literature, whether good or bad, is to be read as 'the notation of the heart', Leyden's is characterised by an absence of affection for the people and country where he worked; as the perceptive Frenchman, Jacquemont observed, indifference of this sort accounted for the boredom of many Englishmen's lives, and the unhealthiness of their relationship to the country. The lack of imaginative sympathy maimed too - perhaps - the poetry Leyden was capable of writing about it.

In fiction as in poetry the first half of the nineteenth century sees the beginning of an Anglo-Indian genre.* In 1826 W. B. Hockley published a novel called *Pandurang Hari, or Memoirs of a Hindoo*. It was republished in 1873 with a preface by Bartle Frere, who, as in many other aspects of his long Indian career, fiercely attacked the popular one-sided view of social relations with the natives. Hockley had written in his introduction to the original edition:

Nothing can be more irksome to the European than the society of the inhabitant of Hindustan. His conversation is monotonous, and little calculated to relieve the tedium caused by the enervating indolence, which, in a tropical climate, overpowers the European, and is also a marked portion of the native character.[12]

Frere retorts:

It never seems to strike the author that the irksomeness to Europeans of the society of natives of India may be as much due to our ignorance of what interests our native visitors, as to their ignorance of what interests us, and that without some common topics of real interest to both parties, there can, in no country, be much pleasure in casual conversation.[13]

Frere as usual took the civilised view, though he understated here the resistance which the British community at large would have raised to sharing any topic, common or otherwise, with a native. The commercial British were doing quite well for themselves without his assistance, and the natives, demoralised by one conquest after another (even if linguistic or economic barriers did not prevent them) lacked the motive for any closer contact with the current master-race than those which business

* There were a few earlier examples such as *Hartly House*, 1789, which was published anonymously.

demanded. And these the Hindu narrator of the novel reveals to be less than nice.

> The Topee Wallah seldom spoke to me, and when he did, it was as if he were adressing a dog. It mattered not, however, as I could never make out a syllable of his bad Hindustanee. I could perceive by his manner, notwithstanding, that he thought me a butt against which he might vent his anger with impunity.[14]

Naturally enough the Hindu looks forward to the day when the Topee Wallah will be driven out of India. The novel also deals with the familiar criticism of the partiality with which justice is administered. A rebellion occurs at Ahmadnagur gaol in which twenty Bheel prisoners are shot dead and twice as many wounded. The narrator does not believe that the English Government will approve this inhuman act; but it soon appears that those in authority are well enough pleased with their officers' conduct. The Topee Wallahs may boast of their desire to do justice, but in any matter which involves a challenge to their authority, they disregard the viewpoint of the natives, who find for their part it is more profitable to conceal than reveal the crimes committed by Europeans. A situation of this sort did not enhance the respect in which either community was held by the other – though the novel as a whole apportions a good deal more blame to the English for lacking the moral standards they are supposed to champion.

In his less ambitious novel of Madras high life, *The English in India*, published two years later, Hockley extended his unfavourable view of his fellow-countrymen abroad to a critique of their feelings for one another, as well as their behaviour to the Indians. The little kindness which exists among them corresponds closely enough to the depiction of the wealthy in novels by Dickens or Thackeray. But Hockley's India is composed of a more doom-ridden vitality in which the emphasis falls upon trying to get rid of a fortune, instead of endeavouring to secure one. The superfluity of servants, the effects of the climate, the daily proximity of death create together the decaying opulence which, in addition to the monotony of life, impresses itself on the mind of the young and newly married Eleanor. She finds her existence neither vigorous nor interesting; and that of her husband and his friends equally futile. The limitations of English society find no compensation in the Indian community with which Eleanor also becomes quickly disillusioned.[15] Here obviously enough are the seeds of catastrophe: imprisoned in one community and seeing no liberty in the other, Eleanor gets by on a kind of indifference and detachment. It is at least encouraging, she discovers, that the moral character of the natives gets worse the farther they live from Company territory: 'Strangers to an enlightened government, guided only by their own bad passions . . .'[16] The rejection of India and its people on moral grounds follows the usual pattern, though here the English, if not indulging in the grosser vices, don't do at all badly in the smaller ones: licentiousness, scandal, snobbery and vulgar ostentation . . .

The table equipage was magnificent; silver curry dishes and tureens, forks and cut-glass decanters seemed without number. The viands were of the most rare and expensive description, all the luxuries of Europe and Asia were combined to grace the table of Captain Jacob Kilderby . . .[17]

In both communities sufficient vice exists to justify rejection; and for all the contact there was between them, except in the matter of servants, they might as well have existed on two different planets. Hockley gets the good-hearted Eleanor out of this pickle, by sending her and her husband away from the wickedness of India to the security of Devonshire where they can look back on their Indian years with happiness. It is a gratifying end, but scarcely an answer to the problems with which British India confronts her citizens. In two later novels of the forties and fifties, Hockley's fairy-tale ending was not resorted to. In them, as the puritanical dislike increased, so the good-humour expired.

Both W. H. Kaye's *Peregrine Pulteney* (1844) and Arnold's *Oakfield* (1854) are valuably illustrative of English society in India before the Mutiny. Neither leave one the least surprised that it occurred (though that is not to suggest that the conditions described in their novels were directly responsible causes). Each is concerned with the social limitations of Anglo-India, and more comprehensively with the effect of Indian life on the individual and his relationships. In fictional method they lack subtlety; but the conviction of their attack upon the attitudes and values of the English in India is not open to doubt. They also apportion a good deal of blame to the kind of place India is, just as Leyden had done. Julian Jenks, one of the central characters in Kaye's novel, declares that India has fulfilled all his expectations of its being 'a confounded hole'.[18] In the later novel all of Oakfield's immediate circle dislike India for various reasons, and look forward to the time of their departure. Active hostility was inevitably a disposing factor towards mutual estrangement between the English and the Indians; and underlying it on the English side Kaye detects a good deal of guilt. Peregrine, a newcomer to India, observes of Jenks's servant: 'Nobody thought of him - nobody sympathised with him - nobody supposed for a moment that he had any feelings, or possibly could have any feelings, like their own.'[19] Psychological unease which characters like Peregrine feel in the Indian context are paralleled in the experiences of sensitive observers, like W. H. Russell, who commented on the unnoted sadness of the punkah-coolie's life.* The shock was most obviously felt by newcomers - at least consciously - but it is arguable that the treatment of servants as less than human was a means of trying to get rid of the guilt and fear which their presence aroused.

But Kaye was concerned with the social problem, not its psychological causes: the lamentable incongruity between the noble structure of Calcutta, and the anything but noble aspect of the living creatures who are seen about it. The squalor which extends to much of European life underlines its heartlessness. Peregrine goes to visit an old friend, Appleby, who is dying in the barracks. He finds him lying in a room irredeemably hideous, with no physical comforts, in terms of medicine, cleanliness or friendship. Peregrine soon discovers that the 'high life' of Calcutta has little to offer in compensation, characterised as it is, by 'flippancy, heartlessness and insin-

---

* punkah-coolie: the servant who pulled the large swinging fan, suspended from the ceiling. W. H. Russell also commented on the unobserved wretchedness of his life: see, Russell, *Mutiny*, p. 196.

cerity.'[20] On these sort of foundations, the English have built their matchwood stage where to the eyes which stare out of the darkness the conquering race is displayed. In this sense the metaphor which Kaye uses of India as a 'sick-room' applies not only to the prevalence of disease, but to that lack of humane feeling which ought to characterise a superior civilisation. Peregrine is compelled to learn this lesson when his life is saved in a critical illness by the loyalty and good offices of Peer Khan; the affection shown him is of a kind which he has not found among his fellow Europeans.

Let none say henceforth, as has often been said, that the natives of this country are the most ungrateful people in the world. They are only ungrateful because not one in a thousand has anything at all to be grateful for.[21]

Contempt and cruelty to the natives, and lack of kindliness and generosity to each other, characterise the ruling race; they scarcely add up to the high civilisation which Macaulay gloried in our possessing, and regarded as our mission to bestow on those less privileged. In Kaye's India, if all else fails, the effect of the climate in inducing inertia, even among those who are morally or aesthetically appalled by what they see, will rot the fibre of resistance, before the long day's fight has begun.

Kaye's style, moderate and balanced in tone, partially conceals the earnestness and concern with which he views the rule of the English. W. D. Arnold's method in *Oakfield*, on the other hand, is more direct. He skilfully contrives a novel of ideas and incident which questions the notions of service and action, as these presented themselves in the context of India to a man of high intelligence. The novel is prefaced by a quotation from Longfellow which asserts a philosophy of progress through action:

> Not enjoyment, and not sorrow,
> Is our destined end or way;
> But to act that each tomorrow
> Finds us further than today.[22]

Oakfield acts upon this philosophy by giving up a distinguished career at Oxford (which would also have involved his being ordained) for service in a native regiment of the Indian army. It does not take his sharp intelligence long to notice the anachronism of an Empire in which the lives of the rulers have so little connection with those whom they rule. It is this estrangement which gives so curious a hue to the idea, previously entertained by Oakfield, that 'every European in India was engaged in the grand work of civilising Asia.'[23] When Oakfield comes to be posted to his regiment, he soon learns that, if that is the intention, the Englishmen he meets don't seem really suited to the job. The officers, in nine cases out of ten, were 'mere animals, with no single idea on any subject in the world beyond their carcasses.'[24] The palpable signs of British civilisation in India remain steamers and roads and canals which, important as they are, have little direct connection with the 'humanisation of man in society,' or the problems of crossing the boundaries of separation in taste, in feeling or in religion. This strikes him with particular force on his arrival at Allahabad: to the Englishman the river is a convenient servant, but to the Indian still a god. Reasonably enough, Oakfield starts to wonder if there can exist a community of feeling with people so different? He also quickly discovers that his fellow-officers don't inflict their minds with such problems; they even consider it 'infra-dig to understand that 'damned black lingo.'[25] The majority of them would in any case not find it useful since the only natives they meet are sepoys or servants. Even Oakfield's friend, Wyckham, has despaired of finding anything likeable in them: 'Well, I do detest the natives; they are a mean, lying, fawning, sordid race; and after ten years' experience, I can say that to call a native "a man and a brother" is a lie.'[26]

As a result of his distinguished service in the Sikh War, Oakfield gets transferred to the civil service and appointed an Assistant Commissioner in the Punjab. He finds there both more intelligence, and practical application to good work; but also how much the basic distinctions of colour and language get enlarged by the more artificial distinctions of rank and money. In his job of magistrate, he soon perceives how far short of a desirable standard in foreign languages even a man of talent and application is likely to fall. But beneath these particular difficulties a more basic objection to the civilisation of Anglo-India is maturing. In Oakfield's concept of service, there is contained that larger view of human relationships which does not depend solely on material things: and this he finds to be wanting in the government of India: 'Our government is purely secular . . . there is an utter want of nobleness in the government of India . . .'[27] Plenty of people come out to make money, and do; there's no lack of physical courage, even intelligence. 'What we want in addition to these is a few bushels of thoughtfulness; of pure, unselfish, nay, if you will, even visionary enthusiasm.'[28] Oakfield's sense of the inadequacy of British rule arises out of the failure of the two communities to find anything more than a secular and material relationship with one another. This invalidates the ruling passion of his essentially religious nature, the idea of service, since it is impossible to serve if you do not exist in a context where service is meaningful.

The break-down of Oakfield's health finally determines his return to England – and the estate which he loves. His disillusion about the nature of English involvement is matched in his friends by a positive dislike of the country; in none by affection or warmth. Oakfield's younger brother is thinking of a career in India, but is advised against it by Wyckham: 'I tell you, Herby, you would hate India; everybody does . . .'[29]

Talents require good soil to develop their natural strength and ability; and for most Englishmen, Arnold's novel implies, the Indian soil and the manner of its administration does not provide the right climate, except to the idle, the stupid, or the indifferent. In varying degrees all three novelists were concerned with a moral critique of Anglo-India, either for the lapses which it encouraged in their fellow-countrymen, or for the vices of the natives, or the mutually corrupting effect of the interaction between the communities. But the effect of Arnold's novel is less depressing than its disillusion suggests. Oakfield's concern for civilisation and its values, and his awareness of the almost insoluble dilemmas which Anglo-India presents, shows at least an appropriate involvement.

Ironically, the legacy of the Mutiny in terms of fiction and verse was not more earnestness, but less. In the second half of the century, burlesque and mild satire predominated as literary forms. Their levity corresponded to the attitude of many administrators that the best policy was one which threatened least trouble. Explosive issues should be avoided, or treated with humour.

In 1871 Iltudus Prichard published his *Chronicles of Budgepore*. These sketches of life in Upper India were intended to show 'the quaint results which an indiscriminate and often injudicious engrafting of habits and ideas of Western civilisation upon Oriental stock'[30] is calculated to produce. From the start Prichard enforces the idea of changes in attitude which resulted from the Mutiny. 'My pistol-case was on the table. I opened it and took up my revolver, and handled it for a moment fondly. It had been loaded ever since 1858.'[31] It is not the fear of renewed violence which Prichard concentrates on (in any case a dangerous theme!) but the irrationality of an imperial democracy which understands, and can hope to understand, nothing of local conditions. New taxes are to be levied at Budgepore by the Municipal Commission, on which the natives - but only the rich natives - have a voice. As a result the taxes are levied on the poor who get sick and die. The ill-effects of municipal corruption reduce a flourishing city to poverty and want; and the installation of drains brings an epidemic of cholera from which thousands die each year. The exaggeration (though in Indian terms not so large) serves to illustrate the point that in a situation where people are working for different ends and with different assumptions things can and do go badly wrong. But Prichard does not sustain the tragic note, or even his mordant irony for long.

'The Budgepore Exhibition,' which becomes the Lieutenant-Governor's pet plan, is intended to show all that the town can produce by way of native art and craft. The latter at least is flourishing; and goes a long way to neutralise the criticism of the English. Those in the service of the English compel the native artisans to give up the work which earns them their daily bread, to manufacture without pay 'trinkets and knick-knacks of all possible and impossible sorts.'[32] Complaints about the absence of pay are rewarded by imprisonment without trial, for 'who was there to see that the law was enforced?'[33] The bribes and lies which anyway form the basis of the British

administration thrive on the potentialities within the Lieutenant-Governor's plan. But the corruption within the native
community is no less palatable than the snobberies among the
English. The Deputy Collector's wife is unable to cooperate
with the wife of a man in a lower grade of the Civil Service.
Rivalries turn the business of organisation into opportunities
for personal vendetta. It's not surprising that the natives are
slow to understand our motives, and cannot trace the connection between the intention or will that prompts, and the resulting actions. Both communities work by mysterious rites
which the wary and the wise know not to tamper with. The
provincial triviality that infects the mind of the newcomer is
only more deplorable in India than England on account of the
tragic results which can arise from the inability of one community to understand what the other is up to.

The trappings of Imperial government also help to widen
the gap, and exacerbate ill-feeling between the communities.
An order is made for a new European barracks at Budgepore:
modern and well-equipped. In the years after the Mutiny, a
show of military strength was a healthy reminder of the
stability and permanence of British rule. But the barracks
provide a bizarre contrast to the Indian labourer's home,
especially if he is regarded as the potential source of trouble:

His dwelling was a hut, built of mud, and about twelve feet square,
plastered inside with mud mixed with cow-dung, and containing for
furniture an old clumsy cot, and an earthen pot for water. His wife
was squatting on the ground near a few embers preparing the
homely dinner, which consisted of a few cakes made of meal; these
she was patting in her hands over the fire. Two small children,
perfectly naked and covered with flies, lay on their stomachs on the
floor beside her. That was the labourer's domestic circle, and the
description of his home will pass for a description of the home of
many tens of millions of the peasantry of India, who, as is well-
known, are so exceedingly well off under British rule.'[34]

Prichard's irony did not only strike at the two nations of
rich and poor in India, but the additional suffering the Indian
peasant had to endure of being beaten for 'crimes' which
neither education nor custom equipped him to understand. The
whip-hand of the superior race could fall with little chance of

retribution – in fact it was one of the regular means by which that superiority was demonstrated, restrained only by fear of the monster whose attention no one wanted to attract: Government.

Prichard described what he saw with an accuracy that was both critical and humorous; but in the absence of much intuitive feeling for the way the native community lived, he inevitably remained the *spectator ab extra*. This impersonality was also symptomatic of a change which the Empire intensified. Some eighteen years after *The Chronicles of Budgepore*, E. H. Aitken published in 1889 another set of pen-portraits of Anglo-Indian life called *Behind the Bungalow*. In these, the natives only appear as curious and not altogether pleasing servants. The word 'Boy' used of the house-servant or waiter expressed the prevailing attitude, reinforced at times by a cuff from master which helped to raise his dignity. One of the many crimes which the servant must not commit is thinking for himself. 'After all,' says the Memsahib, 'I think we could put up with the *Hamal** if only he would not try to think. This is his crowning vice. In vain I try to impress upon him that I engaged him to obey orders, and would rather do the thinking myself.'[35] Servants are identified by the jobs they do, with honesty or dishonesty, adequacy or inadequacy. What other life they enjoy is no concern of the sahib.

The increasing distances between the English and Indian communities was apparent at many levels during the second half of the century – not least in the relationship between ruler and ruled. In 1880 Aberigh-Mackay published his *Twenty-one days in India*; in style and poise he was the master of Prichard and Aitken:

When you consider the matter philosophically, there is nothing *per se* ridiculous in a Raja. Take a hypothetical case: picture to yourself a Raja who does not get drunk without some good reason, who is not ostentatiously unfaithful to his five and twenty queens and five and twenty grand duchesses, who does not festoon his thorax and abdomen with curious cutlery and jewels . . .[36]

The Viceroy is also not left unscathed:

* *Hamal*: a porter.

He is the centre of a world with which he has no affinity . . . He who is the axis of India, the centre round which the Empire rotates, is necessarily screened from all knowledge of India . . . He lisps no syllable of any Indian tongue.[37]

But he is well supported by his Aide who

. . . disapproves of the Indian people, though he condones their existence . . .[38]

Aberigh-Mackay succeeds in turning the provincial comedy of his predecessors into an imperial farce. He gives glimpses of abysses of ignorance just below the surface on almost every Indian topic, while skimming his way gracefully through unpalatable truths and happily phrased exaggerations. In this blitheness there exists an element which is profoundly disquieting - characteristic of a certain detachment in the Anglo-Indian which it is difficult to regard as healthy or good. The sharpest example of this (and the last) occurs in a poet whose close affinities to Kipling, in the use of characterisation and verse narrative, are at once apparent. Aliph Cheem's *Lays of Ind* (1883), already mentioned as the work of W. Yeldham, illustrate with particular vividness the indifference of an invariable good-humour, whatever the topic. In 'Le Beau Sabreur' he tells the tale of Colonel McMurther who enjoys nothing more than a prolonged engagement with the enemy:

> Having slaughtered the most of this cavalry band,
>   To ease my old mare I alighted;
> And on Infantry Sepoys I practised my hand,
>   And – I think I was getting excited;
>
> For they stood pretty close, and my cuts took effect:
>   Heads flew like round-handers at cricket
> It was glorious only to swipe, and neglect
>   Altogether to think of your wicket![39]

He makes much the same kind of fun out of the problems of race and Empire:

> 'Come fraternise, be one of us!
>   We cry: "what harm can skin do?"
> And yet our ladies make a fuss
>   At dancing with a Hindoo . . .

> You say we hold the land in trust,
>   And for a little span, sir,
> The truth is, that we'll hold it just
>   As long as e'er we can, sir!'[40]

It is curious, though true, how radically tone can alter the importance which seems to be attached to a theme; what would have acted as sufficient cause for a character in a novel by Arnold or Kaye to form a lasting dislike for India comes in Yeldham to be little more than a whiff of passing grape-shot. Kipling - whether he knew Yeldham's verses or not (and it seems almost inconceivable that he didn't) - recognised from the beginning that the most serious things in life could often only be said lightly; and yet his lightness was of a kind that did not prevent his language from being as sharp as a sword when he wanted it to hurt:

> A scrimmage in a Border Station -
>   A canter down some dark defile -
> Two thousand pounds of education
>   Drops to a ten-rupee *jezail* -
> The Crammer's boast, the Squadron's pride,
> Shot like a rabbit in a ride!
>
> No proposition Euclid wrote,
>   No formulæ the text-books know,
> Will turn the bullet from your coat,
>   Or ward the tulwar's downward blow.
> Strike hard who cares - shoot straight who can -
>   The odds are on the cheaper man.[41]

The tone of Kipling controls his theme; and though there is little pity here, as in W. H. Owen's greater war poetry, the pun on the word 'cheaper' goes straight home. The lack of finer feeling is consistent too with the kind of coarse-grained society Anglo-India has shown itself to be: by choice, masculine, muscular and unmarried: puritanical and good-humoured, enjoying the club-man's joke. Confronted by Maggie with the choice between 'little whimpering love', and his cigars, the Kipling man chooses the better of the two - at least as a public attitude:

A million surplus Maggies are willing to bear the yoke;
And a woman is only a woman, but a good Cigar is a Smoke.[42]

In spite of the objectivity, Kipling's verse stimulates a response:
indifference to the attitudes its characters express, and the
issues it raises, is scarcely possible. By making the language of
caricature take the place of an overt moral earnestness, and the
levity appear part of a proper masculine public attitude, Kipling
fuses these two extremes into a questioning and probing of
Anglo-Indian life which involves the reader, whether he will
or not. In the novels and short stories, Kipling was to take up
the craft of his verse in a more extended and exploratory form
where those in the magic circle round him could not help but
listen:

> We cleansed our beards of the mutton-grease
> We lay on the mats and were filled with peace,
> And the talk slid north, and the talk slid south,
> With the sliding puffs from the hookah-mouth.
> Four things greater than all things are, –
> Women and Horses and Power and War.
> We spake of them all but the last the most.[43]

The shape that his imagination gave to the landscape of Anglo-
India must wait the next chapter. Now we must turn to that
very different tradition which culminated in the work of
Rabindranath Tagore. The contrast between Kipling and Tagore
will then emerge as a measure of the great gulf which still
separated the Eastern and Western worlds, as they moved from
the 'wonderful century' into the darker waters of the twentieth,
and the First World War.

*

Rabindranath Tagore was born in 1861, the fourteenth child of
a family that had for two generations been among the most
illustrious in Bengal. His art cannot be dissociated from his
background: the great anglicised Bengali families were inevitably involved with the relationship between Eastern and
Western worlds, and the implications of this for the culture of
Bengal. Although the origins of Tagore's art were no less
deeply personal than that of Kipling - an aspect of the comparison between them which I shall expand upon later - its

shafts were often more sharply directed at practical issues seen from this highly personal view-point, than Kipling's ever were. One of the more interesting paradoxes in the contrast between them arises from the fact that Kipling who wrote so much about men of action neither promoted nor practised the active life; and Tagore, the mystic and dreamer, became increasingly involved in practical educational schemes that were the product of his dreams, and which survive him today.

Rabindranath's grandfather, Dwarkanath Tagore, had established himself as a great merchant prince, who became the scientific and literary Maecenas of Calcutta. A close friend of Ram Mohun Roy, he gave his support to the creation of the first Bengali newspaper, the *Samchar Darpan*; later he became the owner of several papers including the one which in 1833 was named *The Englishman*. Among the first Indian members of the 'Bengali Asiatic Society' and a patron of the arts, he was respected by the English and aimed, as Ram Mohun Roy had done, to improve relations between the communities. As already mentioned (on p. 144) the Governor-General, Lord Auckland, showed the respect in which he was held by going to dine at his house. From the time when the family rose to eminence, its fortunes had in this way been closely linked with those of the English in Calcutta.

Dwarkanath's son, Devendranath, was born in May 1817, and educated at Ram Mohun Roy's school and the Hindu College in Calcutta. Brought up in an atmosphere of extravagant luxury, he came - under the influence of his grandmother - a deeply religious woman to whom he was devoted - to reject worldly wealth which had in any case served precociously to convince him of the unreality of all material things. Hostile also to the idolatry of Hinduism, he found in the Upanishads what he took to be the central truth of religion in the worship of Brahma. He says in his *Autobiography*, 'as soon as I came to understand that God was without form or image, a strong antipathy to idolatry arose in my mind.'[44] Out of this was born a conviction of the importance of English education in dispelling the darkness of ignorant superstititions, and an intense desire to preserve those aspects of the Hindu religion which he believed to contain the essential truth. In particular, he was opposed to the efforts of Christian missionaries, and by his institution of a free school attempted to prevent further conversions to Christianity through missionary education. The collapse of his father's business when he was thirty deprived the family of much of its wealth and confirmed him in that asceticism and religious devotion which became increasingly the centre of his life and teaching. 'The pure in spirit, enlightened by wisdom, sees the holy God by means of worship and meditation . . .'[45]

The centrally religious nature of the experience recorded in the work and life of Devendranath Tagore (or his contemporary Keshub Chandra Sen) indicates a kind of sensibility unlike that which dominated the culture of the West at this time, and produced a form of literature that could scarcely have been more different from that discussed in the earlier part of this chapter. Even in the poetry of Wordsworth, emotion was not rejected for some other and ultimate realisation of truth. In the case of Devendranath Tagore it was; and for the rest of his life he alternated periods of retreat and meditation, with others in which he applied himself to the more practical problems of administering the family estates, and bringing up his numerous children. But he was convinced that immortality could only be attained by renunciation; and not by wealth, good deeds or succession. 'I saw God,' he wrote, 'not with fleshy eyes, but with the inner vision, from these Himalayan hills, the holy land of Brahma.'[46] A belief that formed through the conjunction of inner vision with the sublimities of actual Nature shows one important aspect of his thinking, however, that was close to Wordsworth and Emerson.

It was by any standards an unusual household into which the poet was born; and his childhood years were no less unique; isolated from all that went on outside the family mansion, and solitary much of the time there too. But Rabindranath was stirred from the earliest days of his childhood by the natural world – by the garden, and the clouds: 'How intimately did the life of the world throb for us in those days! Earth, water, foliage and sky, they all spoke to us and would not be disregarded.'[47] The young boy behind the shutters spent much of his time observing the trees and the 'tank' where people came to bathe. The life of Nature was for him a world of presences which could not be disregarded; but unlike Wordsworth they contained no fear. The pervasive quality of his childhood was its stillness; and although he suffered in terms of affection from the size of his family, his character was not formed like Kipling's under the influence of any deeply wounding experience.

The intense inner consciousness of the poet did not respond well or easily to formal education. He found the discipline irksome; and the teaching lacked the significance of his more personal experiences. His pleasures were derived from his brothers' children, and the company of men like Srikantha Babu who knew no English and encouraged his early attempts to write poetry. His own schooling in English only began 'after we had made considerable progress in learning through the medium of Bengali.'[48] Of far greater importance to him than any formal education was the atmosphere at his home 'Jorasanko', dominated by literature and the arts, in which several members of the family besides Rabindranath, were to distinguish themselves, though to a lesser degree. The seclusion of his childhood, however, gave special significance to his visits away from home, and in particular his journey with his father to the Himalayas. The land of the snows was a holy place, the throne of the gods, the abode of devils . . . later Rabindranath was to find the source of his own inspiration in a far less dramatic setting.

In spite of his secluded childhood, it was decided that Rabindranath should be shipped off to England at the age of sixteen, so that he could study law and return to earn his living as a barrister. The decision reflected the unusual temperament of his father, who combined the detachment of the mystic, with the practicality of a man of property. Idiosyncratic in behaviour, he would return unread a letter written to him in English;* but still send his son to England for a professional training. Inconsistencies of this sort, however, were not peculiar to Rabindranath's father; they reflected once more the

---

* See also S. Datta, *The World of Twilight*, Oxford, 1971, pp. 56–7. Devendranath Tagore, was not alone in this ambivalence of behaviour and attitude.

anomalous position of English, and the English, in Bengal – partly admired, and partly hated for their haughty and often ignorant behaviour.

It was not until he got to England that Rabindranath for the first time came under the influence of English literature – especially Shakespeare, Milton and Byron; they impressed him by the passion in their works which contrasted sharply with his own experience of literature and life:

The frenzy of Romeo and Juliet's love, the fury of King Lear's impotent lamentation, the all-consuming fire of Othello's jealousy, these were the things that roused us to enthusiastic admiration. Our restricted social life, our narrower field of social activity was hedged in with such monotonous uniformity that tempestuous feelings found no entrance: all was as calm and quiet as could be.[49]

But monotonous though the quietness may have been, the passion which Tagore experienced in the greatest English writers came to appear to him a partial account of human experience and, as the end of literary endeavour, inadequate:

Human emotion is only one of the ingredients of literature and not its end, – which is beauty of perfect fulness consisting in simplicity and restraint. This is a proposition which English literature does not yet fully admit.[50]

Simplicity and restraint are arguably characteristics of Kipling's style; but of that more absolute experience indicated in the phrase 'beauty of perfect fulness', Kipling shows little knowledge. The raw materials of Kipling's art are to be found in the keenness of his observation of a social scene, and the economy of his analysis of individual behaviour. The stuff of Tagore's poetry originates in a particular and private experience which he alone lived through; but of which he left a permanent and public record. Although he had written poetry consistently since his youth, it was only with the following experience that his poetic personality started to achieve maturity; it began early one morning as he was watching the sun rise from the verandah of a house in Calcutta:

All of a sudden a covering seemed to fall from my eyes, and I found the world bathed in a wonderful radiance, with waves of beauty and joy swelling on every side . . .[51]

He found that neither men nor things seemed commonplace any more; and their ultimate significance was impressed on his mind.

The experience lasted some four days; he thought at first it might be recovered by going, as his father had done, to the Himalayas. Then he recognised the experience belonged to the everyday world of Calcutta, and its essential characteristic consisted in the perception of the Infinite in the finite. A vision of this sort conforms to a well-documented kind of mystical experience:

The basic experience is an overwhelming conviction that the objects confronting (the subject) have a numinous significance and importance, that the existence of everything he is aware of is holy. And the basic emotion is one of innocent joy, though this joy can include, of course, a reverent dread.[52]

A vision of just this sort became the determining factor in Tagore's developing poetic consciousness, and the object of his subsequent poetic quest. To this experience may be attributed his sensation of joy in the life of the artist, and his indifference to much in the material (including the political) world. Especially where politics were concerned, the difference between his and his father's time is strikingly evident. Less and less could the Indian uncommitted to the preaching of the politics of nationalism retain any public authority; and within families too the issue caused conflict and disruption – a theme with which Tagore dealt in his novel, *Home and the World*, to be discussed below.

It is not easy to assess, or eliminate, the importance of Tagore's upbringing and family in terms of the kind of poetry which he wrote. The precedent of his father's life made him aware from his early years of the possibility of mystical experience; but whatever value is attached to its recurrence in Tagore's own life, it does not provide a complete account of his poetic success and popularity, especially in Bengal. A great deal is owed to the revival of Bengali which Tagore aided through his knowledge of dialects – for instance, that of the Baül fishermen. A contemporary put it like this:

We have other poets, but none that are his equal; we call this the epoch of Rabindranath. No poet seems to me as famous in Europe as he is amongst us. He is as great in music as in poetry, and his songs are sung from the west of India into Burma wherever Bengali is spoken.[53]

W. B. Yeats offered at least one convincing explanation of this: 'The work of a supreme culture, they yet appear as much the growth of the common soil as the grass and the rushes.'[54] It was what Wordsworth had been after, and never really succeeded in capturing (perhaps because the English language had become literary by that time); and what Yeats himself sought in the mythology of Ireland. Again, Tagore's environment in childhood had played a central role in the development of this part of his talent: in particular, he was indebted to his elder brothers for his knowledge of Bengali and its dialects: and his reference to this points once again to that transitional period just before nationalism became an inescapable issue.

Love of country was . . . by no means . . . a characteristic of the times of which I am writing. Our educated men then kept at arm's length both the language and thought of their native land. Nevertheless, my elder brothers had always cultivated Bengali literature.[55]

In this respect, as in others, Tagore might be seen as the culminating spirit of that eclectic tradition which started with R. M. Roy. 'Roy realised,' Tagore wrote, 'that truth can never be foreign, that money and material may exclusively belong to the particular country which produces them, but not knowledge, or ideas, or immortal forms of art.'[56] In this respect men like his father, and Chatterjee, had remained true to the ancient Indian ideals in spite of their westernisation.

The pursuits and interests to which Rabindranath had been accustomed throughout his childhood at Jorasanko could scarcely have been more remote from that of the majority of Anglo-Indians, most of whom were, as Alfred Lyall put it, 'too busy running the affairs of a continent to give much thought to the life of the mind.'[57] But remote as Tagore was in temperament and personality - and in spite of the fact that his poetry is generally acknowledged to lose almost everything in translation* - his poetry brings a much-needed relief to anyone who approaches it through the verse written in English by Indians in the earlier part of the century; and briefly, it is in this other tradition that he needs to be set before a more detailed comparison between his achievement and Kipling's is attempted.

In the poetry of Henry Derozio, Michael Madhusadan Dutt, the later Dutt sisters, and Manmohun Ghose, the failure to find a natural and easy mode of expression was conspicuous: theirs was a twilight world much influenced by the English romantic tradition, Wordsworth, Southey and Byron; and in Ghose's case by the poetry of the nineties. As in M. M. Dutt's long poem, *The Captive Ladie* (1849) the setting was often Indian, and sometimes, as in this case, historical; but the result was no more authentic than Southey's *The Curse of Kehama* (1809) or *Lallah Rookh* (1817).† Of these poets Toru Dutt who taught herself Sanskrit, after travelling widely in Europe, and absorbing in particular a great deal from the French nineteenth century poetic tradition, came closest to a new synthesis, of which the effect could at times be strikingly odd:

> When first my casement is wide open thrown
>   At dawn, my eyes delighted on it rest;
> A grey baboon sits statue-like alone
>   Watching the sun-rise . . .[58]

Tagore's translations, however inferior to the original and remote in temperament, are marked by a deliberate and masterful self-awareness which quickly establishes an identity of its own. It is not the absence of poetry in the translations of Tagore which is striking, but the presence of a different kind of poetry: the product of a thorough-going subjectivism, itself very different in tone and effect to the English romantic poets.

Both as an Indian poet writing in English, and as a visionary whose perception of the All-in-One endowed all things with a

---

* '. . . it is really impossible to translate Rabindranath's works . . . though he is incomparable in intellect, he is by nature a dealer in the affairs of the heart: and as the ways of expressing aesthetic emotion in Bengali are in many respects different from those in English, the success of the English *Gitanjali* . . . is entirely accidental.' S. Datta, 'An Introduction to Rabindranath's genius', *The World of Twilight*, Oxford, 1971, p. 233.

† See Datta also, p. 163, for an assessment of M. M. Dutt's importance as a Bengali poet. He pioneered the revival which led to Tagore.

significance of which they were also the source, Tagore's artistic achievement stands out as of a different order to that of his predecessors in the nineteenth century, whether poets or mystics. The instinctive dislike of many Europeans for his kind of writing emphasises once more the magnitude of the problems which stood in the way of any real understanding in British India. It is that same lack of clarity about what is being said, a rhetoric which does not appear to be directed towards any end, and the truth of which appears elusive even to the poet himself, that reflects suspicions and irritations as old as the relationship itself.

As the following chapter illustrates, Tagore was not satisfied with the exploration of his own inner experience; he saw in it a means to create, or at least to work for, a real encounter between East and West which would be to their mutual advantage. When the details of this intention are placed beside the view of Anglo-India that Kipling presented, the full nature of the differences in cultural outlook (as these had emerged by the beginning of the present century) can be seen to constitute the challenge of a world in which even the distant glimmer of understanding is only to be won by the hardest endeavour and the utmost restraint.

Chapter 10

Kipling and Tagore

The horror, the confusion, and the separation of the
murderer from his comrades, were all over before I
came. There remained only on the barrack-square the
blood of men calling from the ground . . .
RUDYARD KIPLING: 'Love o' women', *Many Inventions*,
1893

. . the meeting of the East and West still remains
concentrated on the surface – it is external. The result
is, all our attention is diverted to the surface where we
are hurt, or where we can only think of material profits.
RABINDRANATH TAGORE: *Letters to a Friend* (*1913–22*),
1938

'IN Northern India stood a monastery called The Chubára of
Dunni Bhagat.'¹ It was there that the storyteller from the
West met Gobind, the holy man. When they grew to know
each other well, Gobind told his tales which were true, but 'not
one in twenty could be printed in an English book, because the
English do not think as the natives do. They brood over matters
that a native would dismiss till a fitting occasion; and what
they would not think twice about a native will brood over till a
fitting occasion: then native and English stare at each other
hopelessly across great gulfs of miscomprehension.'² What
Kipling wrote here in the 'Preface' to *Life's Handicap*, he
reiterated in many different forms elsewhere. No writer about
Anglo-India realised more keenly than he did how fast an
Englishman got out of his depths, or how dangerous the
consequences of this could be. The sharply drawn figures of his
landscape exist in a country which none but the foolish or
unwary claim to understand, and where the boundaries between
the permissible and impermissible can be fatal, and concealed.

It is a country of instability, of quick entrances and dead exits, of soon-forgotten loves.

The tales of Kipling's India belong to the last two decades of the nineteenth century. By the time of the First World War, the India which he wrote about no longer existed. Kipling himself, though he often talked of returning, did not go back after 1891. Of the twenty-six years of his life, almost fourteen had been spent there. In the first six of his childhood he had lived with something of the freedom of Kim, picking up native talk with the accurate ear he was later to show in the dialogue of his fiction, and observing with that retentiveness which never allowed him to forget a name or a face. His second spell in India came immediately at the end of his English schooling in 1882, when he returned at the age of seventeen for what he called 'seven years hard', as an editor of English newspapers in Lahore and Allahabad. By the time those years were over, Kipling's reputation was established, both in verse by *Departmental Ditties* (1886) and in prose by *Plain Tales from the Hills* (1888) written to fill up columns in the newspaper; the second ranks among the most extraordinary productions of a young talent, for its inventiveness of character and event, which in a few brief pages summon up much that is central to life without losing grip of the fact that the art of story-telling lies in its ability to entertain. To some, the young Kipling appeared a good deal too knowledgeable about the weaknesses of his elders and betters; he also seemed to understand more than was decent about the natives, which led to rumours of there being 'black blood in his veins.' Like many such tales, this derived from a wrongly stated truth. Undoubtedly, Kipling's childhood experiences gave him much of that intuitive feeling for Anglo-Indian life which he used to considerable effectiveness in his early fiction. But the real blackness in his blood was not the product of some passing affection so much as the permanent damage of hate. When not yet seven, Kipling returned to England with his parents, who left him at the start of his education in what was to become the famous 'House of Desolation' in Southsea. There, he learned from his new custodian, 'the woman', all that a young and sensitive nature needed to of physical cruelty, suspicion, and vindictiveness, posing as a kindly desire to instruct the young. Of that time he was later to write, 'When young lips have drunk deep of the bitter waters of Hate, Suspicion, and Despair, all the Love in the world will not wholly take away that knowledge.'[3] It could scarcely have been a formative experience further removed from that of Tagore; and its precise relationship to the development of Kipling's talent cannot be spoken about with certainty – except that it perhaps helped to mature, at an early age, his perceptiveness concerning human motive and behaviour.

Kipling's diverseness, humour and brevity also protected him from the hostility of his Anglo-Indian critics. And in spite of the fact that his portraits of the English in Simla and elsewhere did them little credit, he was often saying something pleasing to English ears; that they were a different kind of being to the native, and it was better for all if this fact were admitted, and acted on. Here, the contrast between W. D. Arnold and Kipling is one of particular interest. In Arnold's view the quality of human relationships, and the civilisation which they go to make up, cannot be divided; the estrangement between black and white in India indicates how far short of civilisation Anglo-India falls; to Kipling the preservation of civilisation is dependent on the recognition of forbidden pathways which a man only takes at the risk of destroying himself, and possibly others as well. The incompatibilities between English and Indian life are to be noted and respected by keeping the distance they imply. In Kipling's India the menace and danger are close to the surface; and often enough they erupt and destroy. A man needs a steady nerve, and a common-sense recognition of his limitations: 'Now India is a place beyond all others where one must not take things too seriously – the midday sun always excepted.'[4] The problems of Kipling's characters begin where Arnold's admit defeat: in the recognition of a racial difference which it is beyond the power of the individual to change. But Kipling also took up his theme in a more interesting and complex way than the writers of the post-Mutiny period, described in the previous chapter. In their work, the natives scarcely existed except as servants. This reflected a social reality, but it was also the product of impoverished imagination. In Kipling no such limitation obtained. The presence of the English in

India related them whether they liked it or not to the native population. The encounter between the races involved the bringing together of attitudes and feelings which had not yet encountered each other. The predictability of cause and event started to break down. Even if it were possible to understand the native mind (and on the whole it wasn't) the assistance could only be partial. It is in the interaction of minds, in the meeting of East and West, that the unexpected and unforeseeable occurs; the resultant is not the mere sum of two forces. A border-land exists between the races; and no one crosses the border without jeopardy.* Crudely expressed, the doctrine might be read as: 'don't get involved; or if you do, don't expect things to turn out in a predictable way; you're tampering with forces you don't understand.' The young writer was greatly impressed by the random effects wrought by his matter-of-fact fellow countrymen. Oddly - for all the later hostility to Kipling as an Imperialist - there was no one who stressed more often than he did that the Englishman in India was vulnerable. Once he attempts to leave the magic circle drawn round British India, he will be subject to forces he cannot perceive, customs he does not appreciate, and religious taboos he would do well not to violate. Only in Strickland and Kim did Kipling conceive characters capable of living both inside and outside the circle with equal ease; and they were both endowed with special resources. Strickland holds 'the extraordinary theory' that 'a policeman in India should try to know as much about the natives as the natives themselves';[5] and he emerges in the early tales as the one figure remotely attuned to the complexity of the situation. To Kim, as to Strickland, knowledge of native languages provides the key to elementary understanding; and few of the English are shown as possessing it. The exclusiveness

* The metaphor of the border-land which must not be crossed, or only at risk, cannot be taken too simply as Kipling's comment on Anglo-India because of its relevance to the creative process. In this the images figured forth are the projections of states of mind and feeling in the artist himself that find their correlative in particular landscapes; they may not therefore be quite the same as his attitudes to it, or his views of it, in a non-fictional world. The problem raised by the nature of the creative process, however, need not be taken too far, since what counts here is the coherence of the view which the Anglo-Indian stories achieve; and the relevance of it to the questions being raised by this book. Undoubtedly, they add a perspective of considerable interest.

(and ignorance) of the English who governed the country both caused the estrangement, and was its symptom. Government by remote control touches the whole situation with a kind of unreality, not apparent in Munro's time. Munro knew how little of India was changed by any English influence; but his own policies were formed under the influence of his own experience. In his first volume of stories, *Plain Tales from the Hills* (1888), Kipling told of a very different style of government in 'Tod's Amendment'. In Olympian Simla, the Viceroy's Supreme Legislative Council is hacking out a bill for the Sub-Montane tracts. They are for the most part less well-equipped than young Tod who at the age of six speaks Urdu, among other 'queer side speeches',[6] and also mixes with the natives. One night, Tod's Mama gives a dinner-party to which the Legal Member of the Council comes; Tod is able to inform him of the flaw in his legislation from his knowledge of native life. The Legal Member's subsequent inquiries confirm Tod's view; and in the rough draft of the Sub-Montane Ryotwary Revised Enactment, the twenty-second clause has pencilled against it 'Tod's Amendment'.[7] The lightness with which the thing is done does not conceal an underlying view of the distance which separates the Legislative Council from those they govern.

In 'The Head of the District' (*Life's Handicap*) the fatal results of Government not understanding local differences are shown when a Bengali, Mr G. C. Dé, is sent to be Commissioner of a Border District. To Tallantire, the assistant Deputy Commissioner, it's a 'piece of cruel folly,' while the Viceroy regards it as part of an enlightened plan to bring a measure of self-government to the people.[8] Trouble soon breaks out in the district; and the newly-appointed Commissioner saves his skin by going on sick-leave; his brother, mistaken for him, is assassinated. The consequences confirm what the narrator has known all along: 'What looks so feasible in Calcutta, so right in Bombay, so unassailable in Madras, is misunderstood by the North, and entirely changes its complexion on the banks of the Indus.'[9] Kipling's view of misunderstanding embraces both the catastrophe which results from a few men trying to govern a vast Empire of which they are mainly ignorant and with the misadventures which derive even from their 'enlightened' efforts to delegate some of their power.

'The Head of the District' forms one of a group of Kipling's Indian stories which tell of a disaster that could have been avoided, if the kind of place India was had been understood, and the workings of the administration subtle enough to take into account the complex community relationships in different parts of the country. The personal tragedy here only illustrates the public event; but in another tale 'Thrown away', Kipling saw rather the waste of an individual life: The Boy who comes out to India and takes things too seriously gets into trouble. 'It is a slack, *kutcha*, country, where all men work with imperfect instruments; and the wisest thing . . . is to escape as soon as ever you can to some place where amusement is amusement and a reputation worth having.'[10] The Boy does not escape and falls, as many did, into debt. He believes himself ruined beyond redemption, and finally kills himself. In India the scale of values is different; it is no use a man thinking he can live by the principles of conduct which operate in England; but there are principles which it's important to know. In India the bankers could have helped the Boy over the money-problems, while nothing can help those who fall over the boundary of race. The Boy's life is 'thrown away'; but in 'Beyond the pale', as the title suggests, there's no longer hope of redemption. Unequivocally, in the first sentence, Kipling states his theme: 'A man should, whatever happens, keep to his own caste, race, and breed. Let the White go to the White and the Black to the Black . . .'[11] The climate has changed a good deal since the care-free days of Hickey; and while Kipling can write, as he does here, with passion and tenderness of the love between man and woman, he regards it as doomed, when race is involved. 'Beyond the pale' is the story of Trejago, a man who took 'too deep an interest in native life; but will never do so again.'[12] Bisesa, a widow at fifteen, prays to the gods to send her a lover; their answer is Trejago. As Bisesa herself knows, their affair cannot end happily: '. . . It's not good that I should have made you dearer than my own heart to me, Sahib. You are an Englishman. I am only a black girl . . .'[13] The price that she pays to Durga Charan in whose house she lives is that of having her hands cut off at the wrists, while Trejago limps slightly from a wound in his groin for the rest of his days. The savageness of the punishment drives home the point made at the opening that the 'sudden, alien and unexpected' may occur when a man does not keep to his own race; and what little control a man does possess over his destiny will slip through his hands.

Although an element of melodrama mars the ending of 'Beyond the pale' (incidentally, a common enough weakness in those of Kipling's stories which fall a little short of his best) the tale's main point is not to be mistaken. In the finer love-story, 'Without benefit of clergy', the element of exaggeration has been replaced by an insistent stress on the transience of all human things – especially in India, where disease strikes often and fatally; and the rains come each year to wash away the vestiges of all that cannot come to good. Holden has from the start to try to conceal a relationship that his superiors would never approve of; and Ameera's mother warns her young daughter of the inevitable end. 'He will go back to his own people in time . . . but by the blessing of God that time is yet far off . . .'[14] The author himself has already stated the warning for us. 'At his feet sat a woman of sixteen, and she was all but all the world in his eyes. By every rule and law she should have been otherwise, for he was an Englishman, and she a Mussulman's daughter . . .'[15] The promised end comes swiftly and absolutely after the fashion of India: their child dies first of autumn fever, then Ameera herself of cholera. In all Kipling's work there are few more direct and penetrating passages than that in which he narrates the return of Holden when Ameera is dying. It is concerned with the isolation of all human beings at the moment of death, but intensified as the inevitable end of their relationship:

Ameera was lying in the room in which Tota had been born. She made no sign when Holden entered, because the human soul is a very lonely thing and, when it is getting ready to go away, hides itself in a misty borderland where the living may not follow. The black cholera does its work quietly and without explanation. Ameera was being thrust out of life as though the Angel of Death had himself put his hand upon her. The quick breathing seemed to show that she was either afraid or in pain, but neither eyes nor mouth gave any answer to Holden's kisses. There was nothing to be said or done. Holden could only wait and suffer.[16]

The shout of joy from the parched city when the rain starts to fall brings news of the life which continues - unaware, indifferent as always to the private grief. Ameera, silent, unresponsive, dies. Holden has to go on - with the memory of the few brief months in which the law and the gods have allowed him his happiness. Once more a few days later, he returns to the rapidly decaying house. He meets the landlord, and offers to keep the house on, in his absence. The landlord refuses: 'When the birds have gone what need to keep the nest? I will have it pulled down - the timber will sell for something always. It shall be pulled down, and the Municipality shall make a road across, as they desire, from the burning ghaut to the city wall, so that no man may say where this house stood.'[14]

Kipling has given to the relationship between Ameera and Holden a kind of completeness - perhaps only possible because of its brevity. Outside the law, they had found a joy that the law could not contain. But their victory, like this, could only be temporary. India, the land of great dissolution, would win in the end - as she always did.

But it was not only in love that Kipling perceived in Englishmen a courage and independence which gave value to their presence in India. What he admired, sometimes amounted to no more than a bloody-mindedness, a refusal to admit defeat when the odds against success were too long - as in the case of Hummil, whose life and death Kipling describes in 'At the end of the passage.'

In a temperature of one hundred and one, 'four men, each entitled to "life, liberty, and the pursuit of happiness," sat at a table playing whist.'[18] They are located in a 'squat four-roomed bungalow that belonged to the assistant-engineer in charge of a section of the Gaudhari State line then under construction . . .'[19] It is one of those places in the East 'where it is not good or kind to let your acquaintance drop out of sight even for one short week.'[20] All the four men are under thirty; and all understand the dread meaning of loneliness. But it is a special and intense kind of loneliness which does not find any

relief in physical comforts or the compensation of large material rewards. Hummil is considered by Lowndes of the Civil
Service a lucky man because he has a kind of roof over his head;
he sees one train daily; he can get 'beer and soda-water and ice
'em when God is good.'[21] He ought to have had the society of
the sub-contractor, but Jevins put a bullet through his own head
the previous week; Hummil calls it an accident because he
knows he himself may need that sort of cover-up one day. He
then admits that he hasn't had ten minutes' sleep since Friday
morning . . . Dinner when it comes after songs on a largely
dismantled piano consists of miserable goat-chops and smoked
tapioca pudding. Hummil's savage humour drives his guests
away; only the doctor remains, and the two men sweat out the
terrible night together. Hummil, again unable to sleep, starts
to crack up. Spurstow reluctantly gives him a shot of morphia;
and goes to the next room to disarm his weapons. To Spurstow
it seems that the man has slipped back into a state of terrified
childhood. He is being hag-ridden by something he can't get
away from. But Hummil refuses to apply for leave. The only
man who could be sent is in his view a fool; and the line must
go on. He intends to stick it out till the rains break. Spurstow
expresses surprise that that kind of attitude is not dead and
done with; but has to go off with the promise he will return in
a couple of days:

Hummil turned on his heel to face the echoing desolation of his
bungalow and the first thing he saw standing in the verandah was
the figure of himself. He had met a similar apparition once before,
when he was suffering from overwork and the strain of the hot
weather . . .[22]

Spurstow is kept from returning by the intensification of an
epidemic among the coolies. He telegraphs to Mottram to go
to the bungalow; but 'Mottram was forty miles away from the
nearest telegraph, and knew nothing of anything save the needs
of the survey . . .'[23] When the men return to the bungalow the
following Sunday, Hummil is dead. 'In the staring eyes was
written terror beyond the expression of any pen.'[24] But the
place in which these men find themselves is in no way normal.
Even the strongest are hard pressed to retain a rational balance.

There may be Heaven – there must be Hell.
Meantime, there is our life here. We . . . ll?[25]

The men have no answer to the question. The natives in this tale appear as servants who have seen men of their own race die in the same sort of way; they remain the silent observers of Hummil's tragedy; but their presence is also to be felt as part of it. Effectively, Hummil is alone with the dark powers which destroy him; practically he is not. The danger to Englishmen of trying to cross the borderline is here reversed: servants cannot cross the borderline to bring any kind of help. Hummil succumbs to the mental horror of his aloneness in a peopled world. He would have been better off with less imagination, but otherwise he showed many of the virtues the Empire demanded: skill in his work, tenacity, and a good deal of indifference to roughing it out till the job had been finished.

The importance which Kipling attached to the right kind of tenacity and loyalty is brought out with particular force by his reiterated dislike of those who went *fantee* or native, as in 'The Man who would be King'. Kipling tells there of two loafers, Peachey Carnehan and Daniel Dravot who earn a precarious living by blackmail in the natives states – referred to 'as the dark places of the earth, full of unimaginable cruelty, touching the railway and the telegraph on one side, and, on the other, the days of Harun al-Raschid.'[26] When their immediate plans are thwarted by the narrator who happens to be, like Kipling himself, the editor of the local newspaper they decide to do a job in Kafiristan on the borders of the Empire where they plan to make themselves Kings. Kafiristan stands on another border too: the Kafiris have their own code, and it is not that of the 'niggers', but one which up to a point both Dravot and Carnehan understood. With a liberal use of bullets and an appeal to native superstitions, Dravot does succeed in establishing his authority among the local mountain tribes who come to believe he is a god. All goes well until Dravot decides he wants a wife. Carnehan reminds him of their bargain to keep clear of women as a potential source of trouble – but Dravot is now too exhilarated by success to be prudent. When the marriage ceremony occurs, the chosen-girl greets her husband-god by biting him in the neck. At the sight of his blood, the crowd who have come to watch the wedding, recognises their God for the mortal being he is. Dravot dies unpleasantly, while Carnehan fails to die after a day of being crucified, and is allowed to make his way back to British India; he carries Dravot's head with him in a black horse-hair bag which he produces for the newspaper editor as proof of their macabre adventure.

'The Man who would be King' works on many levels – not least as a tale of hubris, in which those who attempt to rival the gods are destroyed. At this level it is a work of a high imaginative order. But Kipling's success in this story rests on his perception of such things within the local and immediate – and in particular his view of the boundaries between East and West. Dravot's success *and* downfall depends on his recognition that the people whose allegiance he gains 'aren't niggers, they're English.'[27] They live by a code of conduct in which the assertion of physical force and the loyalty it can inspire is well understood; they are responsive to the brutality and violence by which he goes about making himself a god and a king. At this level, Dravot understands them too; but in his pride at his success with them, fails to recognise the precariousness of his divine authority, which only requires a direct challenge of the kind the girl makes for its destruction. But the initial distinction between the Kafiris and the niggers reflects the distinction between Muslim and Hindu, with the former arousing in the Englishman a sympathy that the latter does not, precisely because his attitudes to life seem more accessible. The code of honour and manliness by which the border tribes-man lives is paradoxically more trustworthy than the adopted personality of the anglicised Bengali. But Kipling's story also makes the opposite point too, that the similarities between tribesman and European are shallow; the man who invokes them runs the risk of being destroyed if he makes a mistake. Or to put it another way, the man who works through the superiority of European arms and organisation has also to recognise the religious element in the submission he wins. In much of Kipling there is to be seen this contrast between the authority, however established, of the European; and the other forces which wait just over the border out of sight, so that neither we, as readers, or the characters themselves, are expecting their attack.* But in the ability to cope, and to quell such situations, Kipling sees also the hall-mark of the European; and he enshrines it in a touching story entitled 'His chance in life'. When a local rising occurs in the absence of the District Officer, the Native Police Inspector who wishes to take no responsibility points out that the half-caste Michele d'Cruze is a Sahib, and the only representative of European authority in the place. This gives him the courage and coolness to restore order. Confronted the following day by the English Assistant Commissioner, Michele finds himself slipping back into his native part:

The tale of the Tibasu riots ended, with the strain on the teller, in an hysterical outburst of tears; the sorrow that he had killed a man; shame that he could not feel as uplifted as he had felt through the night, and childish anger that he could not do justice to his great deeds. It was the White drop in Michele's veins dying out, though he did not know it.[28]

Taken literally of course this is dangerous nonsense; but part at least of the White Man's power consisted in the ability to contain situations by decisive and organised action; and in this sense Michele lived up to the code.

Both Kipling's full-length novels about India, the *Naulahka* (1892) and *Kim* (1901) exemplify in an expanded form the tale where catastrophe does not occur – although on several occasions it very well might. *The Naulahka*, which Kipling wrote jointly with Wolcott Balestier, is a poor piece of work and does not merit much attention, except that as the sub-title, 'a story of east and west,' indicates, its theme is especially relevant to this book. Kipling, by making the hero of the novel an American, gives him a freedom in conversation and action, which would not have been possible for an Englishman. Nicholas Tarvin is taken to Rajputana by two equally questionable motives: to procure a 'fabulous necklace' that hangs round the

* Other, and very different, treatment of similar themes is to be found in 'The Tomb of his Ancestors' and 'The Bridge-Builders' (*The Day's Work*, 1898). Both are considerable achievements.

neck of an idol; and to pursue the girl he wants to marry who has gone there with the intention of devoting her life to improving the lot of Indian women. Tarvin soon discovers 'how entirely the life, habits, and traditions of this strange people alienated them from all that seemed good and right to him.'[29] The impotence of Western philanthropy to improve matters is also illustrated in the failure of Kate's mission, because she does not understand the strength of the traditions and his habits of life opposed to her success. The popular fear that her new medicines are part of a plot to 'make us lose our religion' leads to the desertion of the hospital, and to her eventual departure from India with Tarvin - still unshaken in her belief that Indian life is degraded. Tarvin speaks for both of them when in the final words of the novel he refers to their stay in India as 'distinctly a side issue.'[30] As far as their personal lives are concerned, India has proved too remote and inaccessible for the experience of it to be anything other than tangential. The East has continued to live as it has always lived; the West has made a sally and been repulsed. If they had stayed, and become involved, they would have released forces far beyond their power to control, or even imagine.

Kim did not appear until a decade after Kipling's last visit to India. The detail of its knowledge, and recollection of idiom is no less sharp for that; but the experience contained within the novel is marked by the maturity of long and deep reflection. What the narrative event of the early stories so often makes clear about the boundaries between East and West, Kim takes up at a higher and more meditated level which does not preclude the same vividness, but makes it subservient to a profounder artistic intention.

Kim himself is a figure from the border-land, dyed with its ambiguities, and hewn from its diverse allegiances:

Though he was burned black as any native; though he spoke the vernacular by preference, and his mother-tongue in a clipped uncertain sing-song; though he consorted on terms of perfect equality with the small boys of the bazaar; Kim was white - a poor white of the very poorest.[31]

When Kim is discovered to be English by the chaplain of his

father's old regiment, the old man's sorrow at losing his *chela**
is tempered by his acceptance of the path he must follow in his
search for the River of the Arrow, while the Boy must be
educated as a Sahib. But Kim will go back to the Lama as often
as he can, while the Lama himself collects money for Kim's
education. The growth of an instinctive understanding between them remains among the book's and Kipling's major
achievements - its concord is strikingly contrasted with the
abrasiveness of other relationships; to the Anglican chaplain,
Father Bennett, the Lama is just a fakir whom he is inclined to
call a sentry to evict.[32] He has long since concluded that the
Oriental mind is not something that can be fathomed. The
Colonel of the Regiment regards the natives as increasingly
unpredictable, the more one knows about them.[33] To the
drummer-boy they are simply 'niggers'.[34] Kim has existed
since his childhood far beyond the limits of such common and
elementary prejudices. His ability to live as a native as well as a
Sahib is made possible by his knowledge of native languages;
and from his adaptability in dress and behaviour. He can eat
with forks in the school; or with his hands in the market. But
the book is concerned with that part of Kim's life before he has
to choose where he belongs. Experience is still self-justifying,
and Kim's open nature makes the most of it:

Now a bed among brickbats and ballast refuse on a damp night, between overcrowded horses and unwashen Baltis, would not appeal
to many white boys; but Kim was utterly happy. Change of scene,
service and surroundings were the breath of his little nostrils, and
thinking of the neat white cots at St Xavier's gave him joy as keen
as the repetition of the multiplication table in English.[35]

The Boy contains a great deal of Kipling's own curiosity and
wonder at the strangeness of things: a gift that was fostered by,
as well as inherited from, his father whose museum in Lahore
(appropriately named 'the Wonder House') dominates the
setting for the early scenes of the novel. But as Kim will learn,
the wonder of the universe and the ruling of India are not at all
the same thing. There, men risk and lose their lives in the services of foreign powers; and the Raj needs its informers to

* chela: disciple.

survive. Only the quest of the Lama from Tibet for freedom
from the wheel of things reveals values unlike those of Mahbub
Khan or St Xavier's. Kim has been taught that 'to abstain from
action was unbefitting a sahib.'[36] The Lama tells him: 'to those
who follow the Way there is neither black nor white, Hind nor
Bhotiyal.* We be all souls seeking escape.'[37]

Not quite all - as the other characters in the novel illustrate.
Mahbub Khan, an Afghan agent for the British, leads a tough,
restless life as a horse-trader which justifies plenty of travel
near the borders of the Empire. As often in Kipling it is in the
ambiance and detail of his environment that individual personality is most sharply caught. 'The horse-trader, his deep
embroidered Bokhariot belt unloosed, was lying on a pair of
silk carpet saddle-bags, pulling lazily at an immense silver
hookah.'[38] In another and more loquacious way he also succeeds
with the Hindu, Hurree Babu. The itinerant drug-vendor with
his blue and white striped umbrella in the Himalayan foothills
(who aspires to be an F.R.S.) is an endearing figure. Tougher
than many had made out the Bengali Babu to be, he takes
pleasure in caricaturing himself: talking the best of English
with the vilest of phrases, just to show off.'[39] His dialogue is full
of memorable mistakes: 'You have - Ha! Ha! - swiped the
whole bag of tricks - locks, stocks and barrels. They told me it
was eight months gone up the spouts. By Jove how they beat
me . . .'[40] But with Mahbub and Hurree, for all their vividness
of presentation, there is something external and less deeply
cut than in the relationship between the Boy and the Lama.
This is a source of wonder to the Lama himself. 'Never was such
a *chela*. I doubt at times whether *Ananda*† more faithfully
nursed our Lord. And thou art a Sahib? When I was a man - a
long time ago - I forgot that. Now I look upon thee often, and
every time I remember that thou art a Sahib. It is strange.'[41]
The crisis for the Lama occurs when, during their journey into
the foothills of the Himalayas, they encounter a Frenchman
and a Russian. A quarrel ensues in which the Russian, to the
horror of the coolies, strikes the Lama and knocks him down.
Kim gets possession of the notebooks and papers which the
Frenchman and the Russian are carrying with them; they turn

* Bhotiyal: Tibet.   † Ananda: the Buddha's disciple.

out to be spies. For the Lama the confrontation with the passion he still finds himself capable of feeling is the beginning of the meditation that leads to his discovery of the River of the Arrow, and his freedom from human illusion: a victory and a liberation which he wrenches his soul back from only to share his deliverance with his *chela*.

Kim is root and branch an English novel – in which there is nothing of intellectual choice – but much of the soil natural and right for the particular tree; as in the words of the Anglo-Saxon poem, 'fate goes ever as it will.' The poignance of the novel arises not from conscious choice but from the separation which diversity of being makes necessary. As in all his work, Kipling does not challenge this; he accepts it as being the way things are. But he does write into it the anguish of a friendship that knows the inevitability of human pathways, and the speed with which they separate from one another. For Kim in his youth, and in his involvement with the wills and intentions of other men, the choice is less clear than for the Lama; but Mahbub Khan's guess that he will enter into Government service seems a shrewd one. How he will like it is another matter! In *Kim*, and especially in the relationship between the Boy and the Lama, one sees in an oblique way perhaps some reflection of what in a more ideal world Kipling would have wished Anglo-India to be. In leading the Lama to the threshold of freedom, Kim is also moving towards a discovery of himself. Kipling creates in the four main characters a toleration and acceptance of man's solitary ways which involves no rejection of what is not one's own. In the best sense of the word, the novel conveys a wonder about people and things, which is not far removed from the detachment the Lama achieves. In the calm and serene air where the Lama's quest ends, Kipling reaches a still point in the turning world which he did not often regain. *Kim* leaves open the question of the Lama's absolute truth in its relevance to those who have not travelled so far.

But the direction of change in Anglo-India since the Mutiny had been towards more distance, not less, as the social conventions among the English became more rigid and exclusive. What Kipling brought to bear on the situation was a psychological penetration that did not permit any illusion about the

great divide between the races, and the disasters that could be
caused when fools rushed in. There was no easy solution
to the conflict between the cultures. In normal circumstances
order and law were means of preserving men from disaster; in
India there were no normal circumstances. Kipling's curiosity
pushed his understanding and his experience as far as it could.
But he would have been the first to admit that even in *Kim*, it
had never pushed him far enough to end the curse written on
the under-side of things. Kipling, unlike Tagore, arrived at no
over-ruling account of human experience; the principles which
he observed to work best were those invented by society for its
own protection:

> Now these are the Laws of the Jungle, and many and mighty
> are they!
> But the head and the hoof of the Law and the haunch and the
> hump is – Obey![42]

Tagore's novel, *Home and the World*, translated in 1919, but
originally published in Bengali in 1916, expresses a comparable
viewpoint, though with explicit criticism of it, and on a specific
political issue. The novel is set in 1905 at the opening of the
swadeshi movement which aimed to encourage native industries,
and radically reduce the sale of imported goods. Tagore con-
ceives and tells his tale through three main characters: Nikhil,
Bimala, his wife, and her anarchist lover, Sandhip. Sandhip
sees India's spirituality as a poison; his passionate nationalism
is his will and his religion:

> I want the western military style to prevail, not the Indian. We shall
> then not be ashamed of the flag of our passion, which mother Nature
> has sent out as our standard into the battlefield of life. Passion is
> beautiful and pure – pure as the lily that comes out of the slimy
> soil . . .[43]

Bimala is moved by the intense convictions of Sandhip, and
alienated from her husband when he refuses to support the
swadeshi movement. Nikhil believes neither in the goal, nor in
the passions which drive men to violence and crime for the
sake of a nationalist freedom that must be won at the price of
somebody else's defeat:

I think I have come to the verge of understanding one thing. Man has so fanned the flame of the loves of men and women, as to make it overpass its rightful domain, and now, even in the name of humanity itself, he cannot bring it back under control. Man's worship has idolised his passion.[44]

Nikhil has what Sandhip calls 'a prejudice in favour of truth'[45] as an objective reality. He believes that 'the day we seek the good of the country along the path of righteousness, He who is greater than our country will grant us true fruition.'[46] The revolutionaries in their violence have become the slaves of their passions, and have submitted to the domination of fear. Nikhil's refusal to worship his country as his god isolates him not only from his immediate household, but from the district at large. Nikhil continues to believe that his pursuit of Truth must determine his political action, and his credibility. 'So long as we are impervious to Truth, and have to be moved by some hypnotic stimulus, we must know we lack the capacity for self-government.'[47] Tagore's presentation of the ideological conflict is weakened by Nikhil's pursuit of an ideal which he can only define by the substitution of other concepts, equally vague:

Where our country makes itself the final object, it gains success at the cost of the soul. Where it recognises the 'Greatest as greater than all, there it may miss success,' but gains its soul.[48]

As Sandhip points out, it is not that it is impossible to understand Nikhil's point of view; but one knows it to be dangerous, because like all forms of faith it is not susceptible to proof or validation.

In this respect Tagore's case is not unlike that of George Herbert in English poetry.* An appreciation of his work both in form and content has repeatedly proved itself not to be confined to Christians alone - in spite of Coleridge's argument to the contrary. In both poets, the power and strength of their affirmation, mediated through a persistent conflict with their

* George Herbert (1593–1633): a poet of the 'Metaphysical school' and contemporary of John Donne. The main body of his verse is collected in *The Temple* (1633); it contains 160 poems, concerned with the 'inner weather' of the poet's spiritual and religious life; but Herbert's artistry makes that relevant to much in the everyday life of his own time, and to the problems of our own.

experience of existence, involves the reader in the dialectic of their position: inevitably, in the prose translations of Tagore, the rhythmical tensions of the verse which control the deeper responses are lost (the subtle variety of Herbert's verse does constitute an important aspect of the pleasure to be derived from him) – but what remains is by no means only the esoteric:

My heart longs to join in thy song, but vainly struggles for a voice. I would speak, but speech breaks not into song, and I cry out baffled. Ah, thou has made my heart captive in the endless meshes of thy music, my master![49]

In this book I intend to confine myself to a detailed look at one work, *Gitanjali, or Song Offerings*, translated and published with an introduction by W. B. Yeats in 1912. There, the connection between the verse, and Tagore's experience in life, particularly in his vision, is direct and explicit. 'When one knows thee, then alien there is none, then no door is shut. Oh, grant me my prayer that I may never lose the bliss of the touch of the One in the play of the Many.' Again, as in Herbert, the poet is concerned with how far short of union or identification he frequently falls; and his poetry is often that of the missed experience; but its potential availability endows the natural and visible world with a special significance which invites the reader not only to appreciate its lyric grace, but to read each poem as a metaphor for the poet's own spiritual state. At its best – and even in translation – the broken narrative of the poem impels the reader into this other world where the association of images and ideas is controlled by a sense of incompleteness; but not that of romantic *sehnsucht*. In Tagore, it is rather the tension that exists between the still and the moving, of the ordinary and the mysterious, the possible and the unfulfilled:

The day is no more, the shadow is upon the earth. It is time that I go to the stream to fill my pitcher . . . I know not if I shall come back home. I know not whom I shall chance to meet. There at the fording in the little boat the unknown man plays upon his lute.[50]

For the poet himself there is no doubt where the signs point, although he recognises that other men will not interpret them as he does: 'from the words of the poet men take what meanings please them; yet their last meaning points to thee.'[51] The pointing, however, is not one that can be perceived without conflict; and it isolates the poet from common human experience. 'In pleasure and in pain I stand not by the side of men, and thus stand by thee. I shrink to give up my life, and thus do not plunge into the great waters of life.'[52] In Herbert's poetry we are often reminded of the court-pleasures and worldly ambitions that he has given up for a higher service; in Tagore the renunciation is a persistent effort, something to be aimed at, or for:

As my days pass in the crowded market of this world and my hands grow full with the daily profits, let me ever feel that I have gained nothing – let me not forget for a moment, let me carry the pangs of this sorrow in my dreams and in my wakeful hours.[53]

He is also close to Herbert in recognising that the Lord whom he serves is not to be found in courts, or in riches:

He is there where the tiller is tilling the hard ground and where the path-maker is breaking stones. He is with them in sun and in shower, and his garment is covered with dust.[54]

The great fair of common human life, in its daily occupations, is the place where his Master is to be found and served. Again, the tension of the poet's experience is most noticeable in the contrast between the quest, and the stillness which always exists but has to be sought by devious means. The traveller has to knock at every alien door to come to his own, and to wander through all the outer worlds to reach the innermost shrine at the end. On the way he knows that the song remains unsung, and the meeting unfulfilled, but the journey is saving him from the 'perils of over-much desire.'[55] At times in the translation the lyric grace and emotional intensity (themselves perhaps the equivalents of stillness and motion respectively) are to be heard, as, for instance, in Poem 17 which begins and ends with the refrain, 'I am only waiting for love to give myself up at last into his hands.'[56] The encompassing unity of the poet's experience is to be observed in the complete freedom with which he moves between everyday things, and his awareness of the presence or absence of the Being who gives them significance:

In the busy moments of the noontide work I am with the crowd, but on this dark lonely day it is only for thee that I hope.
     If thou showest me not thy face, if thou leavest me wholly aside, I know not how I am to pass these long rainy hours.[57]

The associations of this with human love-poetry make it accessible in an immediate way; and even where so obvious an association does not exist, Tagore's thought may often be followed with the intellect alone; but it is the characteristic of poetry, like music, to touch deeper levels in us than thought, to involve us in the apprehension of truths, not to inform us of their existence. In this respect the translation of *Gitanjali* succeeds only in a limited way; nonetheless, it does strikingly give a sense of being a work constructed with an unusual degree of mastery, by someone with a clearly defined poetic personality. Moreover, *Gitanjali* contains so powerful and unusual a degree of affirmation, of yea-saying, that this alone identifies the poet as someone whose experience is worth consideration. In Poem 41, the poet is sitting by the roadside, when the men go home from work. They fill him with shame; but he knows he cannot explain for whom he is waiting. 'I sit on the grass and gaze upon the sky and dream of the sudden splendour of thy coming . . .'[58] Gradually the poet makes us feel the expectation is part of the awareness of his existence, not, as in the case of Samuel Beckett's *Godot*, of his non-existence.

Many a song have I sung in many a mood of mind, but all their notes have always proclaimed, 'He comes, comes, ever comes.'
     In the fragrant days of sunny April through the forest path he comes, comes, ever comes . . .[59]

When the encounter occurs in Poem 50, it leads to an intensification of the poet's sense of joy:

Ah, the light dances, my darling, at the centre of my life; the light strikes, my darling, the chords of my love; the sky opens, the wind runs wild, laughter passes over the earth.* [60]

---

* The sensuous, and ever erotic element, in this poetry is apparent, as in much mystic poetry.

As often in Tagore's work, the connection between joy and children is immediate and close.

On the seashore of endless worlds children meet. The infinite sky is motionless overhead and the restless water is boisterous. On the seashore of endless worlds the children meet with shouts and dances.[61]

The rhythm here conveys something of the contrast between the infinite and motionless, and the moving and material. The poet's experience of the world involves both; and also reconciles them through his coherent view of the universe: 'Thou art the sky and thou art the nest as well.'[62] It is not the world as such that he renounces, but the illusions with which it is viewed. 'No, I will never shut the doors of my senses. The delights of sight and hearing and touch will bear thy delight.

'Yes, all my illusions will burn into illumination of joy, and all my desires ripen into fruits of love.'[63] What might strike us at first as self-consciousness of a rather indulgent kind comes to establish itself as a poetic *persona* which is shaped by contact with the reality it comes to possess:

I was tired and sleeping on my idle bed and imagined all work had ceased. In the morning I woke up and found my garden full with wonders of flowers.[64]

The process of life is illuminated by the experience of the poet, not merely his place in it. There is here something of that special view or role ascribed to poets, particularly by themselves, in the early part of the nineteenth century. The 'gift' with which the poet is endowed makes him the instrument for the expression of the significance of things through their part in the pattern of the whole. 'In this playhouse of infinite forms I have had my play and here I have caught sight of him that is formless . . .'[65]

The final poems in *Gitanjali*, from Poem 90, are concerned with the poet's eventual death. His songs, he says, have taught him all the lessons he ever learnt. 'They guided me all the day long to the mysteries of the country of pleasure and pain, and, at last, to what palace gate have they brought me in the evening at the end of my journey?'[66] At his going out he wishes his whole life to pay its homage and salutation to God.

It is not possible to accept the value of Tagore's verse in a partial way. His attitude to life, to the role of the poet, and to the value of his songs is self-consistent and inclusive. The experience which they contain (as much as what they omit) will inevitably prove unsympathetic to many readers. But it is the very nature of this difference, which proves of interest in the contrast, to which I shall shortly return, with Kipling.

First, however, I want to make brief mention of the relationship between the themes of Tagore's poetry, and his practical views on other matters. Aldous Huxley once observed that the poetry of Tagore meant little to him, and that he was primarily interested in Tagore's ideas about education in which what was aimed at was an education of the whole child, an education of all his senses, as well as his intellectual and verbal responses. What came to be Tagore's social and educational methods which he put into practice at Santiniketan and Sriniketan evolved directly out of the kind of poet that he was, and the nature of his poetic experience. In fact, it would appear a radical misjudgment of what Tagore stood for to consider that experience in isolation from his practical application of it. His concept of One World - a real meeting and union between East and West - and the educational projects which he launched in his schools reflect a basic and unwavering allegiance to his Vision. It assumed such significance for him that he attempted to create its correlative in the external world; he tried to make inner and outer cohere, and in doing so followed a path which Kipling implicitly rejects.

The tragic event often occurs for Kipling because there is no possibility of the conjunction between individual necessity and the Laws of Society. To Tagore the possibility exists because of the underlying unity which coordinates all forms of experience if only it could be perceived. His Vision became a way of life recorded both in his poetry and his work as a teacher. Or - to put it in another way - his life became a constant attempt to recapture the perfection and unity he had glimpsed. To proclaim the existence of a truth meant the failure to find it again. As he said in a letter to his friend, C. F. Andrews: 'I am praying to be lighted from within, and not simply to hold a light in my hand.'[67] What was needful to this inner light was a peaceful detachment from the passions and conflicts of the world, so as to bring one face to face with one's own inner being and the deeper reality of the world. 'The cure for all the illness of life is stored in the inner depths of life, access to which becomes possible when we are alone.'[68] It was this sense of unity perceived from within that led to his belief in the idea of world-brotherhood, his rejection of the dangerous untruth in the idea of European superiority, and refusal to support *swa-raj*. ('What is swa-raj?' he was to ask. 'It is *maya*; it is like a mist that will vanish, leaving no stain on the radiance of the Eternal.')[69] In the British Raj, he saw an alienation of man from man that depended on the illusion of difference:

What is radically wrong with our rulers is this: they are fully aware that they do not know us, and yet they do not care to know us. And in consequence, thorny hedges are springing up of unscrupulous intermediaries between the rulers and the ruled, giving rise to conditions which are not only miserable, but unspeakably vulgar.[70]

The All which he had seen was the key to the improvement in all human relations. As a result of the First World War, Tagore conceived the idea of forming at Santiniketan a home of brotherhood and peace, 'where East and West might meet in common fellowship of study and work . . .'[71] He saw that an encounter had taken place between East and West; but 'so far has produced only our pitiful politics, because it has not yet been turned into truth.'[72] He loved India - but as an idea, not a geographical expression: he wanted it to stand for the cooperation of all the people of the world. Like Yeats's 'Innisfree' - a poem which Tagore greatly admired - Santiniketan was to be both a place, and something which existed in 'the deep heart's core.' Out of the encounter between East and West which had so far proved superficial, he believed it was possible that 'there would mature the seed of a great future of union.'[73] In the place of the present commercial exploitation of India by Europe, which encouraged all the baser passions of man, East and West must join together in a common spiritual pilgrimage.

But the application of Tagore's educational and cultural theories lie in the period after the First World War. By then the society which Kipling had written about had crumbled, if not entirely disappeared. The Raj itself in the Montagu-Chelmsford reforms of 1919 had effectively let a time limit be set on its existence. The civilisation of the pre-1914 world, with its belief in steady progress towards a millennium, had fallen in the general ruin; and in its place the politics of black versus white, in the literal and metaphorical senses, had forced men to choose not to sit on the fence. It was indicative of the spirit of the time that Tagore quarrelled with Gandhi in his attack on Ram Mohun Roy as 'a pigmy' compared with those Indian leaders who had never had any contact with the West. Tagore was not inspired by reform, to reform himself. However antediluvian, he did not believe in any side which did not start from the assumption that the only progress must lie in the advancement of all men towards Truth. Remote as this sounds from the politics of the inter-war years, it was perhaps no more so than the life and society depicted in Kipling's *Departmental Ditties* (1886) and *Barrack-room Ballads* (1892), which earned him fame and fortune. Their very success indicated the kind of audience to whom they first appealed in India; that in itself was part of the skill with which they were conceived. The poem called 'The Galley-Slaves', which was not included till the third edition, and was in fact Kipling's valediction to India, caught a part of its tone exactly:

> But today I leave the galley. Shall I curse her service then?
> God be thanked – whate'er comes after, I have lived and
> toiled with Men![74]

The belligerent self-assertion of these lines stands in another corner of the world from the quiet self-effacement of Tagore at about the same time: 'Nothing is more beautiful or great than to perform the ordinary duties of one's daily life simply and naturally.'[75] It is possible to take exception to elements in both points of view; but they have nothing to say to each other.

Kipling's feeling for the idiosyncratic Anglo-Indian temperament – for its oddities of vocabulary and conventions – also accounted for his popularity: its rites could only be fully shared by those who had been in the country, whether the tone was mocking:

> If down here, I chance to die,
>   Solemnly I beg you take
> All that is left of 'I'
>   To the Hills for old sake's sake
> Pack me very thoroughly
>   In the ice that used to slake
> Pegs I drank when I was dry –
>   This observe for old sake's sake.[76]

or nostalgic:

I am sick of endless sunshine, sick of blossom-burdened bough,
Give me back the leafless woodlands where the winds of Springtime
   range –
Give me back one day in England, for it's Spring in England now.[77]

Of the everyday and ordinary feeling *Gitanjali* contained almost
nothing: there, the conflict lay in the nature and quality of the
experience, or its realisation. Kipling's robustly healthy ir-
reverence enjoyed a vulgarity which Tagore deplored. The lack
of asylum in any aesthetic or religious belief also left Kipling
with the hard problem of values – of what they were, and how
they should be preserved:

> The black shall mourn for hoof and hide,
>   The white man for his brother.
> 'Tis war, red war, I'll give you then,
>   War till my sinews fail;
> For the wrong you have done to a chief of men
>   And a thief of the Zukka Kheyl.[78]

The brotherhood of fighting men undoubtedly had its attrac-
tion for Kipling; but such brotherhood only lasted when built
on the severe code of endurance and self-discipline which he
expressed in a poem written on the outbreak of the First
World War; and which expressed much of the austerity by
which the Anglo-Indians of the mid-century, like the Law-
rences, had ruled their lives:

> No easy hope or lies
> Shall bring us to our goal
> But iron sacrifice
> Of body, will and soul. . .[79]

The largeness of Tagore's vision in his pursuit of a meaning-ful concord between East and West, and the value of his hope that it might be achieved stands beyond question. But in his poetry, as in his life, the centrality of his vision of that unity short-circuited altogether those passions, desires and sorrows which motivated, as he once saw, Romeo and Juliet, Lear and Othello. Tagore's vision of a unified world was not dissimilar to Shakespeare's in his final plays. In Shakespeare, however, the general arises from the particular. Individual men of sin pay the price of their wickedness; redemption when it comes comes to individuals. And although its availability makes a comment upon the world in which we live, its significance, if not its relevance, is confined to those who attain it. It was freedom from this world of pain and illusion which Tagore sought in the All; and it was the translation of that All back into the world of men which he worked for in the idea of human brotherhood. It was a great idea. But the problem did not exist only in the failure of the West to understand the East, as in the failure common to both worlds to find a *via media* which would harmonise the forces in each that led to hostility and mutual destructiveness. In a very different sense Tagore brings us back to Kipling:

But there is neither East, nor West, Border, nor Breed, nor Birth,
When two strong men stand face to face, though they come from the
    ends of the earth.

Epilogue

The contrast between Kipling and Tagore of the last chapter outlines a major distinction between the two cultures as they stood in relation to one another before the start of the disintegration of Western civilisation in the First World War. As well as the consequences of that in the West, it was in the postwar years that the *swa-raj* movement, under the increasing authority and influence of Gandhi, started to dissolve the unity of Anglo-India, and threw it into a state of conflict which only ended in 1947. In Kipling and Tagore we can see reflected for the last time in calm and undistorted waters some of the basic differences and obstacles to understanding which had existed since the seventeenth century. It is not an encouraging vision as the product of three hundred years' relationship. The Western man sees mainly the necessity for each race sticking to its own kind; and any attempt at fusion leading only to confusion, except in the case of the individual and exceptional pilgrimage which, as in Kipling's *The Miracle of Purun Bhagat* (*The Second Jungle Book*), or in *Kim* leads men to cross boundaries as the only means to self-discovery. By this act, the first of the great questors, Thomas Coryat, had discovered the strength of his own convictions, and his abhorrence of paganism; later, less dogmatic spirits, like James Forbes, had found the same confirmation of their own personal beliefs, but learned to regard them as relative to the equally strongly held convictions of other men. Where he saw a possible gain in human happiness or understanding, Forbes saw no reason for reticence about putting forward his own ideas; but it was no longer a matter of dogma, so much as aspiration and will to leave life in the country where he worked a little better, more enlightened, prosperous and free from civil strife.

The literature of Anglo-India has been shown to contain the records of many such lives, spent neither on an imperial dream, nor a desire to impose the culture or religion of the West on others, out of a belief in its innate superiority. But the story of Anglo-India cannot be separated from its dynamic; and in a survey of the long historical moment, the causes for hope are less strongly written. By the first decade of the present century a man so perceptive as Sudhindranath Datta* recorded that the English had 'begun to be hated';[1] and he gave as reasons both the attitude to, and treatment of, men whose skin was a different colour. Whatever their talents, abilities, powers, colour alone brought them humiliation and contempt. An Indian could not visit the homes of the English 'except as a suppliant carrying propitiatory gifts; if business demanded his attendance at their clubs, he could only enter by the servants' door; he was not allowed to stray into the part reserved for them in the best public park; and to eat in their restaurants he had to borrow their clothes, or be thrown out.'[2] Statements like this make one question the good sense of Malcolm Muggeridge's dismissal in the introduction to Datta's book: 'Already most people have forgotten there was a British raj, which after all only lasted a very short time, and had a very trifling impact . . .'[3] It was not a trifling impact on those who experienced it; and the fact that it has been forgotten, if true, embodies a state of things questionably desirable. Although exactly similar situations will not arise again, the Raj exemplifies much that gives pause for thought about the relationship between Eastern and Western worlds, about the hardness of attaining even an elementary understanding of any person whose cultural background is radically different; and of the very real barriers which this can create to the attainment or preservation of high civilisation. The exclusive and restrictive nature of Anglo-Indian life – however justified by the caution which Kipling advocates – with its sharply prescribed boundaries between ruler and ruled did not create an environment in which much progress could be made with the 'humanisation of man in society,' any more than the exclusively commercial pursuits of the majority of Company

---

* Datta, who died in 1960, was among the most celebrated Bengali poets of this century; he was also an essayist, journalist, and man of letters.

servants in the eighteenth century were likely to encourage it.

But reflection on the civilisation of Anglo-India makes it impossible also to overstate the importance of the attitudes and ruling passions by which men are guided when confronted by things and situations beyond their immediate understanding, and with which habit and custom have not made them familiar. In such new situations the influence of the most articulate in the community becomes of special importance. The denigration of all things Hindu by the elder Mill set the tone for the predominant English attitude in the later part of the nineteenth century; it was bolstered by Macaulay and endorsed by the Mutiny. In turning away from the attitudes and knowledge pioneered by Warren Hastings and William Jones the English restricted their horizons, and in doing so, denied the chance for anything except the provincial to flourish in their soil. In this respect the civilisation of Anglo-India got the culture it deserved.

No one would wish to underestimate the magnitude of the difficulties involved – except that no good reason existed why the relationship should have resolved itself into hate. It might be argued that the period of the British presence was both too long and too short: too short for the points of contact to become natural and instinctive, considering the number and size of the obstacles to understanding on both sides; too long for the relationship to remain as superficial as it did without hurt. Together with physical privations and the hardship of exile, these difficulties were enough to arouse dislike. In addition, the rapid change in Western attitudes which arose out of the increasing domination of science, and the endorsement this gave to the English liking for the practical, served to widen the gap between the two civilisations in the nineteenth century, when long acquaintance might have drawn them closer together. Since this change ran parallel to an intensifying sense of Empire, and racial superiority, it left little room for the forces of enlightenment to work in a context where large differences of thought, feeling and style of living already made understanding especially hard. But at the same time the nature of the challenge was unique. A stranger to all that he saw and experienced, the Englishman was involved in a situation which offered every possibility for increasing men's humanity, and improvement in human affairs through the mutual benefit to be derived from the widened understanding that close contact with other cultures could bring. The success of many Indians in assimilating what they wanted from the West without losing a sense of their own cultural and national identity is conspicuous by comparison.

The question from which I began concerning the nature of the differences between East and West as these expressed themselves in the prolonged relationship between Britain and India has revealed the necessity for attempting an answer in the specific context, and moment of time. All human conflicts, however wide and general their base, are made of this sort of concreteness. But I hope also to have caught something of the ebb and flow of minds towards and away from each other in the complex process of inter-cultural relationship, because it is, I believe, the broader view of the pattern which enables us to look forward as well as back. The death of imperialism has done nothing to solve the problems of ignorance and mis-understanding.

By 1914 it was clear that the Empire was not only threatened on those frontiers which Lord Curzon had been so zealous to guard; but from the internal forces which the British presence had fostered. At the same time not even these were simple in their substance or their effect. While the relationship between the English and the Indians had become increasingly strained in the two decades around the turn of the century, the willing-ness of the Indians to fight 'for the Empire' in the First World War showed how complex and differentiated the feelings beneath the surface still were. In the years to come the problem of loyalties was to impose strains under which many without the belief or detachment of men as great as Tagore and Gandhi were to break. The Englishman was to turn against his own kind, either because he remained loyal to the idea of our right to maintain possession of the richest jewel in the Imperial Crown, or because he denied it. The anglicised Indian was to find it impossible to forgo the deep conviction which he had formed of the fundamental benefits to be derived from the continuing relationship with English life and civilisation; at the same time he was unable to deny the claims of those who saw all causes as unimportant till India was once more freed from foreign rule. But the triumphs and tragedies of those conflicts are, as Kipling would have said, another story.

Notes

INTRODUCTION

1. Rudyard Kipling, *Verse* (Definitive edition), 1969, p. 238. (Hereafter Kipling, *Verse*.)
2. W. D. Arnold, *Oakfield; or Fellowship in the East*, 2 vols., 1854, I, p. 160.
3. 'Passages from India', *Adam*, Nos. 355–360, 1971, p. 14.

CHAPTER ONE: *A Kind of Permanence*

1. W. H. Russell, *My Diary in India, in the years 1858-9*, 2 vols., 1860, I, p. 122. (Hereafter, Russell, *Diary*.)
2. J. W. Kaye *The Life and Correspondence of Lord Metcalfe*, 2 vols., 1858, I, p. 285. (Hereafter, Kaye, *Metcalfe*.)
3. E. Eden, *Up the Country*, 2 vols., 1866 (2nd edn.), II, p. 116.
4. J. Beames, *Memoirs of a Bengal Civilian*, 1961, p. 115.
5. Sitā Rāma, *From Sepoy to Subadar*, trans. by Lt.-Col. Norgate, Calcutta, 1911, p. 21.
6. A. Mayhew, *The Education of India*, 1926, p. 94. (Hereafter Mayhew, *Education*.)
7. R. Tagore, *My Reminiscences*, 1917, p. 52. (Hereafter Tagore, *Reminiscences*.)
8. John Fryer, *A new account of East India & Persia, being nine years travels, 1672-81*, Hakluyt Society, 3 vols., 1909-15, I, p. 165.
9. J. Douglas, *Book of Bombay*, Bombay, 1883, p. 556 (quoting from N. Macleod, *Peeps at the Far East*, 1871).
10. Quoted by Dennis Kincaid in *British Social Life in India, 1608-1937*, 1938, p. 240.
11. 'Wanderings in India', *Household Words*, Nov. 14, 1857, Vol. XVI, p. 459.
12. E. M. Forster, *The Hill of Devi*, 1967, p. 106.
13. J. H. Grose, *A Voyage to the East Indies, begun in 1750 with observations continued till 1764*, 1766 (2nd edn.), p. 89.
14. Tagore, *op cit.*, pp. 188–9. See also Mildred and W. G. Archer, *Indian Painting for the British 1770-1880*, Oxford, 1955, p. 13. The

lack of 'perfection' among Indian *artists* in contrast to their European contemporaries of the late eighteenth and early nineteenth centuries is commented on.

15. Grose, *op. cit.*, p. 235.
16. Chaudhuri, *op. cit.*, p. 31.
17. W. Hodges, *Travels in India, during the years 1780–3*, 1793, p. 10.
18. V. Ball, *Jungle Life in India; or the Journeys and Journals of an Indian geologist*, 1880, p. 93.
19. Eden, *Up the Country*, I, p. 23.
20. Mayhew, *Education*, p. 97.
21. The limited appeal of the 'Nautch' depended on different tastes in music and dancing; and the perennial problem of language remained unsolved.
22. *Household Words*, Oct. 3, 1857, Vol. XVI, p. 321.
23. *Early Travels in India*, ed. by W. Foster, Oxford, 1921, p. 328. (Hereafter, Foster.)
24. ibid.
25. Eden, *Up the Country*, I, p. 187.
26. Viscountess Falkland, *Chow Chow*, 2 vols., 1857, I, p. 36.
27. Quoted in Aldous Huxley's *Jesting Pilate*, 1926, p. 121.
28. Marchioness of Dufferin and Ava, *Our Viceregal Life in India, 1884–8*, 2 vols., 1889, II, p. 38.
29. E. Eden, *Letters from India*, 2 vols., 1872, I, p. 148.
30. W. B. Hockley, *The English in India*, 3 vols., 1828, I, p. 302.
31. quoted in *The Sahibs*, ed. by Hilton Brown, 1948, p. 40.
32. R. Kipling, 'At the end of the passage', *Life's Handicap*, 1891, p. 172.
33. J. W. Kaye, *Life and Correspondence of Sir John Malcolm*, 2 vols., 1856, I, 208. (Hereafter Kaye, *Malcolm*.)
34. Kaye, *Metcalfe*, I, p. 246.
35. R. Heber, *Narrative of a Journey through the Upper Provinces of India, 1824–5*, 3 vols., 1828, I, p. 246.
36. G. Graham, *Life in the Mofussil; or, the Civilian in Lower Bengal*, 2 vols., 1878, I, p. 93.
37. A. Lyall, *Poems*, 1908, p. 103.
38. Kipling, *Verse*, p. 164.
39. G. Orwell, *Collected Essays*, ed. by Sonia Orwell and Ian Angus, 4 vols., 1968, II, p. 100.

CHAPTER TWO: *The Single Spies*

1. Vincent Smith, *Akbar, the Great Moghul*, Oxford, 1917.
2. Kipling, *Verse*, p. 521.
3. see, in particular, Percival Spear, *Twilight of the Mughuls: Studies in late Mughul Delhi*, Cambridge, 1951. (Hereafter, Spear, *Twilight*.)
4. see, for a full account, R. Hakluyt, *Principal Navigations*, 12 vols., 1903–5, VII, p. 116.
5. Foster, *op. cit.*, p. 17.
6. *ibid.*, pp. 21–2.
7. *ibid.*, p. 23.
8. *ibid.*, p. 24.
9. *ibid.*, p. 56.
10. *ibid.*, p. 65.
11. John Jourdain, *Journal*, Hakluyt Society, 1895, p. 162.
12. Foster, *op. cit.*, p. 83.
13. *The Embassy of Sir Thomas Roe*, ed. by W. Foster, 2 vols., Hakluyt Society, 1894–9, I, p. 113ff.
14. *ibid.*, p. 116.
15. *ibid.*, p. 114.
16. *ibid.*, p. 120.
17. *ibid.*, 'Introduction', p. xlii.
18. *ibid.*, p. 123ff.
19. *ibid.*, p. 246.
20. *ibid.*, II, p. 490–1.
21. *ibid.*, p. 358, fn. 1.
22. Foster, *op. cit.*, p. 325.
23. *ibid.*, p. 325.
24. Roe, *op. cit.*, I, p. 138.
25. Foster, *op. cit.*, p. 266.
26. *ibid.*, p. 269.
27. *ibid.*, p. 287.

CHAPTER THREE: '*A Company of base quarrelling people*'

1. Spear, *Twilight*, p. 13.
2. Clive's victory at Arcot in 1751 put an effective end to French ambitions in India, confirmed by the replacement of Dupleix in 1754.
3. 900 square miles of territory south of Calcutta.
4. Fryer, *op. cit.*, I, p. 180ff.

5. J. Ovington, *A Voyage to Surat in the year 1689*, 1696, p. 230. (Here-after, Ovington.)
6. John Burnell, *Bombay in the Reign of Queen Anne*, Hakluyt Society, 1933, p. 25.
7. Kincaid, *op. cit.*, p. 41.
8. Grose, *op. cit.*, p. 82.
9. Smith, *Akbar*, p. 147.
10. Thomas Bowrey, *A Geographical Account of Countries round the Bay of Bengal, 1669–79*, Hakluyt Society, 1905, p. 224.
11. W. Hedges, *Diary of*, Hakluyt Society, 3 vols., 1887–9, Vol. II, p. xc.
12. quoted in W. W. Hunter, *Thackerays in India*, 1897, p. 36.
13. Hedges, *op. cit.*, I, p. 177.
14. Hedges, *op. cit.*, III, p. lxxx.
15. *ibid.*, p. cxxviii.
16. Alexander Hamilton, *A new account of the East Indies*, ed. by W. Foster, 2 vols., 1930, I, p. 79.
17. *ibid.*, p. 143.
18. Quoted by Philip Woodruff, *The Men who ruled India*, 2 vols., Cape paperback, 1963, I, p. 106.
19. Fryer, *op. cit.*, I, p. 235.
20. Ovington, *op. cit.*, p. 404.
21. E. Ives, *A Voyage from England to India in 1754*, 1773, p. 68.
22. J. Forbes, *Oriental Memoirs* (revised by his daughter), 2 vols., 1834, II, pp. 77 and 269ff.
23. Kincaid, *op. cit.*, p. 11.
24. J. Talboys Wheeler, *Early Records of British India*, Calcutta, 1878, p. 53.
25. quoted by Surendranath Banerjea, *A Nation in the Making*, Oxford, 1925, p. 163. (Hereafter, Banerjea.)
26. Ovington, *op. cit.*, p. 400.
27. C. Lockyer, *An Account of the Trade in India*, 1711, p. 24.
28. Ives, *op. cit.*, pp. 29–30.
29. *ibid.*
30. Fryer, *op. cit.*, II, p. 217.
31. Wheeler, *op. cit.*, p. 360.
32. T. B. Macaulay, *Critical and Historical Essays*, ed. by F. C. Montague, 2 vols., 1903, II, p. 410.
33. S. G. Hossein Khan, *Seir Mutaqherin*, 4 vols., Calcutta, no date, III, p. 29. (First edn. in Persian, 1786.) (Reprint of Raymond' translation of 1789.)

34. W. Mackintosh, *Travels in Europe, Asia, Africa*, 2 vols., 1782, II, p. 23 – Letter dated Nov. 18, 1779.
35. Douglas, *op. cit.*, p. 107.
36. Fryer, *op. cit.*, p. xxxvi.
37. Hamilton, *op. cit.*, I, p. 7.
38. Fryer, *op. cit.*, I, p. 218.
39. W. Hickey, *Memoirs*, 4 vols., New York, 1923–5, II, p. 153.
40. Ovington, *op. cit.*, p. 397.
41. Ives, *op. cit.*, p. 47.
42. *ibid.*
43. *ibid.*, p. 21.
44. Hickey, *op. cit.*, IV, p. 366.
45. *Francis Letters*, ed. by B. Francis and E. Kean, 2 vols., 1901, I, p. 219. (Hereafter, Francis.)
46. Hickey, *op. cit.*, III, p. 277.
47. C. R. Wilson, *Early Annals of the English in Bengal*, 4 vols., 1895–1917, p. 62.
48. Woodruff, *op. cit.*, I, p. 155.
49. Kincaid, *op. cit.*, p. 51.
50. Douglas, *op. cit.*, p. 85.
51. Hedges, *op. cit.*, II, p. ccix–x.
52. *ibid.*, I, p. 142.
53. Hamilton, *op. cit.*, II, p. 11.
54. Hickey, *op. cit.*, III, p. 327.
55. R. Kipling, 'Beyond the Pale', *Plain Tales from the Hills*, 1888, p. 147.
56. Kincaid, *op. cit.*, p. 90.
57. Hickey, *op. cit.*, II, p. 163.
58. Hickey, *op. cit.*, II, p. 169.
59. Wheeler, *op. cit.*, p. 192.
60. For a detailed account of Bolts' activities, see Woodruff, *op. cit.*, I, p. 104ff.
61. Quoted by Keith Feiling, *Warren Hastings*, Papermac, 1966, p. 31.
62. Lord Clive's Speech in the House of Commons on the motion made for an Inquiry into the 'Nature, State, and Condition of the East India Company, etc.', 1772, p. 9 and p. 19.
63. *ibid.*, p. 42.
64. *ibid.*, p. 45.
65. Hickey, *op. cit.*, I, p. 115.
66. Forbes, *op. cit.*, I, p. 96.

67. *ibid.*, I, p. 42.
68. *ibid.*, p. 130.
69. *ibid.*, p. 325.
70. *ibid.*, p. 491.
71. Forbes, *op. cit.*, II, p. 245.

CHAPTER FOUR: *An Age of Enlightenment*

1. Quoted in David Kopf, *British Orientalism and the Bengal Renaissance, The Dynamics of Indian Modernisation, 1773–1835*, University of California Press, 1969, p. 18. (Hereafter, Kopf.) I wish to acknowledge a particular debt to David Kopf's work for its many illuminating insights and quotations.
2. *ibid.*
3. Feiling, *op. cit.*, p. 41.
4. *ibid.*, p. 138.
5. *ibid.*, p. 85.
6. *ibid.*, p. 103.
7. *ibid.*, p. 86.
8. Quoted in *The British Discovery of Hinduism in the Eighteenth Century*, ed. by P. J. Marshall, Cambridge, 1970, p. 189.
9. *ibid.*, p. 142.
10. *ibid.*, p. 189.
11. *ibid.*, p. 107.
12. *ibid.*, p. 48.
13. *ibid.*, p. 50.
14. Kopf, *op. cit.*, p. 30.
15. James Rennell, *Memoir of the Map of Hindoostan*, 1788, p. iii.
16. Forbes, *op. cit.*, I, pp. 461–2.
17. W. Jones, *Letters*, ed. by Garland Cannon, 2 vols., Oxford, 1970, II, p. 740.
18. *ibid.*, p. 741.
19. *ibid.*, p. 766.
20. S. N. Mukherjee, *Sir William Jones, a study in Eighteenth Century British attitudes to India*, Cambridge, 1968, p. 141.
21. Samuel Foote, *The Nabob*, A Comedy in 3 Acts, Dublin, 1773, p. 288.
22. *ibid.*, p. 289.
23. *ibid.*, p. 308.
24. Woodruff, *op. cit.*, I, p. 146.
25. Edmund Burke, *Works*, 6 vols., 1893, II, p. 182.

26. *ibid.*, pp. 194–5.
27. *ibid.*, III, p. 132.
28. *ibid.*, p. 193.

CHAPTER FIVE: *The Awakening of Giants*

 1. Charle Cornwallis, 1st Marquess, *Correspondence*, ed. by Charles Ross, 3 vols., 1859, I, p. 388.
 2. C. Grant, *Observations on the State of Society among the Asiatic subjects of Great Britain, written chiefly in 1792* (revised in 1813), p. 62.
 3. John Shore, Lord Teignmouth, *Memoirs of the Life and Correspondence of*, ed. by his son, 2 vols., 1843, I, p. 35.
 4. *ibid.*, I, p. 85.
 5. *ibid.*, II, p. 142.
 6. Grant, *op. cit.*, p. (i).
 7. *ibid.*, p. 43.
 8. *ibid.*, p. 71.
 9. *ibid.*, p. 222.
10. Quoted in F. G. Hutchins, *The Illusion of Permanence*, Princeton, 1967, p. 6.
11. *ibid.*, p. 6.
12. Quoted in A. T. Embree, *Charles Grant and British Rule in India*, 1962, p. 274.
13. A. Mayhew, *Christianity and the Government of India*, 1929, p. 93. (Hereafter, Mayhew, *Christianity*.)
14. Kopf, p. 80.
15. Mayhew, *Christianity*, p. 109.
16. *ibid.*, p. 170.
17. *ibid.*, p. 236.
18. W. Hunter, *The Old Missionary*, Oxford, 1895, p. 24.
19. Heber, *op. cit.*, I, p. 110.
20. *ibid.*, II, p. 344.
21. *ibid.*, III, p. 350.
22. Douglas, *op. cit.*, p. 270.
23. Embree, *op. cit.*, p. 192.
24. Viscount Valentia, *Voyages and Travels to India, Ceylon in the years 1802–6*, 4 vols., 1811, I, 192.
25. T. Twining, *Travels in India a hundred years ago*, ed. by W. H. G. Twining, 1893, p. 484.
26. Quoted by G. D. Bearce, *British Attitudes towards India, 1784–1858*,

Oxford, 1961, p. 75, from Mill's *History*, 6 vols., 1826, VI, pp. 216–17.

27. P. Spear, *The Nabobs*, 1932, p. 139.
28. Kincaid, *op. cit.*, p. 107.
29. Kopf, *op. cit.*, pp. 88–9.
30. *ibid.*, p. 131.
31. *ibid.*, p. 235.
32. Mayhew, *Education*, p. 10.
33. Kopf, *op. cit.*, p. 182.
34. Kopf, *op. cit.*, p. 259.
35. James Mill, *History of British India* (Fourth edn., with notes and contributions by H. H. Wilson), 8 vols., 1848, II, p. 155 and p. 164.
36. *ibid.*, I, p. 467 and p. 476.
37. *ibid.*, II, pp. 517–18.
38. S. D. Collet, *Life and Letters of R. M. Roy* (ed. by H. C. Sakkar), Calcutta, 1914, p. 250.
39. Quoted by Thomas Metcalf, *The Aftermath of Revolt, India 1857–70*, Princeton, 1965, p. 20.
40. Collet, *op. cit.*, p. 96.
41. *ibid.*, p. 228.
42. Hunter, *op. cit.*, p. 119.
43. Valentia, *op. cit.*, I, p. 109.
44. *ibid.*, p. 336.
45. Valentia himself speaks of their 'desire to throw off our yoke' (p. 336).
46. J. Bradshaw, *Thomas Munro* (Rulers of India), Oxford, 1894, pp. 36–8.
47. Sir Thomas Munro, *Selections from his Minutes and other Official Writings*, ed. by A. J. Arbuthnot, Madras, 1886, p. cxxiv.
48. Woodruff, *op. cit.*, I, p. 195. In these pages on the 'great four' I am greatly indebted to Philip Woodruff.
49. Bradshaw, *op. cit.*, p. 182.
50. *ibid.*, p. 181.
51. Munro, *op. cit.*, pp. 489–50.
52. Woodruff, I, *op. cit.*, pp. 189–90.
53. Kaye, *Malcolm*, I., p. 23.
54. Sitā Rāma, *op. cit.*, p. 15.
55. Kaye, *Malcolm*, II, p. 362.
56. J. S. Cotton, *Mountstuart Elphinstone*, Oxford, 1892, p. 128.
57. *ibid.*, p. 124.
58. *ibid.*, p. 186.

59. *ibid.*, p. 190.
60. *Bearce, op. cit.*, p. 134.
61. Kaye, *Metcalfe*, II, p. 15.
62. *ibid.*, p. 124.
63. *ibid.*, p. 148.
64. *ibid.*, p. 149.
65. *ibid.*, I, p. 122.
66. M. Elphinstone, *History of India*, 6 edn., 1874, p. 753.
67. Maria Graham, *Journal of a Residence in India*, 1812, p. 28.
68. *ibid.*
69. *ibid.*, p. 133.
70. *ibid.*, p. 136.
71. *ibid.*, pp. 133-4.
72. V. Jacquemont, *Letters from India*, trans. with an introduction by C. A. Phillips, 1936, p. xxv.
73. *ibid.*, p. 23.
74. *ibid.*, p. 309.
75. *ibid.*, p. 335.
76. Kincaid, *op. cit.*, p. 177.
77. Jacquemont, *op. cit.*, p. 10.
78. E. Stokes, *The English Utilitarians in India*, Oxford, 1959.
79. Bearce, *op. cit.*, p. 162.
80. Hilton Brown, *op. cit.*, p. 250.
81. John Clive, *Macaulay, the Shaping of the Historian*, 1973, p. 236.
82. *ibid.*, p. 365.
83. *ibid.*, p. 372.
84. T. B. Macaulay, 'The Government of India', A Speech in the House of Commons on July 10, 1833 (Reynard Library), 1952, pp. 704-5.
85. *ibid.*
86. *ibid.*, p. 717.
87. *ibid.*, p. 718.
88. T. B. Macaulay, 'Indian Education', Minute of Feb. 2, 1835 (Reynard Library), p. 723.
89. *ibid.*, p. 727.
90. *ibid.*, p. 728.
91. *ibid.*, p. 729.
92. *ibid.*, p. 730.
93. Bearce, *op. cit.*, p. 171.
94. Kopf, *op. cit.*, p. 250.
95. Mayhew, *Christianity*, p. 176.

96. Kopf, *op. cit.*, p. 291. He is quoting from Girish Chandra Ghose, a leading Calcutta journalist, who was writing on January 6, 1862.
97. Quoted in A. Greenberger, *The British Image of India, 1880–1960*, Oxford, 1969, p. 75, from F. A. Steel's *The Hosts of the Lord* (1900).

CHAPTER SIX: *The Birth of the 'Nigger'*

1. quoted in Mayhew, *Education*, p. 32.
2. G. E. Trevelyan, *Macaulay*, 2 vols., 1876, I, p. 410.
3. Jacquemont, *op. cit.*, p. 102.
4. Eden, *Up the Country*, I, p. 183.
5. *ibid.*, II, p. 96.
6. Russell, *Diary*, II, p. 120.
7. *ibid.*, p. 149.
8. C. Acland, *Popular Account of the Manners and Customs of India*, 1847, pp. 129–30.
9. Eden, *Letters from India*, I, p. 215.
10. *ibid.*, p. 260.
11. Marquess of Dalhousie, *Private Letters*, ed. by J. G. A. Baird, 1910, pp. 22–3 and 31–2.
12. Sitā Rāma, *op. cit.*, p. 16.
13. Eden, *Letters from India*, II, p. 252.
14. J. W. Kaye, *Peregrine Pulteney, or Life in India*, 3 vols., 1844, III, p. 27.
15. G. F. Atkinson, *Curry and Rice*, 1859 (no pagination, 'Our Cook Room').
16. Russell, *Diary*, I, p. 103.
17. *ibid.*, p. 180.
18. *ibid.*, p. 143.
19. *ibid.*, p. 148.
20. F. J. Shore, *Notes on Indian Affairs*, 2 vols., 1837, Vol. I, p. 2.
21. see Kipling, 'Tod's Amendment', *Plain Tales from the Hills*, 1888.
22. Shore, *op. cit.*, p. 211.
23. *ibid.*, p. 13.
24. *ibid.*, p. 127.
25. *ibid.*, II, p. 424–5.
26. *ibid.*, p. 503.
27. Meadows Taylor, *The Story of my Life*, ed. by his daughter, 1878 (2nd edn.), pp. 259–60. (Hereafter, Taylor, *Life*.)
28. See Michael Edwardes, *The Necessary Hell*, 1958, p. 45ff.

29. H. B. Edwardes, *Life and Letters*, 2 vols., 1886, I, p. 303.
30. *ibid.*, II, p. 214.
31. Edwardes, *The Necessary Hell*, p. 74.
32. Arnold, *Oakfield*, II, p. 223.
33. Russell, *Diary*, I, 356.
34. quoted in Edwardes, *Life and Letters*, II, p. 192.
35. Falkland, *op. cit.*, II, p. 47.
36. W. Sleeman, *Rambles and Recollections of an Indian Official*, ed. by V. Smith, 2 vols., 1893, II, p. 205. [First published 1844.] (Hereafter Sleeman, *Rambles*.)
37. *ibid.*, I, p. 131.
38. *ibid.*, p. 205.
39. J. L. Kipling, *Beast and Man in India*, 1891, p. 15.
40. F. Parkes, *Wanderings of a Pilgrim in search of the Picturesque*, 2 vols., 1850.
41. *ibid.*, I, p. 146.
42. *ibid.*, p. 355.
43. *ibid.*, p. 396.
44. *ibid.*, II, p. 17.
45. *ibid.*, p. 434.
46. *ibid.*, p. 439.
47. *ibid.*, I, p. 149.
48. Russell, *Diary*, I, p. 386.
49. Aliph Cheem (W. Yeldham), *Lays of Ind*, 1883, p. 141.
50. G. Campbell, *Memoirs of my Indian career*, ed. by Charles Bernard, 2 vols., 1893, I, p. 11.
51. Michael Holroyd, *Lytton Strachey* (paperback edn.), 1971, p. 32.
52. Philip Mason, *Prospero's Magic*, 1962, p. 28.
53. Taylor, *Life*, p. ix.
54. *ibid.*, p. 251.
55. *ibid.*, p. 232.
56. *ibid.*, p. 370.
57. *ibid.*, p. 425.
58. *ibid.*, p. 435.
59. *ibid.*, p. 464.
60. Sleeman, *Rambles*, I, p. 72.
61. *ibid.*, p. 214.
62. *ibid.*, II, p. 51.
63. *ibid.*, p. 334.
64. W. Sleeman, *Journey through the Kingdom of Oudh in 1849-50*, ed. and abridged by P. D. Reeves, Cambridge, 1971, pp. 275-6.

65. *ibid.*, p. 233.
66. *ibid.*, p. 228.
67. *ibid.*, p. 225.
68. 'Preface' to 1858 edn. of Sleeman's *Journey*, p. xxi.
69. Brigadier-General John Jacob, *The Views and Opinions of*, ed. by Lewis Pelly, 1858, p. 2.
70. *ibid.*, p. 220.
71. H. B. Edwardes, *op. cit.*, I, p. 166.

CHAPTER SEVEN: *Mutiny*
1. Taylor, *Life*, p. 340.
2. H. Martineau, *Suggestions towards the future Government of India*, 1858, p. 13.
3. Metcalf, *op. cit.*, p. 60.
4. *ibid.*, p. 85.
5. Michael Edwardes, *Red Year, The Indian Rebellion of 1857*, 1973, p. 46.
6. *ibid.*, pp. 89–90.
7. Quoted by *Woodruff*, I, p. 361.
8. Alfred Lyall, *Letters*, MS. EUR F.132 (Lyall Collection), May 12, 1857.
9. *Household Words*, Vol. XVII, 1858, pp. 348–50.
10. W. H. Russell, *My Indian Mutiny Diary*, ed. by Michael Edwardes, 1957, p. 45. (Hereafter, Russell, *Mutiny*.)
11. *ibid.*, p. 87.
12. *ibid.*, p. 97.
13. *ibid.*, p. 101.
14. *ibid.*, p. 86.
15. Woodruff, *op. cit.*, I, p. 358.
16. *ibid.*
17. *ibid.*, pp. 361–2.
18. Taylor, *Life*, p. 350.
19. Russell, *Mutiny*, p. 8.
20. *ibid.*, p. 129.
21. *ibid.*, p. 166.
22. *ibid.*, p. 287.
23. Mark Thornhill, *The Personal Adventures and Experiences of a Magistrate during the rise, progress and suppression of the Indian Mutiny*, 1884, p. 2.
24. *ibid.*, p. 7.

25. *ibid.*, p. 87.
26. *ibid.*, p. 321.
27. H. B. Edwardes, *Life & Letters*, I, p. 45.
28. W. S. Blunt, *Ideas about India*, 1885, p. 172. (Hereafter, Blunt, *Ideas.*)
29. Russell, *Diary*, II, pp. 272–3 and p. 398.
    R. Kipling, *Soldiers Three* (Indian Railway Library), Allahabad,
30. 1888, p. 77.
31. *ibid.*, p. 89.
32. Hutchins, *op. cit.*, p. 99.

CHAPTER EIGHT: *The Wide Arch of Empire*
 1. Russell, *Diary*, II, p. 283.
 2. *ibid.*, p. 272.
 3. K. Rose, *Superior Person*, 1969, p. 343.
 4. Bholanauth Chunder, *Travels of a Hindoo to various parts of Bengal and Upper India*, 2 vols., 1869, I, p. 229.
 5. *ibid.*, pp. 165–6.
 6. *ibid.*, p. 283.
 7. *ibid.*, p. 375.
 8. E. A. King, *The Diary of a Civilian's Wife in India, 1877–82*, 2 vols., 1884, I, p. 137.
 9. G. O. Trevelyan, *The Competition Wallah*, 1864, p. v.
10. *ibid.*, p. 58.
11. *ibid.*, pp. 252–3.
12. *ibid.*, p. 278.
13. *ibid.*, p. 280.
14. *ibid.*, p. 281.
15. *ibid.*, p. 444.
16. *ibid.*, p. 451.
17. Bartle Frere quoted in *Ladies in the Sun*, ed. by J. K. Stanford, 1962, p. 127.
18. G. Campbell, *op. cit.*, II, p. 391.
19. E. Lear, *Indian Journal*, ed. by Ray Murphy, 1953, p. 181.
20. Quoted by Anil Seal, *The Emergence of Indian Nationalism*, Cambridge, 1968, p. 144.
21. Hutchins, *op. cit.*, p. 99.
22. Quoted in Stanley A. Wolpert, *Tilak and Gokhale, Revolution and Reform in the Making of Modern India*, University of California Press, 1962, p. 223.

23. W. S. Blunt, *My Diaries, 1888-1914*, with a preface by Lady Gregory, 1932, p. 598.
24. Martineau, *op. cit.*, p. 95.
25. Val Prinsep, *Imperial India, an Artist's Journal*, 1879, p. 37.
26. *ibid.*, p. 38.
27. R. Carstairs, *Little World of an Indian District Officer*, 1912, p. 161.
28. *ibid.*, p. 279.
29. Yeldham, *op. cit.*, p. 188.
30. Beames, *op. cit.*, pp. 63-4.
31. *ibid.*, p. 151.
32. *ibid.*, pp. 173-4.
33. *ibid.*, p. 216.
34. *ibid.*, p. 225.
35. *ibid.*, p. 237.
36. Graham, *op. cit.*, II, p. 210.
37. Beames, *op. cit.*, p. 264.
38. *ibid.*, p. 277.
39. Andrew Frazer, *Among Indian Rajahs and Ryots*, 1911, p. 42.
40. *ibid.*, p. 65.
41. *ibid.*, p. 105.
42. *ibid.*, p. 250.
43. *ibid.*, p. 294.
44. *ibid.*, p. 274.
45. *ibid.*, p. 360.
46. Lala Lajpat Rai, *Autobiographical Writings*, ed. by V. C. Joshi, Delhi, 1965, p. 121.
47. W. S. Blunt, *Ideas*, p. 29.
48. *ibid.*, p. 47.
49. *ibid.*, p. 48.
50. Kaye, *Metcalfe*, II, p. 125.
51. Blunt, *Ideas*, p. 45.
52. Heber, *op. cit.*, III, p. 373.
53. Kincaid, *op. cit.*, p. 151.
54. *ibid.*, p. 143.
55. King, *op. cit.*, I, p. 41.
56. *ibid.*, p. 87.
57. *ibid.*, p. 156.
58. *ibid.*, p. 178.
59. *ibid.*, II, p. 14.
60. *ibid.*, p. 33.
61. *ibid.*, p. 24.

62. *ibid.*, p. 167.

63. M. Diver, *The Englishwoman in India*, 1909, p. 135.

64. *The Englishwoman in India*, by a lady resident, 1864, p. 106.

65. Metcalf, *op. cit.*, p. 308.

66. *ibid.*, p. 318 and p. 320.

67. Quoted in *The Concept of Empire, Burke to Attlee, 1774–1947*, ed. by George Bennett, 1953, p. 240.

68. 'Letter' to *The Times*, 1 March, 1883.

69. Kincaid, *op. cit.*, p. 195.

70. *Englishman*, 28 April 1883 (quoted in Seal, *op. cit.*, p. 166).

71. *ibid.*, p. 170.

72. Banerjea, *op. cit.* p. 336.

73. G. F. I. Graham *Life and Work of Syed Ahmad Khan*, 1885, pp. 183–4.

74. Seal's book deals with both these themes profoundly, brilliantly and lucidly. In style and material his book is a model for anyone interested in this period.

75. A. E. Mason, *The Broken Road*, 1907, p. 99.

76. Banerjea, *op. cit.*, p. 21.

77. *ibid.*, 'Appendix A', p. 409. (Reprinted from A. O. Hume's article in *India*, 1893.)

78. see Seal, *op. cit.*, pp. 145–7, for a further discussion of Lytton's policies.

79. *ibid.*, p. 73.

80. *ibid.*

81. *ibid.*, p. 67.

82. *ibid.*

83. Quoted in Wolpert, *op. cit.*, p. 111.

84. *ibid.*, p. 112.

85. Banerjea, *op. cit.*, p. 156.

86. *ibid.*, p. 187.

87. *ibid.*, p. 196ff.

88. *ibid.*, p. 312.

89. *ibid.*, p. 308.

90. Rai, *op. cit.*, p. 4.

91. *ibid.*, p. 132.

92. *ibid.*, p. 100.

93. *ibid.*, p. 121.

94. Wolpert, *op. cit.*, p. 102.

95. *ibid.*, p. 80ff.

96. *ibid.*, p. 97.

97. *ibid.*, p. 100.
98. *ibid.*, p. 239.
99. *ibid.*, p. 206.
100. Seal, *op. cit.*, p. 140.
101. E. M. Forster, *op. cit.*, p. 18.
102. Wolpert, *op. cit.*, p. 175.
103. quoted by David Dilks, *Curzon in India*, 2 vols., 1969, I, p. 28.
104. *ibid.*, p. 63.
105. Rose, *op. cit.*, p. 345.
106. Wolpert, *op. cit.*, p. 175.
107. *ibid.*
108. *ibid.*, p. 176.
109. To Balfour in 1901, quoted in Rose, *op. cit.*, p. 349.
110. *ibid.*, p. 344.
111. Kincaid, *op. cit.*, p. 239.
112. Dilks, *op. cit.*, I, p. 199.
113. *ibid.*, p. 211.
114. *ibid.*, p. 237.
115. *ibid.*, p. 245.
116. *ibid.*, p. 246.
117. Rose, *op. cit.*, p. 339, n.

CHAPTER NINE: *The Foothills of the Himalaya*

1. B. C. Chatterjee, 'A Popular Literature for Bengal', reprinted with *Rajmohan's Wife*, ed. by S. J. C. Bagal, Calcutta, 1969, p. 100.
2. *ibid.*, pp. 97–8.
3. Bearce, *op. cit.*, p. 292.
4. Arnold, *op. cit.*, 'Preface' to second edn., 1854, pp. ix–xii.
5. Kipling, *Verse*, p. 18.
6. Prinsep, *op. cit.*, p. 20.
7. Aberigh-Mackay, *op. cit.*, p. 142.
8. John Leyden, *Poetical Remains*, with memoirs of his life by J. Morton, 1819, p. lxv.
9. *ibid.*
10. *ibid.*, p. lxxvii.
11. *ibid.*, p. 164.
12. W. B. Hockley, *Pandurang Hari, or Memoirs of a Hindoo*, with an introductory preface by Sir H. Bartle Frere, 2 vols., 1873, p. 17.
13. *ibid.*, p. viii.
14. *ibid.*, p. 87.

15. W. B. Hockley, *The English in India, a novel of Madras high life*, 3 vols., 1828, II, p. 58.
16. *ibid.*
17. *ibid.*, III, p. 230.
18. J. W. Kaye, *Peregrine Pulteney, or Life in India*, 3 vols., 1844, I, p. 12.
19. *ibid.*, p. 27.
20. *ibid.*, p. 103.
21. *ibid.*, III, p. 27.
22. Arnold, *op. cit.*, p. i.
23. *ibid.*, p. 16.
24. *ibid.*, p. 39.
25. *ibid.*, p. 230.
26. *ibid.*, II, p. 138.
27. *ibid.*, p. 223.
28. *ibid.*, p. 234.
29. *ibid.*, p. 192.
30. Iltudus Prichard, *The Chronicles of Budgepore or Sketches of life in Upper India*, 2 vols., 1880, I, p. v (first published 1871).
31. *ibid.*, p. 20.
32. *ibid.*, p. 60.
33. *ibid.*, p. 63.
34. *ibid.*, II, p. 267.
35. E. H. Aitken, *Behind the Bungalow*, 1889, p. 65.
36. G. Aberigh-Mackay, *21 Days in India, being the Tour of Sir Ali Baba, K.C.B.*, 6th edn., 1896.
37. *ibid.*, p. 4.
38. *ibid.*, pp. 11–12.
39. Yeldham, *op. cit.*, p. 119.
40. *ibid.*, p. 115 and p. 117.
41. Kipling, *Verse*, p. 45.
42. *ibid.*, p. 49.
43. *ibid.*, p. 248.
44. Devendranath Tagore, *Autobiography*, translated from the Bengal by Satyandranath Tagore, and Indira Devi, 1916, p. 54.
45. *ibid.*, p. 162 (quotation from the Upanishads).
46. *ibid.*, p. 252.
47. Tagore, *Reminiscences*, p. 22.
48. *ibid.*, p. 40.
49. *ibid.*, pp. 181–2.
50. *ibid.*, p. 184.

51. *ibid.*, p. 216.
52. 'Introduction' by W. H. Auden to *The Protestant Mystics*, ed. by Anne Fremantle, Mentor Books, 1965, p. 20.
53. R. Tagore, *Gitanjali*, trans. by the author, with an introduction by W. B. Yeats, 1921, p. viii.
54. *ibid.*, p. xiv.
55. Tagore, *Reminiscences*, p. 140.
56. Gilbert Murray and Rabindranath Tagore, *East and West*, League of Nations, 1935, p. 53.
57. Alfred Lyall, quoted in L. Cornell, *Kipling in India*, 1966, p. 77.
58. Toru Dutt, *Ancient Ballads and Legends of Hindustan*, with an introductory memoir by Edmund Gosse, 1885, p. 137.

CHAPTER TEN: *Kipling and Tagore*

1. R. Kipling, 'Preface', *Life's Handicap*, 1891, p. vii.
2. *ibid.*, pp. viii–ix.
3. C. Carrington, *Rudyard Kipling, his life and work* (paperback edn.), 1970, p. 52.
4. Kipling, 'Thrown away', *Plain Tales from the Hills*, Calcutta, 1888, p. 14.
5. 'Miss Youghal's Sais', *ibid.*, p. 23.
6. 'Tod's Amendment', *ibid.*, p. 168.
7. *ibid.*, p. 173.
8. 'The Head of the District', *Life's Handicap*, p. 110.
9. *ibid.*, p. 115.
10. 'Thrown away', *Plain Tales*, p. 15.
11. 'Beyond the Pale', *ibid.*, p. 147
12. *ibid.*
13. *ibid.*, p. 152.
14. 'Without benefit of clergy', *Life's Handicap*, p. 132.
15. *ibid.*, p. 131.
16. *ibid.*, pp. 154–5.
17. *ibid.*, p. 158.
18. 'At the end of the passage', *Life's Handicap*, p. 159.
19. *ibid.*, p. 160.
20. *ibid.*
21. *ibid.*, p. 164.
22. *ibid.*, p. 179.
23. *ibid.*
24. *ibid.*, p. 180.

25. *ibid.*, p. 184.
26. 'The Man who would be King', *Under the Deodars*, 1892, p. 173.
27. *ibid.*, p. 199.
28. 'His chance in life', *Plain Tales*, p. 71.
29. *The Naulahka*, 1892, p. 177.
30. *ibid.*, p. 276.
31. *Kim*, 1901, p. 1.
32. *ibid.*, p. 138.
33. *ibid.*, p. 158.
34. *ibid.*, p. 150.
35. *ibid.*, p. 195.
36. *ibid.*, p. 303.
37. *ibid.*
38. *ibid.*, p. 26.
39. *ibid.*, p. 260.
40. *ibid.*, p. 398.
41. *ibid.*, p. 386.
42. Kipling, *Verse*, p. 560.
43. R. Tagore, *Home and the World*, 1919, p. 113.
44. *ibid.*, p. 124.
45. *ibid.*, p. 185.
46. *ibid.*, p. 188.
47. *ibid.*, p. 45.
48. *ibid.*, p. 112.
49. Tagore, *Gitanjali*, p. 3.
50. *ibid.*, p. 69.
51. *ibid.*, p. 70.
52. *ibid.*, pp. 71-2.
53. *ibid.*, p. 73.
54. *ibid.*, p. 9.
55. *ibid.*, p. 12.
56. *ibid.*, p. 14.
57. *ibid.*, p. 15.
58. *ibid.*, p. 33.
59. *ibid.*, p. 37.
60. *ibid.*, p. 52.
61. *ibid.*, p. 54.
62. *ibid.*, p. 62.
63. *ibid.*, p. 68.
64. *ibid.*, pp. 75-6.
65. *ibid.*, p. 88.

66. *ibid.*, p. 92.
67. R. Tagore, *Letters to a friend*, edn. with an introduction by C. F. Andrews, 1931 (Letters written 1913–22), p. 47.
68. *ibid.*, p. 55.
69. *ibid.*, p. 128.
70. *ibid.*, p. 76.
71. *ibid.*, p. 81.
72. *ibid.*, p. 164.
73. *ibid.*
74. Kipling, *Verse*, p. 75.
75. Quoted by K. Kripalani, *Rabindranath Tagore*, 1962, p. 145.
76. Kipling, *Verse*, p. 31.
77. *ibid.*, p. 78.
78. *ibid.*, p. 270.
79. *ibid.*, p. 330.

EPILOGUE
1. Datta, *op. cit.*, p. 59.
2. *ibid.*, p. 81.
3. *ibid.* ('Foreword' by Malcolm Muggeridge), p. vi.

Bibliography

The place of publication for the following works is London, unless otherwise stated. Dates in square brackets refer to date of the first edition, where different and relevant.

PRIMARY SOURCES

Aberigh-Mackay, G., *21 Days in India, being the Tour of Sir Ali Baba, K.C.B.*, 6th edn. with illustrations, 1896.

Acland, C., *A Popular Account of the Manners and Customs of India*, 1847.

Aitken, E. H., *Behind the Bungalow*, 1889.

[Aliph Cheem], *Lays of Ind.*, 1883.

Arnold, E., *The Light of Asia, or The Great Renunciation*, 1885.

Arnold, W. D., *Oakfield; or Fellowship in the East*, 2 vols., 1854.

Atkinson, G. F., *Curry and Rice or the Ingredients of Social Life at 'Our' Station in India*, 1859.

Aurobindo, Sri, *Letters* (1st Series) (Bombay), 1947.

Baber, *Memoirs*, trans. F. G. Talbot, 1909.

Ball, V., *Jungle Life in India; or the Journeys and Journals of an Indian geologist*, 1880.

Banerjea, S., *A Nation in the Making* (Oxford), 1925.

Beames, John, *Memoirs of a Bengal Civilian*, 1961 [mainly written 1875–8].

Bernier, François, *Travels in the Mogul Empire, A.D. 1654–1668* (revised trans. Archibald Constable), 1891.

Best, Thomas. *The Voyage of*, Hakluyt Society, 1934.

Bhagavad Gita, with a commentary by R. C. Zaehner, Oxford, 1969.

Bignold, R. F., *Leviora: Being the shyness of a successful competitor* (Calcutta), 1888.

Blunt, W. Scawen, *My Diaries: Being a personal narrative of events 1888–1914*, 1932.

——, *India Under Ripon: a private diary*, 1909.

——, *Ideas about India*, 1885.

Bonnerjee, S., *The Life of W. C. Bonnerjee, First President of the Indian National Congress* (Calcutta), 1944.

Bowrey, T., *A Geographical Account of Countries round the Bay of Bengal, 1669–79*, Hakluyt Society 1905.

British Discovery of Hinduism in the Eighteenth Century, The, ed. by P. Marshall, Cambridge, 1970.

Burke, Edmund, *Works*, 6 vols., 1893.

——, *Selections* (Oxford), 1966.

Burnell, John, *Bombay in the Reign of Queen Anne*, Hakluyt Society, 1933.

Campbell, G., *Memoirs of my Indian career*, 2 vols., ed. Charles Bernard, 1893.

Campbell, W., *My Indian Journal*, Edinburgh, 1864.

Carstairs, R., *Little World of an Indian District Officer*, 1912.

Chatterjee, B. C., *Rajmohan's Wife*, ed. S. J. C. Bagal (Calcutta), 1969.

Chaudhuri, N., *The Continent of Circe*, 1967.

Chunder, Bholanauth, *Travels of a Hindoo*, 2 vols., 1869.

Churchill, W. S., *My early life*, 1930.

Chutney Lyrics, The: A Collection of Comic pieces in Verse on Indian subjects (Madras), 1871.

Clive, John, *Thomas Babington Macaulay, the Shaping of the Historian*, 1973.

Clive, R., *Speech in the House of Commons*, 1772.

Colesworthy, Grant, *Rural Life in Bengal*, 1860.

Collet, S. D., *Life and Letters of R. M. Roy*, ed. by H. C. Sarkar, Calcutta, 1914.

Cornwallis, C., 1st Marquess, *Correspondence of*, ed. Charles Ross, 3 vols., 1859.

Coverte, Robert, *The Voyage and Travels of*, Harleian Society, Vol.II, 1745.

Crawford, F. Marion, *Mr Isaacs: A Tale of Modern India*, 1882.

Cunningham, H. S., *Chronicles of Dustypore*, 1875.

Curzon, N. G., 'Frontiers', Romanes Lecture, 1907.

——, *Leaves from a Viceroy's Notebook*, 1926.

Dalhousie, Marquess of, *Private Letters*, ed. J. G. A. Baird, 1910.

Datta, S., *The World of Twilight* (Oxford), 1971.

Derozio, H., *Poems* (Calcutta), 1871.

Diver, Maud, *Honoria Lawrence*, 1936.

——, *The Englishwoman in India*, 1909.

Douglas, J., *Book of Bombay* (Bombay), 1883.

——, *Glimpses of Old Bombay and W. India*, 1900.

Dufferin and Ava, Marchioness of, *Our Viceregal Life in India, 1884–1888*, 2 vols. 1889.

The Dutt Family Album, 1870.

Dutt, M. M., *The Captive Ladie*, 1849.

Dutt, Toru, *Ancient Ballads and Legends of Hindustan*, 1885.

Early Travels in India, ed. by William Foster (Oxford), 1921.

Eden, Emily, *Letters from India*, 2 vols., 1872.

——, *Up the Country*, 2 vols., 1866.

Edwardes, H. B., *Life and Letters*, 2 vols., 1886.

——, 'The Safety of a Christian Policy in India', a speech, 1860.

Englishwoman in India, The, by a lady resident, 1864.

Evelyn, J., *Diary*, 3 vols., 1906.

Falkland, Viscountess, *Chow-Chow; being Selections from a Journal kept in India*, 2 vols., 1857.

Fay, Mrs Eliza, *Original Letters from India, 1779–1819*, with introductory and terminal notes by E. M. Forster, 1925.

First Englishmen in India, ed. J. Courtenay Locke, 1930.

Foote, Samuel, *The Nabob, A Comedy in 3 Acts* (Dublin), 1773.

Forbes, J., *Oriental Memoirs, the Narrative of 17 years' Residence in India*, 2 vols., 1834.

Forster, E. M., *The Hill of Devi*, 1967.

Francis, P., *Letters*, ed. by B. Francis and E. Kean, 2 vols., 1901.

Frazer, A., *Among Indian Rajahs and Ryots*, 1911.

Fryer, John, *A New Account of East India and Persia, being nine years travels, 1672–81*, Hakluyt Society, 3 vols., 1909–15.

Ghose, Aurobindo, *Thoughts and Glimpses* (Calcutta) 1920.

Ghose, M., *Love Songs and Elegies*, 1898.

——, *Songs of Love and Death*, ed. with an introduction by Lawrence Binyon (Oxford), 1926.

Gleig, G. R., *Memoirs of the Life of Warren Hastings*, 2 vols., 1841.

Graham, G., *Life in the Mofussil; or, the Civilian in Lower Bengal*, 2 vols., 1878.

Graham, G. F. I., *Life and Work of Syed Ahmad Khan*, 1885.

Graham, Maria, *Journal of a Residence in India*, 1812.

Grand, G. F., *The Narrative of the Life of a Gentleman long resident in India*, ed. W. K. Firminger (Calcutta), 1910.

Grant, C., *Observations on the State of Society among the Asiatic Subjects of Great Britain, particularly with respect to Morals, written chiefly in 1792*, and revised in 1813.

Grose, J. H., *A Voyage to the East Indies, begun in 1750 with observations continued till 1764*, 2nd edn., 1766.

Hakluyt, Richard, *Principal Navigations etc.*, 12 vols. (Glasgow), 1903-5.

Hamilton, Alexander, *A new account of the East Indies*, ed. by W. Foster, 2 vols., 1930 [1727].

Hastings, Marquess of, *Private Journal*, ed. by his daughter, 2 vols., 1858.

Heber, Reginald, *Narrative of a Journey through the Upper Provinces of India, from Calcutta to Bombay, 1824-25*, 3 vols., 1828.

Hedges, W., *Diary of*, Hakluyt Society, 3 vols., 1887-9.

Hickey, William, *Memoirs*, 4 vols., New York, 1923-5 [mainly concerns 1775-1809].

Hobson-Jobson, see Yule, H.

Hockley, W. B., *The English in India*, 3 vols., 1828.

——, *Pandurang Hari, or Memoirs of a Hindoo*, with an introduction by Bartle Frere, 2 vols., 1873.

Hodges, William, R. A., *Travels in India, during the years 1780-3*, 1793.

Hooker, J. D., *Himalayan Journals: or Notes of a Naturalist*, 1854.

Household Words (ed. by C. Dickens), Vols. XVI-XVII, 1857-8.

Hunter, W. W., *India of the Queen, and other essays*, 1903.

——, *The Old Missionary* (Oxford), 1895.

——, *Thackeray in India*, 1897.

Huxley, Aldous, *Jesting Pilate*, 1926.

Ives, Edward, *A Voyage from England to India in the year 1754*, 1773.

Jacob, John, *The Views and Opinion of Brigadier-General*, ed. by Lewis Pelly, 1858.

Jacquemont, V., *Letters from India*, trans. by C. A. Phillips, 1936.

Jourdain, John, *Journal of, 1608-17*, Hakluyt Society, 1895.

Jones, William, *Letters*, ed. Garland Cannon, 2 vols. (Oxford), 1970.

Kalidasa, *Sacontala*, trans. by W. Jones, 1790.

Kaye, J. W., *The Life and Correspondence of Lord Metcalfe*, 2 vols., 1858.

——, *Life and Correspondence of Sir John Malcolm*, 2 vols., 1856.

——, *Peregrine Pulteney*, 3 vols., 1844.

Khan, Hossein S. G., *Seir Mutaqherin*, trans. by Raymond, 1789, 4 vols., no date.

King, E. A., *The Diary of a Civilian's Wife in India, 1877-82*, 2 vols., 1884.

Kipling, John Lockwood, *Beast and Man in India*, 1891.

Kipling, Rudyard, *Departmental Ditties*, 1886.

——, *Plain Tales from the Hills*, Calcutta, 1888.

——, *Soldiers Three*, 1888.

——, *Life's Handicap*, 1891.

——, *The Naulahka*, 1892.

——, *Barrack-room Ballads*, 1892.

——, *Under the Deodars*, 1892.

——, *Wee Willie Winkie*, 1892.

——, *Many Inventions*, 1893.

——, *The Jungle Book*, 1894.

——, *The Second Jungle Book*, 1895.

——, *The Day's Work*, 1898.

——, *Kim*, 1901.

——, *Just So Stories*, 1902.

——, *Something of Myself*, 1937.

——, *Verse* (Definitive Edn.), 1969.

Lajpat Rai, Lala, *Autobiographical Writings*, Delhi, 1965.

Lawrence, H. M., *Adventures of an Officer in the Punjab*, in 2 vols., 1846.

Lear, Edward, *Indian Journal*, ed. by Ray Murphy, 1953 [1873].

Letters of Warren Hastings to his Wife, introduced by Sydney Grier, 1905.

Leyden, John, *Poetical Remains*, 1819.

Linschoten, John Huyghen van, *Voyage to the East Indies*, Hakluyt Society, 1885.

Lockyer, C., *An Account of the Trade in India*, 1711.

Lushington, Mrs Charles, *Narrative of a Journey from Calcutta to Europe, 1727-8*, 1829.

Lyall, Alfred, *Poems*, revised and slightly enlarged from 'Verses written in India', 1908.

Macaulay, T. B., 'The Government of India', a speech in the House on July 10, 1833 (Reynard Library), 1952.

——, 'Indian Education', a Minute of February 2nd, 1835.

——, *Critical and Historical Essays*, ed. by F. C. Montague, 2 vols., 1903.

Macgregor, C. M., *Wanderings in Balochistan*, 1882.

Mackintosh, W., *Travels in Europe, Asia, Africa*, 2 vols , 1782.

Malabari, B. M., *The Indian Muse in English* (Bombay), 1876.

Malcolm, J., *Central India*, 1823.

Mallinson, G. B., *Recreations of an Indian Official*, 1872.

Manucci, Niccolo, *Memoirs of the Moghul Court*, ed. by Michael Edwardes, 1967.

Martineau, H., *Suggestions towards the future Government of India*, 1858.

Martyn, H., *Journals and Letters*, ed. S. Wilberforce, 1839.

Marx, K., *Letters on India* (Lahore), 1936.

Mason, A. E. W., *The Broken Road*, 1907.

Master, Streynsham, *Diaries, 1675–80*, ed. R. C. Temple, 2 vols., 1911.

Mill, James, *History of British India*, with a continuation by H. H. Wilson, 8 vols., 1848.

Moore, Thomas, *Lalla Rookh – an Oriental Romance*, 1826.

Munro, Sir T., *Selections from his Minutes and Other Official Writings*, ed. A. J. Arbuthnot (Madras), 1886.

Murray, G. and R. Tagore, *East and West*, League of Nations, 1935.

Oaten, E. F., *European Travellers in India during the 15th, 16th, 17th centuries*, 1909.

Orme, R., *History of the Military Transactions of the British Nation in Hindustan from 1745*, 3 vols. (Madras), 1861 [1763].

Orwell, G., *Collected Essays*, ed. by Sonia Orwell and Ian Angus, 4 vols., 1968.

Ovington, J., *A Voyage to Surat in the year 1689*, 1696.

Pai, N. W., *Stray Sketches in Chakmapore* (Bombay), 1894.

Parkes, F., *Wanderings of a Pilgrim in search of the Picturesque*, 2 vols., 1850.

'Passages from India', *Adam*, Nos. 355–60, 1971.

Prichard, Iltudus, *The Chronicles of Budgepore or Sketches of life in Upper India* [first published 1871].

Prinsep, A., *The Babu, and other Tales descriptive of Society in India*, 2 vols., 1834.

Prinsep, Val C., *Imperial India, An Artist's Journal*, 1879.

Purchas, Samuel, *Purchas his Pilgrimes*, 20 vols. (Glasgow), 1905.

'Records', *Geological Survey of India*, vol. XX, 1887.

Rennell, James, *Memoir of a Map of Hindoostan; or the Mogul Empire*, 1788.

Roe, Sir Thomas, *The Embassy of*, ed. by W. Foster, Hakluyt Society 2 vols., 1894–9.

Russell, W. H., *My Diary in India, in the years 1858–9*, 2 vols., 1860.

——, *My Indian Mutiny Diary*, ed. by M. Edwardes, 1957.

Scott, Walter, *The Surgeon's Daughter*, 1827.

Sen, K. C., *Autobiography*, trans. from Bengali (Calcutta), 1915.

Shore, F. J., *Notes on Indian Affairs*, 2 vols., 1837.

Shore, John (later Lord Teignmouth), *Memoirs of the Life and Correspondence of*, by his son, 2 vols., 1843.

Sherwood, Mrs, *The History of Little Henry and his Bearer* (Wellington, Salop.), 1822.

Sitā Rāma, *From Sepoy to Subadar*, trans. by Lt-Col. Norgate, Calcutta, 1911.

Sleeman, W., *Journey through the Kingdom of Oudh in 1849–50*, ed. and abridged by P. D. Reeves, Cambridge, 1971.

——, *Rambles and Recollections of an Indian Official*, 2 vols., ed. by V. Smith, 1893 [1844].

Stephen, James Fitzjames, *Liberty, Equality, Fraternity* (Cambridge), 1967.

Tagore, D., *Autobiography*, trans. from the Bengali by S. Tagore and E. Devi, 1916.

Tagore, Rabindranath, *Collected Poems and Plays*, 1967.

——, *Gitanjali, Song Offerings*, with an intro. by W. B. Yeats, 1921 [1912].

——, *Letters to a Friend*, ed. with two introductory essays by C. F. Andrews, 1931.

——, *Home and the World* (Author's revised translation), 1919.

——, *Broken Ties and other stories*, trans. by the author, 1925.

——, *My Reminiscences*, 1917.

Taylor, Meadows, *Confessions of a Thug*, new ed., 1873.

——, 'Introduction' to *Tara*, 1863.

——, *The Story of my Life*, ed. by his daughter, 1878.

Thackeray, W. M., *Burlesques*, 1869.

Thornhill, Mark, *The Personal Adventures and Experiences of a Magistrate during the rise, progress, and suppression of the Indian Mutiny*, 1884.

Tod, James, *Annals and Antiquities of Rajasthan*, 3 vols. (Oxford), 1920 [1829–32].

Trevelyan, G. E., *Macaulay*, 2 vols., 1876.

Trevelyan, G. O., *The Competition Wallah*, 1864.

Tuzuk-i-Jahangir, or Memoirs of Jahangir, trans. A. Rogers and ed. H. Beveridge, 2 vols., 1909 and 1914.

Terry, Edward, *A Voyage to the East Indies*, 1655.

Twining, T., *Travels in India*, a hundred years ago, 1893.

Valentia, Viscount, *Voyages and Travels to India, Ceylon, in the years 1802, 1803, 1804, 1805 and 1806*, 4 vols., 1811.

Waterfield, William *Indian Ballads, and other poems*, 1868.

Wheeler, J. Talboys, *Early Records of British India* (Calcutta), 1878.

Wilson, A., *The Abode of Snow*, 1875.

Wilson, C. R., *Early Annals of the English in Bengal*, 4 vols., 1895–1917.

Yeldham, W., see under Aliph Cheem.

Yule, H. and Burnell, R. E., *Hobson-Jobson, a glossary of colloquia. Anglo-Indian words and phrases*, ed. by W. Crooke, 1969.

SECONDARY SOURCES

Archer, M. and W. G., *Indian Painting for the British, 1770–188c* (Oxford), 1955.
Archer, M., *British Drawings in the India Office Library*, 2 vols., 1969.
——, '*Company' drawings in the India Office Library*, 1972.
Bearce, G. D., *British Attitudes towards India, 1784–1858* (Oxford) 1961.
Bengal Past and Present, Vol. LXXXIV, July–December, 1965.
Bradshaw, J., *Thomas Munro* (Oxford), 1894.
Brown, Hilton (ed.), *The Sahibs*, 1948.
Carrington, Charles, *Rudyard Kipling, his life and work*, 1970.
Chakravarty, Aniya, *A Tagore Reader*, 1961.
Concept of Empire, The, Burke to Attlee, 1794–1947, ed. by G. Bennett, 1953.
Cornell, L., *Kipling in India*, 1966.
Cotton, J. S., *Mountstuart Elphinstone* (Oxford), 1892.
Cronin, Vincent, *A Pearl to India* (The Life of Roberto de Nobili). 1959.
Dilks, D., *Curzon in India*, 2 vols., 1969.
Diver, Maud, *Honoria Lawrence*, 1936.
Edwardes, Michael, *British India*, 1967.
——, *High Noon of Empire*, 1965.
——, *The Necessary Hell*, 1958.
——, *Red Year, The Indian Rebellion of 1857*, 1973.
Elphinstone, M. *History of India*, 1874 [1841].
Embree, A. T., *Charles Grant and British Rule in India*, 1962.
Feiling, K., *Warren Hastings* (Papermac) 1966.
Frazer, R. W., *A Literary History of India*, 1898.
Garratt, G. T., *The Legacy of India* (Oxford), 1967.
Greenberger, A., *The British Image of India, 1880–1960* (Oxford), 1969.
Grierson, H. J. 'Edmund Burke', *Cambridge History of English Literature*, Vol. XI, 1922.
Holroyd, M., *Lytton Strachey*, 1971.
Hutchins, F. G., *The Illusion of Permanence, British Imperialism in India*, Princeton, 1967.
Iyengar, Srinivasa, *Indian Writing in English* (Bombay) 1962.

Kincaid, Dennis, *British Social Life in India, 1608-1937*, 1938.
Kipling's Mind and Art – essays ed. by Andrew Rutherford, 1964.
Kopf, David, *British Orientalism and the Bengal Renaissance, The Dynamics of Indian Modernisation, 1773-1835* (Univ. of California Press), 1969.
Kripalani, K., *Modern Indian Literature* (Bombay), 1968.
——, *Rabindranath Tagore*, 1962.
Ladies in the Sun, ed. by J. K. Stanford, 1962.
Maclagan, Edward, *The Jesuits and the Great Moghul*, 1932.
Malleson, G. B., *Lord Clive*, Oxford, 1893.
Marshall, P. (ed.), *Problems of Empire: Britain and India, 1757-1813*, 1968.
——, *The Impeachment of Warren Hastings*, Oxford, 1965.
Martin, Briton, Jnr., *New India, 1885*, California, 1969.
Mason, P., *Prospero's Magic, Some Thoughts on Class and Race*, 1962.
Mayhew, A., *The Education of India*, 1926.
——, *Christianity and the Government of India*, 1929.
Metcalf, Thomas, *The Aftermath of Revolt, India 1857-70* (Princeton), 1965.
Mukherjee, S. N., *Sir William Jones, A Study in Eighteenth Century British Attitudes to India* (Cambridge), 1968.
Protestant Mystics, The, ed. by Anne Fremantle, 1965.
Rawlinson, H. G., *India, a short cultural history*, 1965.
Rose, Kenneth, *Superior Person*, 1969.
Saul, S. B., *Studies in Overseas Trade, 1870-1914*, 1960.
Seal, Anil, *The Emergence of Indian Nationalism* (Cambridge), 1968.
Sencourt, Robert, *India in English Literature*, 1923.
Sewell, Robert, *A Forgotten Empire* (Vijayanagar), 1924.
Singh, Bhupal, *A Survey of Anglo-Indian Fiction*, 1934.
Sitwell, C., *Reform to Flowers and Elephants*, 1929.
Smith, Vincent, *Akbar, the Great Mogul* (Oxford), 1917.
Smith, Vincent, *Oxford Student's History of India*, revised by H. G. Rawlinson, 1962.
Sorabji, Cornelia, *India Calling*, 1934.
Spear, P. *Twilight of the Mughuls* (Cambridge), 1951.
——, *The Nabobs*, 1932.
Stewart, J. I. M., *Rudyard Kipling*, 1966.
Stokes, E., *The English Utilitarians in India* (Oxford), 1959.
Sutton, Denys, *Tiger of Mysore: Life and Death of Tipu Sultan*, 1970.
Thackeray, W. M., *The Newcomes*, 1855.
Thompson, Edward, *Life of Charles, Lord Metcalfe*, 1937.

Tompkins, J. M. H., *The Art of Rudyard Kipling*, 1959.

Wolpert, Stanley A., *Tilak and Gokhale, Revolution and Reform in the Making of Modern India* (Univ. of California Press), 1962.

Woodruff, Philip, *The Men who ruled India*, 2 vols. (Cape paperback), 1963.

Index

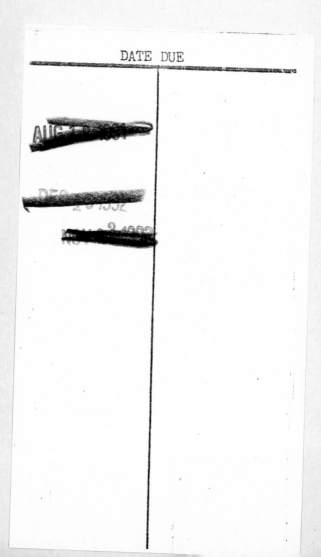